A Kiss Is Still a Kiss

Roger Ebert

A Kiss Is Still a Kiss

Andrews, McMeel & Parker
A Universal Press Syndicate Company
Kansas City • New York

Library of Congress Cataloging in Publication Data

Ebert, Roger.
A kiss is still a kiss.

1. Moving-picture actors and actresses--Biography--Miscellanea. I. Title.
PN1998.A2E25 1984 791.43'028'0922 [B] 84-16953
ISBN 0-8362-7926-3

For my parents

Contents

Prologue

... no matter what the future brings

Not Being There

Like most other people whose tastes began to form before television became the dominant entertainment medium, I have a simple idea of what it means to go to the movies. You buy your ticket and take a seat in a large dark room with hundreds of strangers. You slide down in your seat and make yourself comfortable. On the screen in front of you, the movie image appears—enormous and overwhelming. If the movie is a good one, you allow yourself to be absorbed in its fantasy, and its dreams become part of your memories.

Television is not a substitute for that experience, and I have never had a TV-watching experience of emotional intensity comparable to my great movie-going experiences. Television is just not a first-class way to watch movies. The screen is too small. The image is technically inferior. The sound is disgracefully bad. As the viewer I can contain television—but the movies are so large they can contain me. I can't lose myself in a television image, and neither, I suspect, can most other people. That is why people are forever recreating movie memories in great detail, but rarely bring the same passionate enthusiasm to made-for-TV films.

I believe, then, that to experience a movie fully you have to go to the movies. I enjoy television for other purposes, and my favorite TV programs are the live ones (sports, news, elections, talk shows), where immediacy compensates for the loss in intensity. Unlike a lot of movie buffs, I am not a fan of "The Late Show." If a movie is good enough to stay up late for, it's too good to be watched through the dilution of television. I'll catch it later at a revival theater or a film society, or, if I never catch it again at least I'll think of it as a movie and not as late-night programming.

Maybe it's no wonder, then, that, with these personal biases, I was disturbed by some of the things I heard a few years ago during a conference I went to in Colorado. The American Film Institute had taken over the Aspen Institute for three days, and invited forty-five people to gather for a discussion of the future of the feature film. By "feature film," they meant both theatrical and made-for-TV features, the latter including docudramas and TV miniseries.

The conference was weighted toward the TV people, among them executives of various pay-cable companies, and although several of us professed an interest in a discussion of content (that is, what movies are *about* these days), most of the talk was about "delivery" (how to sell television programming at a profit). What actually went out on the airwaves or cable systems would presumably take care of itself.

Many panelists' remarks were couched in a technological Newspeak that I had trouble understanding at first. *Software,* for example, was the word for TV programming—software to feed the hardware of our new home video entertainment centers. ("Software?" they said. "You know. That's a word for product." Product? I asked. "Yeah. Like a movie.") *Television consuming units* was another expression that gave me trouble until I realized it was a reference to human beings. *Windows* was a very interesting word. It referred to the various markets that a new movie could be sold to (or "shown through") once it was made. First there would be the theatrical window, a traditional booking in a movie theater. Then came the network window—sale to commercial television. After that the windows came thick and fast: the pay-cable window, video cassette window, video disc window, airline in-flight window, and so on. In the hierarchy of these windows, the traditional practice of showing the movie in a theater seemed furthest from everybody's mind; the theatrical run was sort of a preliminary before the other markets could be carved up.

One of the enticing things about all the windows, I learned, was that a new movie could now be in the position of turning a profit before it was made. The pre-sales of subsidiary viewing rights would take the risk out of the initial investment.

The chilling thought occurred to me that, if a movie was already in profit, actually showing it in theaters could be risky because promotion, advertising, and overhead would be seen as liabilities instead of (in the traditional view) as an investment risk with a hope of profitable return. But no, I was assured, that was wrong. Movies would still have to play in theaters because the theatrical run "legitimatized" them: they thus became "real" movies in the eyes of people buying them on cassettes or over pay cable.

Wonderful, I thought. The theatrical feature film, the most all-encompassing art form of the twentieth century, has been reduced to a necessary marketing preliminary for software.

If this was a pessimistic view, it was mild compared to some of the visions of the future held by the conference participants. An important TV writer-producer, one of the most likable people at the conference, calmly predicted that in ten years people would be sitting at home in front of their wall-size TV screens while (and I am indeed quoting) "marauding bands roam the streets." I thought he was joking, until he repeated the same phrase the next day.

What about going out to the movies? Another television executive said he used to go, but he had stopped. "You have to stand in line and be crowded in with all those people. And it's too expensive."

Well, apart from the fact that he could no doubt afford to buy a ticket for everyone in line, and that higher ticket prices only reflect general inflation, his view overlooked the fact that video cassettes and pay cable can be as expensive as going out to the movies, especially when you consider the initial "hardware" investment. And for your money, you get to watch a TV image made up of dots arranged in 625 lines—an image that, even assuming your set has perfect adjustment and color control, does not and cannot approach the quality of an image projected by light through celluloid.

But those technical considerations aside, why did this man and some of his colleagues have such a distaste for going out to the movies? I do it all the time. I feel it adds something to a movie-going experience to share it with other people. It's communal. A lot of the fun of seeing a movie such as *Jaws* or *Star Wars* comes, for me, from the massed emotion of the theater audience. When the shark attacks, we all levitate three inches above our seats, and come down screaming and laughing.

Watching *Jaws* on network TV isn't a remotely comparable experience. And watching a *comedy* in isolation can actually be a depressing experience. Our laughter during a movie comedy is an act of communication; an audience roaring with laughter is expressing its shared opinion about what's funny. I've watched comedies while I was alone in a room, and I've noticed that I don't laugh at all. Why should I? Who's to hear? And, perhaps because I don't laugh, those comedies don't seem as funny. Maybe it's essential to comedy that we're conscious of sharing it with other people; maybe, in human development, the first communication was a scream and the second was a laugh, and then they got around to words.

As anyone who has seen one knows, giant TV screens aren't the answer because they further dilute the already washed-out TV image. The TV signal has only 625 lines to contain its information no matter *how* large the screen is, and so a larger screen means a faded picture. TV retail outlets report that consumers seem to understand this, and that seventeen- and nineteen-inch sets are preferred to twenty-one- and twenty-four-inch screens because of the sharper image.

What is clearly happening is very alarming.

A superior system of technology—motion pictures—is being sold out in favor of an inferior but more profitable system—pay video hardware/software combinations. The theatrical motion picture, which remains such a desirable item that it's used to sell home cassette systems, is in danger of being held hostage. Truly daring and offbeat film subjects will become increasingly risky because they can't easily be presold for showing through other "windows."

The two edges that movies have enjoyed over television are greater quality and impact of image, and greater freedom of subject matter. Now television is poised to absorb and emasculate the movies, all in the name of home entertainment. It will serve us right, as we sit in front of our fuzzy giant-screen home video systems ten or twenty years from now, if there's nothing new or interesting to watch on them. Count me in with the marauding bands.

one

A sigh is just a sigh

Robert Mitchum remembers this conversation with his wife:

"Dorothy, why do they take it so seriously? Why do they want my autograph? What's the big deal?"

"Bob, it's because when you're up there on the screen they're smaller than your nostril."

Mitchum is my favorite movie actor. I am not talking here about some form of objective analysis in which I compare the virtues of Brando, De Niro, Cagney, Tracy, Mastroianni and the other contenders. I make no analysis at all. Mitchum is my favorite because when I went to see Heaven Knows, Mr. Allison, *I realized that there was something in him that was more than character and more than story; it was style.*

I met him for the first time in 1968, on the Dingle Peninsula in Ireland, where he was filming Ryan's Daughter. *We sat around in the cottage he had rented, and he played Marty Robbins records and boasted that when David Lean asked if he could do an Irish accent, he had answered, "Come on, David. Which county?"*

With Mitchum, you do not ask questions, or at least you do not expect answers. He speaks in free association, and has gotten a reputation for being a bad interview when in fact he is one of the best, if you go with the conversational flow. The other subjects of this chapter, Michael Caine, Mel Brooks and

Walter Matthau, are poets of conversation. The idea in their interviews is just to listen carefully.

I don't use a tape recorder when I do interviews because it gets in the way: It inspires the subject to start dictating, and puts him on guard with every word. The notepad is much more confidential. When you think the subject is about to elaborate on an indiscretion, you keep writing, so that the silence hangs in the air and must be filled. During moments of revelations and confidences, you don't write at all. But you remember.

The Day That Marilyn Died

She was here, she was sort of a wraith,
she was just passing through.
Los Angeles, 1982

Sometimes you wake up with the clock radio completing a sentence from one of your dreams. On the morning of Friday, August 6, I was dreaming about Robert Mitchum. In my dream, he was discussing one of his movies with a class at the University of Chicago. Then a disc jockey was saying: *Another Leo birthday today is Robert Mitchum, who is sixty-five. And on this date in history, Marilyn Monroe died in 1962.*

"Died" is the proper word for Monroe's death, all right, irrefutable and incontrovertible. Hollywood folklore has by now limited the other possibilities to "committed suicide," or "was murdered."

The coroner's report in 1962 suggested that Monroe killed herself with an overdose of barbiturates, but dying by your own hand of booze or pills, accidentally or intentionally, is such a humdrum way to die in Hollywood that after twenty years people still want to believe there was more to it than that. And so there is irony in the fact that the Monroe autopsy, which first brought fame to former Los Angeles County coroner Thomas Noguchi as "coroner to the stars," is now being defended by Noguchi against what he terms publicity seekers.

On the twentieth anniversary of Marilyn Monroe's death, the *Los*

Angeles Herald Examiner was giving front-page play to a story the *Los Angeles Times* chose to ignore, about a "veteran Hollywood private investigator" named Milo Speriglio, who was offering a reward of ten thousand dollars for a mysterious "red diary" he claimed has been missing ever since Monroe's death. The diary would show, he said, that she was murdered by a "dissident faction of the CIA," which feared she would reveal secrets confided to her by Robert F. Kennedy, then the attorney general.

Reading about the "red diary," I drank my morning coffee beside the pool of the Sunset Marquis Hotel. For the first time in years, I found myself remembering the day of Marilyn Monroe's death. The news that day in 1962 came over a car radio, and my first thought was I had not yet met her, and meeting Marilyn Monroe was one of the things I had planned to do in my lifetime.

Since there has not been a sex symbol like Marilyn Monroe since she died, younger readers may not realize how important Monroe once was, as a symbol, as an image, even as a name—*Marilynmonroe,* pronounced as if it were one word by twelve-year-old boys to whom *Marilynmonroe* summed up in five syllables all they knew about lips and legs and breasts and blondes. How could death invade such a dream?

I showered, shaved and drove my rented Toyota out to the Malibu Colony, that long stretch of real estate where stars, agents and best-selling authors buy million-dollar "cottages" on the Pacific Ocean. I was driving out to Malibu to interview Sylvia Kristel, who was the nearest thing we had in the 1970s to a sex symbol like Monroe. Kristel starred in *Emmanuelle,* the best-selling sex movie of the decade, and the critics wrote that she had a Monroe kind of innocence about her, a disingenuous way of approaching a sex scene so that it seemed as new to her as it did to us.

Monroe, of course, never made many "sex scenes" per se. Her specialty was comedy and the infinite possibilities in a smile. Perhaps, I reflected, turning onto the Pacific Coast Highway, perhaps Sylvia Kristel was really more like Brigitte Bardot than like Monroe, more like a standard-issue sex kitten than like a woman who became an American symbol and married Joe DiMaggio and Arthur Miller and once sang "Happy Birthday" to Jack Kennedy in Madison Square Garden. Still, Sylvia Kristel was the nearest thing to a sex symbol that I personally was going to interview today, and so I determined to make the best of it. After all, I still had Robert Mitchum's birthday party to look forward to.

I turned off the highway and down a little road into a private cove. Kristel's house looked, from the street, like a modest bungalow, and, from the beach, like the headquarters of one of James Bond's enemies. I rang the bell and was ushered into the living room by a Mexican maid who offered me a Tab and brought me a Sunkist orange.

The room was two stories high, filled with sun and fresh flowers, overlooked by a balcony and overlooking the ocean. Two women walked in and introduced themselves: Sylvia's aunt and niece, from Holland, enjoying their first visit to America and, oh yes, still excited by their trip to Disneyland. I shook hands and settled myself and noticed, above the fireplace, the famous Andy Warhol portrait of Marilyn Monroe, the portrait that makes Warhol's statement that portraits and trademarks are interchangeable in a world where everything is marketed like a can of soup.

Sylvia Kristel appeared after a while, looking younger than she had a few mornings earlier, when I had seen her new movie, *Lady Chatterley's Lover*. She looked not only young but fresh, with curly brown hair and a peaches-and-cream complexion, and she talked in short, enthusiastic bursts, like a schoolgirl afraid of being cut off. Yes, I thought to myself, I see where they get the notion that she has a kind of innocence about her.

I was just admiring your Warhol, I said.

"Marilyn," she said, in a slight Dutch accent. "I think you can see that she was short-sighted too, just like me. I sometimes think that was what gave her such an open look—the fact that she could not really see anything without her glasses on."

She sat at the opposite end of a long couch and curled her feet beneath her. As she leaned forward to take a cigarette from a pack on the coffee table, I could see her breast through the open side of her white peasant blouse. She leaned back, blew out smoke, and looked up at the portrait again.

"They called her the love goddess," she said. I said nothing, because I wanted to see how this would go. "I have been called the love goddess, too," she said. "If you make a list of love goddesses, it is very long, I think. Now the love goddess of the 1980s is Brooke Shields. I am growing old. I am over thirty. I am tired of making pictures. For *Lady Chatterley's Lover*, I ran around naked in the cold mud while the crew was dressed for an Arctic expedition. I may retire. Or perhaps I'll try comedy. The sex symbols get younger and younger, you know. I saw a portrait the other day of Barbara Mandrell's daughter, made up to look exactly like her mother. It was uncanny. She's five years old."

Marilyn would have been fifty-six, I said.

"It's better that she died young," Kristel said. "Can you imagine Marilyn Monroe at fifty-six?"

Well, I said, not unreasonably, what about yourself? Can you imagine yourself at fifty-six?

"Heavens, yes, but then I'm not like Monroe. First of all, I would not like to be dead and miss the end of the world. I'm a curious person. I don't know how curious Marilyn was. I wonder if she could see beyond her own problems. Of course, who would not be neurotic under the circumstances?"

They're offering ten thousand dollars for a diary she was supposed to have kept, I said. They say it proves the CIA murdered her because Bobby Kennedy told her all of his secrets.

"They say she died of a coronary," Kristel said. "But I believe she died of an injection. That's what I heard. Yet no needles or syringes were ever found in her room. If you knew who removed the needle, you'd know a lot more about her death than they want you to know."

Who is they?

"I don't know. I was only ten when she died. But that's what I've heard."

Chapter One

Watching you in *Lady Chatterley's Lover* the other day, I said, I was sort of reminded of Marilyn in the scene where you looked at the naked body of the game-keeper, as he bathed himself in a clearing. The closeup shots as you watched him seemed very sensuous, very suggestive, and yet I couldn't see you *doing* anything to make them so.

"I had to fight for that," she said. "The director kept asking me to 'look excited.' Of course, when you try to look excited, you only look ridiculous. It is much better to use the other image—the naked man—to prepare the viewer's mind for what they *think* you are thinking, and then to go into a sort of trance when you hear the word *action*."

Do you think Marilyn did something like that?

"I don't know. Whatever she did, she did it wonderfully well."

Just then Kristel's husband came into the room and staged an interesting little scene. Pretending not to notice that she was being interviewed, he delivered a long complaint about how he was going to have to drive all the way into town to plant some bushes in front of one of his buildings, because it was impossible to hire competent help who would put the bushes in the right place.

I had heard of this husband earlier. Kristel had asked that I keep his name out of the article: "He wants to keep a low profile." They had just returned from their honeymoon a few weeks earlier. He wore standard-issue uniform: running shoes, no socks, white pants, sportshirt worn outside the pants, curly hair, mustache, sun visor and sunglasses.

"I have to go into Beverly Hills anyway, to pick up some money," he said.

Then he noticed me. He learned that I was from Chicago. "I'm in the financial business," he said. "I made my biggest deal with Northwest Federal. You ever heard of it? Largest financial institution in the state of Illinois. I've only been in Chicago two times and I know more about it than you do. Isn't that funny!"

I was seized by an almost irresistible compulsion to reply that, despite their difficulties, the Continental and First National banks were still among Illinois' many financial institutions that were larger than Northwest Federal. But prudence prevailed and I grinned ruefully, playing the pupil from Chicago. By now Kristel's husband had redirected his attention from me to the maid: "Haven't you warmed up the car yet? Am I speaking another language or something? Why can't anyone follow my instructions?"

Then he was gone. Sylvia Kristel and I sat down on the couch again, but the air was still heavy with aggression, egotism and unhappiness. I reflected that it was against the rules for me to lean forward and say, *Speaking quite frankly, Sylvia, how can you stand that pompous ass?* So I said, instead, that I'd asked all the questions I could think of, and really appreciated her taking the time to talk with me.

"He still sends roses, after all this time," Sylvia said as she showed me to the door.

Your husband?

"No. Joe DiMaggio."

Driving back north on the Pacific Coast Highway, I stopped at the Malibu Colony Florist and bought a bouquet of flowers for a sick friend. The shop was owned by a tall, pretty woman named Maggie. I asked her if anyone had bought flowers for Marilyn's grave.

"Well," she said, "you wouldn't know what the flowers were for, would you? Still, isn't it a nice idea?"

Back on the road, I remembered an *Esquire* magazine article written many years ago by Gay Talese, about the flame that still burned in Joe DiMaggio's heart for Marilyn Monroe. The article was about fame, and how those two American legends had handled it. It had one of the greatest headlines in the history of *Esquire.* It referred to Monroe's trip to Korea to entertain American troops:

"Joe," said Marilyn, "you've never heard such cheering."
"Yes I have," said DiMaggio.

I drove back east on the Santa Monica Freeway, six lanes of cruise control with an FM radio soundtrack. I got off at La Cienega, took Melrose to Los Palmas, and found a parking space right in front of Francis Ford Coppola's Zoetrope Studios, where

Robert Mitchum was working on the twentieth anniversary of Monroe's death.

On the one and only occasion when I visited the Cinematheque Francais in Pàris, they were showing Otto Preminger's *River of No Return* (1954), starring Mitchum and Monroe. It was part of an homage to Otto Preminger, and during the film I made a key critical discovery. Keeping your mind on Preminger in a movie starring Robert Mitchum and Marilyn Monroe is like saying your prayers in a strip joint.

Mitchum was working on Stage 6: He was starring as the coach in the long-delayed film version of *That Championship Season,* Jason Miller's Pulitzer Prize-winning play about an aging coach and four middle-aged survivors of a state championship basketball team. The other four cast members were Bruce Dern, Stacy Keach, Martin Sheen and Paul Sorvino. They were all major movie actors. Mitchum was a star. Standing in the shade of a fake tree on a phony lawn outside a set of a Pennsylvania frame house, I watched Mitchum light a Pall Mall and I made a mental note: *Remember this moment. Right now, this moment, is just as historic as if you were on a Hollywood soundstage forty years ago watching Humphrey Bogart lighting a Chesterfield, because Bob Mitchum is the last of the old lions. He is as close as you're going to get in this lifetime to a legend like Monroe.*

Mitchum was walking through a rehearsal of a shot in which he approaches one of the cast members and fearlessly takes a loaded shotgun out of his trembling hands. It is the sort of scene Mitchum does with an authority that cannot be learned. When the scene was right they handed it over to the lighting men, the cinematographer and the stand-ins, and Mitchum went to change shirts in his dressing room across the street.

Inside, in the full blast of an air conditioner, Mitchum lit another cigarette and paged through his dialogue.

"I think this is my favorite line," he said. "The one guy is accusing the other guy of having an affair with his wife. The one guy says, *I wanna know if my wife is a good lay.* The other guy answers, *That's none of your business!"*

He laughed a soft, head-shaking, bemused Mitchum laugh.

Happy birthday, I said.

"What? Oh. Yeah."

Do you have any thoughts on your birthday? Any profound reflections?

"Only that tomorrow is Saturday."

Today is also the twentieth anniversary of Marilyn Monroe's death, I said.

"And also, they dropped the atomic bomb on Hiroshima," Mitchum said. "All sorts of things happened on my birthday."

What do you think it would be like if she were still alive? If we had twenty more years of Marilyn Monroe roles to talk about?

Mitchum blew out a long, weary plume of smoke. "How can you answer that?" he said. "What can you say? She was here, she was sort of a wraith, she was just passing through. I knew her very well. I knew her for a long time. She was always normal with me. She had the peculiar psychic condition where people are afraid of people and places. What's it called? Agoraphobia. She'd go to the hairdresser early in the morning, and then go home and not leave her home all day. They were always talking about her perfect complexion. God, it was beautiful, all right. Until the director said *action,* that is. Then she'd immediately break out in a rash. My theory is, she started to menstruate whenever the camera started to roll. She was that vulnerable."

He drew circles in the ashtray with the end of his cigarette.

"What I found most fetching about Marilyn," he said, "was that women loved her. They simply adored her."

An assistant director came to call Mitchum back to the set. He worked another two hours, going through different camera angles of the same scene. Then it was 7:30 P.M., a wrap on a thirteen-hour day. The assistant director stood self-consciously in the middle of the set and said, "Ladies and gentlemen, we have a special occasion today. It is the coach's birthday."

The lights went up behind the frame house, and everybody

walked around to the back of the set, where a big birthday cake was flanked by bottles of champagne. Mitchum made a short speech ("Thank you, everybody") and then, while the champagne was being poured, a blonde woman in a brief red dress appeared. She was carrying a large wrapped present.

"Special delivery for Mr. Mitchum," she said.

She put the present down and Mitchum unwrapped it. The box contained a large portable tape player. The woman pushed a button and the machine played "The Stripper." She started to do a strip tease. Everybody laughed at Mitchum, who sat down in a director's chair and pretended to review the performance dispassionately. After the blonde had stripped down to panties and a bra, she sat on Mitchum's lap and kissed him. Mitchum was at pains to make her feel less awkward. "You're very nice," he told her. "Thank you, everybody."

The blonde stood up and passed out her business card, for Strip-O-Gram Inc. "I also act," she said. It was possible that this engagement would be the closest she would ever get to a Hollywood movie, but then again, maybe not. What ambitions ran through Marilyn's head on the day she posed for the nude calendar shot?

Much later that night, up on Sunset Strip, Russ Meyer went to see Kitten Natividad perform at the Body Shop. Meyer is known as the King of the Skin Flicks. He has spent the last twenty-three years making comedies about sex, and Kitten Natividad is the star of two of his films.

The announcer introduced Kitten Natividad as "the sex symbol of the 1980s." Meyer sat in the back row of the club, next to a meek little man who introduced himself as "Kitten's number one fan."

You did a lot of cheesecake photography in your early days, I said to Meyer. Did you ever shoot Marilyn Monroe?

"Only once," he said. "I was an assistant to another guy. It would have been before she became famous. All I can remember is that she was a very nice girl, very quiet, and when you developed the pictures she had something. She had something with the camera."

You could tell that even then?

"Oh, most definitely."

This was at about the time of the nude calendar shot?

"Sometime around there, probably. Before or after. I can't remember."

The next day's editions of the *Herald Examiner* carried stories saying that the ten thousand dollar offer for the "red diary" by private investigator Milo Speriglio had been upstaged by a Hollywood rare book dealer, who called a press conference to offer one hundred thousand dollars for the same diary. It was a safe enough offer, since the diary probably did not exist, and, if it did, would probably be worth a hundred thousand to somebody if it contained the revelations Speriglio said it did.

A smaller story said that several dozen people visited Marilyn Monroe's grave on the twentieth anniversary of her death, including several women dressed as Marilyn look-alikes. A young man who described himself as "Marilyn's number one fan" said he left because the scene had been turned into a circus. The story was illustrated with a photograph showing a bouquet of red roses that had been delivered early in the day. There wasn't any card or, if there had been a card, someone had taken it. Somewhere there's probably a market for a card signed "Joe."

Robert Mitchum

While you're resting, would you mind carrying these anvils upstairs?

McKeesport, Pa., 1971

The sky hung low and dripping over the Sheraton Motor Inn, and Robert Mitchum hunched his shoulders against it and scooted around to the other side of the Mercury, slamming the door against the rain.

"I bought some of that lime spray," he told his friend Tim Lawless, who was in the driver's seat. "Maybe she'll go for some of that lime spray."

"Lime spray," Tim said. Then he started the car and guided it down a ramp and onto a highway, turning left, which was, as it turned out, a fateful decision.

"This is, I would say, relaxing work," Mitchum said. "They don't push you too hard. *While you're resting,* they say, *would you mind carrying these anvils upstairs?"*

"Jesus, what a lousy, crummy day," Tim said.

"And here it is only two in the afternoon," Mitchum said. "Reflect on the hours still before us. What time is the call for?"

"They're looking for you around 2:30, quarter to three," Tim said. "You got it made."

"You know the way?" Mitchum said.

"Hell yes, I know the way," Tim said. "I was out here yesterday. Sons of bitches, picking locations way the hell the other side of hell and gone ..."

"Look at those kids," Mitchum said. Three or four kids had parked their motorcycles at an intersection and were sitting backwards on the seats, in the drizzle, watching traffic. "Kids hanging around street corners," Mitchum said wonderingly, as if that were a sight he didn't see much anymore. "Oogling, drooling ..."

"Drooling," Tim said.

"Oogling," Mitchum said. "What do we gotta shoot this afternoon? We gotta jam our butts into those little cells again?"

"Those are the smallest cells I've *ever* seen," Tim said. "Can you imagine pulling solitary in one of those?"

"I did five days of solitary once, when I was a kid," Mitchum said. "In Texas. Of course, in Texas, you might as well be in as out ..."

"You did solitary?" Tim said.

"I *liked* it," Mitchum said. "You read about Alvin Karpis, up in Canada, they finally let him out after forty years or something? Son of a bitch walks outside, and the guy who put him in is still there. J. Edgar. Son of a bitch does forty years, the least we could do for him is not have J. Edgar still sitting there when he gets out a lifetime later ...."

"Karpis?" Tim said.

"I guess he was a real mean mother at one time," Mitchum said.

The wipers beat back and forth against the windshield, and on the sidewalks people put their heads down and made short dashes between dry places. We were in Pittsburgh now, and the smoke and fog brought visibility down to maybe a couple of blocks.

"I'm glad we're shooting inside today," Tim said.

Mitchum whistled under his breath, and then began to sing softly to himself: *"Seventy-six trombones led the big parade ...."*

"With a hundred and ten cornets in the rear," Tim sang, banging time against the steering wheel.

"A hundred and ten? Is that right?" Tim said after a while.

"All I know is the seventy-six trombones," Mitchum said. "I don't have time to keep pace with all the latest developments."

So how long you been in Pittsburgh? I asked.

"I was born here," Mitchum said, "and I intend to make it my home long after U.S. Steel has died and been forgotten. I intend to remain after steel itself has been forgotten. I shall remain, here on the banks of the Yakahoopee River, a grayed eminence ... I used to come through here during the Depression. I don't think the place has ever really and truly recovered ..."

He reached in his pocket for a pipe, filled it carefully, and lit up. "I find myself talking to the kids," he said. "And they say ..."

He broke off as a Mustang with two girls in it pulled up next to the Mercury at a stoplight. Through the window on his side, he mouthed a warm suggestion. "Hey, baby, you want to ..." The Mustang pulled away. "They don't have lip-readers worth a damn in this town," Mitchum said. "But the kids. I was talking about the kids. They say they figure they owe the community about two more years, and then they're pulling out, before they're flung headlong into despair."

"I don't think we went through a tunnel yesterday," Tim said.

"Well, we're going through a tunnel now," Mitchum said.

"Are you sure we're supposed to be on seventy-nine, and not seventy-six?" Tim said.

"I think I'm sure," Mitchum said. "We were either supposed to sing 'Seventy-six Trombones' to remind us to *take* seventy-six, or to remind us *not* to, I'm not sure which ...."

"You're not leading me down the garden path, are you, Bob?" Tim said.

"Route 79," Mitchum said. "Maybe it was seventy-six. Or ... Route 30?"

"This is the goddamn airport road," Tim said. "Look there."

"Steubenville, Ohio," Mitchum said. "Jesus Christ, Tim, we're going to Steubenville, Ohio. Maybe it's just as well. Make a left turn at Steubenville and come back in on the Pennsylvania Turnpike ...."

"Ohio's around here somewhere," Tim said.

"I've always wanted to make a picture in Ohio," Mitchum said. "Maybe I have. I was bitten by a rowboat once in Columbus ...."

There were three lanes of traffic in both directions, and Tim held grimly to the wheel, trying to spot a sign or an exit or a clue.

"The Vesuvius Crucible," Mitchum said. "Pull off here and we'll ask at the Vesuvius Crucible. If anybody ought to know where they are, the Vesuvius Crucible ought to."

Tim took the next exit and drove into the parking lot of the Vesuvius Crucible. Mitchum rolled down the window on his side and called to a man inside the office: "Hey, can you tell us how to get to the Allegheny County Workhouse?" Mitchum said.

"The *what?*" the man said.

"The Allegheny County Workhouse," Mitchum said.

"Hell, they closed that down back here six months ago," the man said. "It's empty now."

"We just want to visit," Mitchum said. "Old times' sake."

The man came out into the yard, scratching himself thoughtfully. "The Allegheny County Workhouse," he repeated. "Well, buster, you're real lost. You turn around here and go right back to downtown Pittsburgh. Take the underpass. When you get to downtown Pittsburgh, ask for directions there."

"How wide are we off the mark?" Mitchum said.

"Buster," the man said, "you're thirty-eight or forty miles away from where you should be."

"Holy shit," Mitchum said.

"I'm telling you," the man said, "they shut the workhouse down back here six, seven months ago. You won't find anybody there."

"Thanks just the same," Mitchum said.

Tim drove up to the expressway overpass and came down pointed at Pittsburgh. "We should have taken Route 8," he said.

"Sorry about that," Mitchum said. "There's a road to Monroeville. Ohio's around here somewhere ..."

"Nice countryside," Tim said. "You ought to buy it and build yourself a ranch."

"I could be the biggest rancher in Pittsburgh," Mitchum said. "Get up in the morning and eat ham and eggs in my embroidered pajamas. Some girl broke into the motel, did you hear about that? With a pair of embroidered P.J.'s?"

"Embroidered?"

"A great big red heart right over the rosette area," Mitchum said. "I've got an idea. Maybe we should hire a cab and have it *lead* us to the Allegheny County Workhouse."

"I don't even think we're in Allegheny County," Tim said.

Mitchum hummed "Seventy-six Trombones" under his breath and filled his pipe again.

This is your first picture since *Ryan's Daughter,* right? I asked him. The picture was *Going Home,* with Mitchum as a man who murdered his wife years ago, gets out of prison, and is confronted by his son.

"There's a funny thing about that," Mitchum said. "At the same time I was reading this script, I was also reading a script about a jazz musician in San Francisco. So I ask myself, do I want to play a jazz musician in San Francisco, or do I want to go out on location in some godforsaken corner of McKeesport, Pennsylvania, and live in a motel for two months? No way. *No* way. So these two guys come in and we have a drink or two, and I sign the contract. On their way out, I say I'll see them in San Francisco. I thought they looked a little funny. Do you know what I did? I signed up for the *wrong fucking movie."*

"Here's Route 8 right now," Tim said.

"That's Exit 8, not Route 8," Mitchum said.

"We're going to be real late," Tim said. *"Real* late."

"They can rehearse," Mitchum said. "They can practice falling off stairs, tripping over lights, and shouting at each other in the middle of a take."

The car was back in the tunnel again now, heading the other way. Tim came down through a series of cloverleafs and found himself back on Route 79, headed for the airport.

"I'm lost," he said. "Baby, I am lost."

In desperation, he made a U-turn across six lanes of traffic and found himself on an up-ramp going in the opposite direction, with a cop walking slowly across the street toward him.

Mitchum rolled down the window. "Roll down your window," he told Tim. "Let's get a breeze in here." He shouted to the cop: "Hey, chief! We're lost! We been forty miles out in the country and here we are headed right back the same way again."

"What are you doing making a U-turn against all that traffic?" the cop said. "You could go to jail for that."

"Hell, chief," Mitchum said, "that's where we're *trying* to go. We been looking for the Allegheny County Workhouse for the last two hours."

"They closed that down back here six months ago," the policeman said.

"We're shooting a movie out there," Mitchum said.

"Hey, you're Robert Mitchum, aren't you?" the cop said.

Mitchum pulled his dark glasses down on his nose so the cop could see more of his face, and said, "We are *so* lost."

"I tell you what you do, Bob," the cop said. "You take this underpass and follow the road that curves off on your left before you get to the bridge."

"Thanks, chief," Mitchum said.

Tim drove onto the overpass, followed the road that curved off on the left before he got to the bridge, and groaned.

"We're back on Route 79 heading for the airport," he said.

"Jesus Christ," Mitchum said. "Screw that cop. Screw that cop and the boat that brought him."

"Now we gotta go *back* through the tunnel," Tim said. "I'm upset. I am really upset."

On the other side of the tunnel, Tim pulled over to a State Highway Department parking lot and backed into it down the exit ramp. A state employee came slowly out of a shed, wiping his hands on a rag.

"Ask that guy," Mitchum said. "Offer him a certain amount to lead us there with a snow-plow."

Tim got out and got some instructions from the state employee. Their essence seemed to be: Go back that way.

Tim tried it again, back through the tunnel, across the bridge, down the overpass to the red light, where a police squad car was stopped in front of the Mercury. Mitchum jumped out of the car and hurried up to the squad car for instructions. He got back just as the light turned green.

"You'll see a sign up here that says Blawnox," he said. "That's what we need. Blawnox."

"I'm out of gas," Tim said.

"I got a letter from John Bryson today," Mitchum said. "John's in Dingle, in Ireland. Where we shot *Ryan's Daughter*?"

"I am really upset," Tim said.

"According to John," Mitchum said, "they've formed a Robert Mitchum Fan Club in Dingle. The membership is largely composed of unwed mothers and their brothers."

"Where the hell are we?" said Tim.

"That's what happens when you shoot on location," Mitchum said. "It's nothing but a pain in the ass."

He began to whistle "Seventy-six Trombones" again, softly, but not too softly.

Michael Caine

I was standing in the lobby of the Beverly Wilshire one day, talking to Cary Grant...

Los Angeles, 1979

Why is everyone looking at me so strangely? I'm sitting quietly, fairly decently dressed, a sweater to guard against the coldest day in Los Angeles history. I'm stirring my Perrier and vodka just like everybody else ... and people are sneaking covert glances out of the corners of their eyes.

But they are not, I realize belatedly, looking at me. They are looking at my table. I am in Ma Maison on Melrose Avenue in Los Angeles. There is no restaurant in town right now that is more in. There are five rows of five tables each. I am seated at the center table of the center row. In my dim way I gradually realize that it is the most important table in the room, and ... this takes me another second or two ... that everyone is wondering who I am meeting for lunch. Michael York is at the next table. Angie Dickinson is right over there. David Janssen is directly behind me. Jacqueline Bisset just walked in. Kirk Kerkorian, the czar of MGM, is against the wall.

In the deep shadow, over there in the corner, dressed entirely in black, the magnificent presence of Orson Welles looms behind the glowing ash of his cigar. A Monte Cristo cigar, no doubt, I think to myself....For a small-town kid, I learn fast. I sip my drink. Maybe I'm not imagining that even ... Orson Welles ... wonders why I am at Table Number One. My mind toys with the memory of a day in August when I went to interview Orson Welles and Kermit the Frog, and only Kermit would talk to me. Now I have Orson Welles' table. Is this arrogance? Have a seat, and I'll tell you how it feels to interview a rayon frog.

"Ha!" says Michael Caine. He shakes my hand, sits down, asks for the wine list. A physically palpable sensation of relief begins all the way over there by Kirk Kerkorian and sweeps, as we say, across the room. It is Michael Caine's table. So that is whose table it is.

You'd like Caine. He occupies Table Number One as if it were overstuffed. He orders a good French wine in good French. "Did you hear," he says, "about the bloke who took this bird out to a French restaurant and ordered everything in perfect French? *Soupe a l'oignon,* the works. The waiter's impressed, the girl's impressed, the waiter asks the guy something in French. *Sorry,* he says, *I only speak food."*

You've moved out here, I hear.

"I had to. When the Chancellor of the Exchequer told the British rich he'd make them scream, what he neglected to realize is that they would be screaming from the south of France, and Beverly Hills. As a result of our tax laws, we have become a great exporting country. We have, for example, exported our film industry."

The wine arrives, is presented, is inspected, is good, is poured, is the occasion of a small nod.

"I would describe myself politically," Caine says, "as a radical right Socialist. I approve of what they're doing *for* the people, but not what they're doing *to* the people. Don't get me wrong. I'm not against the country. I'm against the regime. I wouldn't approve of a place where the children were starving while I had ten times more than I needed. On the other hand, I do not intend to starve in my old age.

"So my wife and I have bought a house here in California, and I'm taking driving lessons. I can't drive, you know. At the age of thirty, I went directly from not being able to afford the lessons to buying a Rolls-Royce and having a chauffeur."

The waiter arrives and Caine orders, speaking excellent food.

"Driving here, I must have passed sixty dirty bookstores," he says. "Do you know: There's not a dirty bookstore in the country I can go into without being recognized. I tried it once in New York. Walked into a place off of Times Square. It was filled with men whose eyes were carefully downcast as they examined the merchandise. No eye contact. So far, so good. The bloke behind the cash register looks up and shouts: *Well! Look who we have here! Michael Caine!*"

A sip of wine.

"Lost a sale, he did. Still, I suppose that's the price of fame. I'd rather be famous than have a pile of dirty books at home. Being recognized is a two-edged blade. I was standing in the lobby of the Beverly Wilshire Hotel one day, talking to Cary Grant, and this woman sprinted across the lobby like an Olympian. *Michael Caine!* she shrieks. *God! I've been in this lobby for three weeks, trying to spot a movie star, and you're the only one I've seen!* She turns to

Cary Grant. *Isn't it terrible?* she says.

"*Terrible,* says Cary Grant."

Dramatic pause. Caine examines the salad that has been placed before him. "At that exact moment in time," he says, "Randolph Scott walked past. I toyed with the notion of introducing them, but, no ..."

And at that exact moment in time, a woman looms over Michael Caine's left shoulder and talks softly, confidentially in his left ear.

"What is the name," she confides, "of the calypso singer who came after Billy Daniels?"

"I'm certain I don't know," Caine says.

"You know, the guy after Billy Daniels."

"I haven't the slightest."

"Oh. Well. Thanks anyway."

She walks away.

"That," says Caine, "is an example of what I was just talking about. Some people will say anything just so they can talk to a movie star. There is no way in the world that woman cares about Billy Daniels."

He's sitting right behind you, I say.

And that leads us to look a bit more thoroughly around the room, at all of the stars exchanging nods and smiles and handshakes and feeling really great, as a matter of fact, because there's nothing quite so nice as half a bottle of chilled good white wine at lunch at a good restaurant filled with beautiful people.

And at that exact moment in time, something interesting happens. You remember that Jacqueline Bisset and Michael York and David Janssen and ... you remember, all the people in the room. They all fall silent at once. Every last one of them stops chatting and eating and waving, and they all simultaneously share a common experience that lasts for almost fifteen seconds. They watch, and think, as Orson Welles, having paid his check, stands up and gravely walks from the room. Their eyes follow him. It is uncanny. They are famous and successful and unawed by celebrity, but he is Orson Welles. Caine finally breaks the hush by clearing his throat.

"Orson Welles," he says. "He was the first human being on earth to say to me, *You'll make it, kid.* I was at the time in a play in London. There were twenty-two people in the audience. One of them was Welles. He came backstage and told me he thought I'd done a good job. That was so important to me I can hardly begin to explain it. I was at the time almost wondering if I should be an actor."

What would you have been?

"A cook. A chef. Wear the white hat. Run an exclusive private hotel like the one in 'The Duchess of Duke Street.' My mother was a cook. She was like Mrs. Bridges on 'Upstairs, Downstairs.' I was raised in enormous houses like that one. My mother *was* Mrs. Bridges. When anything terrible happened, she'd always make tea. That's a British thing. Monty Python does it all the time: The world is ending! Put on the kettle!"

He smiles.

The meal has been good. The day has been good. It is even going to get better.

The waiter appears.

"Tea," says Caine.

Mel Brooks

I bite my dog. I grab his jowl in my teeth
and pull him across the floor.
Los Angeles, 1983

"Everything's a casserole! We are standing next to a sheer drop of one thousand feet! I'm talking to an English girl's navel! Her father was a viscount!"

Mel Brooks is talking about his lawyer's housewarming.

"All of his clients are English except me! You know how tall English girls are! I'm the only short Jew in the room! My wife is a health food nut and all these casseroles are driving her crazy! She won't eat sugar, she won't eat white flour, she won't eat salt, and for all she knows these casseroles are made out of nothing else! Meanwhile, buzz-words are swarming in the background: *So cold ... my cat ... chiropractor ... '60 Minutes' ... buzz, buzz.* I'm going nuts!"

Mel Brooks is doing this routine in the hallway at Twentieth Century-Fox. Inside his office door are gathered various secretaries, writers, friends and assistants. Outside in the hallway his audience includes a kid from the mail room and two secretaries belonging to somebody else. Brooks calls them all "sweetie."

"I brought him some wine. A magnum of a very nice Pommard. And what does he serve me? Nouveau Beaujolais 1983. A very old nouveau. And my lawyer's house! He broke through some walls and came up with one of these California houses where you look through any window and it's a sheer, heart-sickening drop to the stones far below. And it has ten thousand sliding doors. He changed them all to French doors. That I approve of.

"If you buy a California house and it has an eighty-foot wall, right away you put in two forty-foot sliding doors. Then you keep them slid *closed* all the time, because they might sneak in and murder you and throw you over the edge. So there's no fresh air, so you put in high ceilings: *I like this house! This house looks big enough to hold enough air for me to breathe to see me through the night."*

It is time for lunch, and Mel Brooks leads a little parade down the hallway of the Fox office building and out into the lot. It is a sunny day in December. We are heading for the commissary. It used to be decorated so that a giant, fierce mural of Darryl F. Zanuck glared directly into the executive dining area. But now, Brooks says, it has been redecorated and everybody's digestion has improved.

Walking down the studio street, he spots Danny DeVito, the "Taxi" cast member who plays Shirley MacLaine's slavishly devoted admirer in *Terms of Endearment.*

"I saw the picture last night!" Brooks tells him. "I thought you were terrific! You only had one line, but you delivered it *perfectly*! No, you were great!"

He walks into the commissary and takes the table by the door.

"Larry, talk to me!"

Larry is the head waiter.

"Larry, tell me what's what. I'm worried about the fish, I'll be perfectly frank with you. It's been a long time since my wife has given me fish for dinner, and I have the strangest little feeling that *tonight*— I get fish! So I better not have fish for lunch. Twice in one day, I have this condition, I could break out."

"How about the roast beef plate?" says Larry.

"All roast beef?"

"For you, maybe we put on a little turkey, eh? And some sliced beefsteak tomatoes?"

"Perfect!"

Brooks looks around the room. "In this business," he says, "you've got to train like an athlete."

In the old days in the executive dining room of the Fox commissary, the tables used to be filled with aging tycoons, nodding to each other over foot-long Cuban cigars. Now a new generation has taken over the movie industry, and the executives all look like they just came from the gym. They wear expensive sports clothing and glowing tans. Over there at the next table is Julia Phillips, the executive producer of *Close Encounters,* with tinted aviator glasses parked on top of her perfectly streaked hair.

Mel Brooks is arguably the oldest person in this room, and he is only fifty-six. He is also the closest thing the Fox executive commissary can boast, these days, to a tycoon. A funny thing happened to him on his way to a career as a maker of comedies. He became a serious producer, almost as a sideline, and in the last few years his Brooksfilms company has produced three critical and box office hits: *The Elephant Man, My Favorite Year* and *Frances.* Include the movies he directed or starred in, like *Young Frankenstein, Blazing Saddles, Silent Movie, High Anxiety* and *The History of the World, Part One,* and he may have the best track record on the lot.

Brooks and his wife, whom he sometimes describes as "the famous actress Anne Bancroft," have just finished a new project. It is a remake of *To Be or Not to Be,* the 1942 Ernst Lubitsch comedy starring Jack Benny and Carole Lombard, and Brooks and Bancroft take the Benny and Lombard roles, playing Warsaw stage actors who impersonate Nazi officers to confuse Hitler's takeover plans for

Poland.

"A lot of people said: *How dare they?*" Brooks said. "*How dare they remake a movie by the great Lubitsch?* Just the other day, in fact, I got a call from a man who wanted to apologize for saying that. He saw our version and he liked it after all. My theory is, you can't remake a drama, because a drama is real, and so it can only be real once. But you can remake a comedy, because a comedy isn't real, and so as long as people laugh, you're safe."

I noticed, I said, that in the opening credits there is a drawing where you are made to look just a little like Jack Benny.

"There are two places in the movie where I salute Benny directly," Brooks said. "One is the name of a street. You see the street sign, and it's Kubelsky Street. That was Benny's real name. Also, later, I steal his delivery. I make an entrance, walking out of a darkened theater, talking to Tim Matheson, and at first I don't see Jose Ferrer ...

Brooks: I stink without a script!

Ferrer (aside): He stinks with *a script.*

Brooks: I heard *that!*

"... just like Benny. He was wonderful. Nobody could take a funny line from wholesale to retail better than Benny."

The roast beef plate arrived, heaped with turkey.

"There's a line in the movie," Brooks said, "that I'm thinking of using in the ad copy: *He's world-famous ... in Poland.* Sort of a Polish joke, maybe, but otherwise there are no Polish jokes whatsoever in the movie, because they're a cheap shot, they aren't funny, and, besides, this is a movie about a bunch of brave, patriotic Polish citizens taking on Hitler. And did *we* study *Polish!*"

At the beginning of the movie, Brooks and Bancroft talk and sing in Polish, until the voice of God comes on and decrees that from now on the picture will be in English, to make it a little easier on everybody.

"We took lessons," Brooks said. "We took from a young lady at UCLA, and *was she strict*! Can you tell the difference between *uh* and *eh*? She can. And I think the Polish-speaking community is going to be a little surprised by the opening of this picture, because Annie speaks a lot of very rude Polish. Then, after we start speaking English, I love the dialogue where my character wants to think only about the theater, not about the Nazis:

Any minute, could be war!

So what? We're in the theater! Sondheim! Send in the clowns!

"And another thing, I like the touch where we gave Annie a gay as her dresser, instead of a woman, which would have been standard. That allowed us to work in the part about how the Nazis weren't just rounding up the Jews, but also the homosexuals and Gypsies, too. I love the line we wrote: *Without fags, Jews and Gypsies, there is no theater!*"

But why, I asked, thinking of Brooks' classic but still sort of touchy "Springtime for Hitler" production number in *The Producers,* why do you think Nazis are funny?

"Because they take themselves so seriously. They don't see how closed-minded they are, so blind to human values, so they're easy to use as objects of scorn and derision. Also, in my own humble little way, in my little corner, I've been trying to even it out for what they did to the Jews. Better to trample them with humor and ridicule than take them seriously like they took themselves. I even have a new 'rap' record about Nazis. It's called "To Be or Not to Be—The Hitler Rap." It goes: *Don't be stupid, be a smarty! Come on and join the Nazi Party!*"

You didn't direct this movie yourself?

"No, because I hired Alan Johnson to direct it. He was the the choreographer of 'Springtime for Hitler' and the Inquisition number in *History of the World.* He freed me for the first time in my life to concentrate on my job as an actor and enjoy it. This was too big a role to be worrying about the directing, too. Besides—my motto—I Only Direct to Protect. So somebody else doesn't miss the good parts. You've heard of hyphenates? Guys who are Producer-Directors, or Producer-Writers, or Director-Stars? I'm the only hyphenate known as a Producer-Comedian."

It was nearing the end of the lunch hour, and as each party got up to leave, its members stopped at the table by the door to check out with Mel. He knew everybody's name, everybody's project, everybody's latest credit, everybody's wife, car, dog and vice.

"How's the pit bulldog?" he asked one executive. "You know, I've got a pit bull, too. Seven years old. His teeth are still growing in. He knows he can kill a Buick. He hates yellow Buicks. This man came to my house. While he wasn't looking, my pit bull rammed his Buick and left a dent in the side. I pretended I didn't see."

Brooks waved goodbye. "Actually," he said, lowering his voice, "I bite my dog. I grab his jowl in my teeth and pull him across the floor."

What does the dog do?

"He looks at me with love."

Walter Matthau

This was in Utah, see. That's why Jack was sucking on a goddamned horehound drop in the first place.

Los Angeles, 1981

Early one morning in Los Angeles, I accidentally overheard a small moment of Walter Matthau's life. I was walking along a back street between the giant sound stages at Metro-Goldwyn-Mayer's Culver City lots, when I heard Matthau's voice emerging from the open door of a portable dressing room.

"The stockbrokers?" he was saying. "The stockbrokers go to *Hawaii,* for Christ's sake!"

I kept right on walking, wondering about that line. Was it dialogue from a movie? A complaint about broker's fees?

Soon I was on the set of *Buddy Buddy,* a Billy Wilder movie in which Matthau played a Mafia hit man, Jack Lemmon played a suicidal producer for "60 Minutes," and Klaus Kinski played a sex therapist who transported Paula Prentiss, Lemmon's wife, to the fourth plateau of sexual excitation. There are nine plateaus. Wilder, Lemmon, Kinski and Prentiss were already on the set, rehearsing. Matthau did not have much to do in this scene, since his character was supposed to be passed out unconscious on the bed. He was just arriving now.

Billy Wilder announced, "Ladies and gentlemen, Walter Matthau." And Matthau, sweeping his arm in a large bow, shambled onto the set.

"Where do I pass out?" he asked.

"On the bed, just as we rehearsed," Wilder said.

The scene they were shooting was rather complicated: After hit-man Matthau threatens to kill Lemmon, who is suicidal because of his wife's affair with sex therapist Kinski, Prentiss and Kinski break into the room to knock out Lemmon with a tranquilizer, but Kinski stabs the needle into Matthau's rear end by mistake, after which a horrified Lemmon discovers that his wife has melted down her golden wedding band into a tiny replica of Klaus Kinski's genitals, for a necklace.

Matthau's role in all of this was to recline on the bed with his rear end sticking up into the air. It sounds like a routine scene, but Matthau made it special. He is perhaps the only actor in movie history with a hangdog expression on his ass. "Please don't take any photographs of this scene," he mumbled to the still photographer, his words muffled because his face was buried in the bedspread. "You know and I know where they will end up: on the front page of the *National Enquirer.*"

"Moan, please, Walter," said Billy Wilder.

"Moan," said Matthau.

"Again."

"Moan."

"More emotion, please."

"Moan!"

"But as if you were unconscious, of course."

Matthau turned over on the bed and rolled his eyes. "That's a new movie phrase that we can coin right here today," he said. "More Emotional Moaning. We'll call it 'M.E.M.' Like the German director who wanted to shoot a scene without sound, and ordered his cameraman to work *Mit out sound,* and to this day they call that 'M.O.S.'"

"Right," said the Vienna-born Wilder. "Everybody knows what that means: Mit out sound."

"Moan," said Matthau, rolling back onto his stomach.

After Wilder was satisfied with the scene, he announced a lunch break, and Matthau pulled up his pants and shambled back to his mobile dressing room. It was an air-conditioned Winnebago with a refrigerator full of mineral water, fruit, yogurt and other California junk food.

"It's tough, that scene," Matthau said. "You play it too fast, you step on the laughs. You play it too slow, everybody looks weird, standing around staring at those tiny golden balls. Every time we played that scene, I was reminded of the Myron Cohen story about the guy who goes up to the street peddler in New York and says, *You got dates? No,* says the peddler. *Then, you got nuts?* And the peddler says, *Listen, mister, if I had nuts, I'd have dates.*"

Matthau began to peel an apple. He squinted with one eye and sighted down the knife at the apple, and then he sliced it, and scrutinized it, and ate it thoughtfully, and I realized that if someone had eaten an apple in exactly that way and asked me who he was imitating, I would have answered: Walter Matthau. He seemed genuinely content with himself.

Do you still gamble? I asked him.

"Hardly at all. For big stakes, that is. Of course I gamble, to make the games interesting. But five hundred dollars a game, tops. Or sometimes a grand. No heart attack bets. I just like to keep track of the game. One of my proudest moments came once when I was in Chicago and they let me throw up the ball at the beginning of the Bulls-Knicks game, and I threw it up behind my back, faking out both clubs. Bill Bradley, who is now our United States senator from New Jersey, gave me a look that meant, *What a ham!*"

You do follow basketball pretty closely, then.

"Pretty closely."

How many games did Indiana lose during the regular season?

"Nine. What scores do you want to know during the regular season?"

Matthau stood up and went over to the trailer's tiny cupboard. "Drink?" he said. "Coffee?"

Are you making coffee?

"I haven't had *coffee*," he said, growling forlornly, "since the pancreas came out. You know, of course, that coffee may be a dilator. Suspected of it, anyway."

A dilator?

"Or a constrictor. There's quite a difference, of course."

Matthau went over to the telephone and dialed a number. "Hello? Dr. Kerwin, please. He's not in? Is this Rachel? I thought so. Well, Rachel, this is Walter. Listen. I need to know, fast: Is coffee a vaso-dilator? It is? OK. Thank you, Rachel."

He hung up the phone. "So now you know," he said. "Any other questions?"

What is it like working with Jack Lemmon and Billy Wilder again?

"Well, since I see Lemmon and Wilder all the time when I'm not working, it's like a party. Wilder is exactly the same at a party as he is on the set—with me, anyway. I fight with him, tout him on horses, correct his English. The only difference when we're making a movie is that Izzy Diamond is always hanging around in the shadows, looking sometimes like Heimlich Himmler, sometimes like a chicken farmer who is about to shoot you."

Izzy Diamond is I.A.L. Diamond, who has collaborated with Wilder on his screenplays for the last twenty years.

Didn't you once say, I asked Matthau, that if I.A.L. Diamond had joined the Black Muslims, his name would have been I.A.L.X.?

"Not me. Sounds more like a Wilder line. I would never say a line like that. It's just not my level."

The telephone rang. Matthau answered it. "Hello? Oh, hello, Dr. Kerwin. No, no. I'm fine. Just curious. Right. Dr. Kerwin, is coffee a vaso-dilator? What? You say coffee is a vaso-*constrictor*? It's not a dilator? Hello? So it's not good for people who have migraine headaches? Check it out, will ya? Look it up. You have the book right on your desk. Right. Thanks." He hung up.

Speaking of constrictors, I said, what about the time Jack

Lemmon almost choked to death in front of your eyes?

"Well, what about it?"

Lemmon once told me you didn't know what was the matter with him. He was turning blue and falling on his knees in front of you, and you were saying, *all right, all right, we'll* go *back to the car.*

"Is that what he said?"

That you didn't even know he was choking.

"Well I'll tell you the straight facts. This was in Utah, see. That's why Jack was sucking on a goddamned horehound drop in the first place. We were being shown through a mansion in Provo. The Mormons don't smoke, they don't drink, they don't even use coffee. They eat a lot of candy. Jack was sucking on a horehound drop and it got stuck in his throat. And then I ..." Matthau stood up and spread his arms in the air. "... I *saved* him! I turned him around and lifted him up, having seen that Heimlich Maneuver somewhere in the past, see, and I squeezed him and saved his life, and hurt my chest, having just had open-heart surgery not long before. So I still had a chest that looked like a Christmas turkey."

He indignantly popped another slice of apple into his mouth. "So he says I didn't save him, huh? Well what does he know? He forgets everything anyway. He gets drunk a lot. Besides, Jack can't possibly admit to me having saved his life because he couldn't handle it, having to walk around with that knowledge. *Plus,* of course, there was no doubt a lack of oxygen to the brain, so no wonder he couldn't remember."

The telephone rang again. Matthau answered. "Hello? Dr. Kerwin calling? Yes, I'll wait. Hello, doctor. What? You gave coffee to your dad when he was having a coronary and he went totally under? Were you a doctor then? You were *studying?* Jesus Christ! And *now* you know what? The vessels overly dilate in a migraine and you *want* to constrict them? What's that? Coffee is a dilator in the heart region and a constrictor in the cranium? Well I'll be a son of a bitch! No, doctor. That's all. No problem. Thanks."

He hung up. There was silence.

I finally spoke. Why do they go to Hawaii?

Matthau looked deeply introspective. "I see," he said after a moment. "I see. Yes, of course, why *do* the stockbrokers go to Hawaii?"

two

Hearts full of passion

I love uninhibited talkers who wave their hands and bare their hearts and hurtle into confessions. With the interviews in this chapter, I walked into situations that were waiting to happen.

Jerry Lewis surprised me by tape-recording the interview himself, maybe for his archives, maybe so he could check up on me. Stallone is one of the most colorful and dramatic speakers in the movies; he always sounds a little like Everett McKinley Dirksen. In an earlier interview with Tony Curtis, I was trying to sneak up on a question about his most famous alleged line of dialogue ("Yondah lies da castle of muh fadder") when he spontaneously volunteered, "I get so tired *of that* yondah lies da castle of muh fadder *shit! I never said that and I never woulda said it."*

Not long after the Dangerfield interview, Rodney came to Chicago to give two concerts at the Auditorium Theater. Afterward, I went along with him to the Pump Room for a late supper. The restaurant is famous for its telephone in Booth Number One. For Dangerfield, they installed a pay phone.

"Ha! Ha! I don't get no respect! Get it?"

During the long dinner, he grew more and more morose. He looked around the room and observed that every man there had a date except for him. What had they done? Why were *they so lucky? At fifteen dollars a ticket, he had filled the Auditorium twice. That was eight thousand times fifteen, or $120,000, which meant that after the house net and expenses, he cleared a hundred grand for two hours work. How come he was the only guy in the room without a broad?*

We closed the room. Outside at the curb, his limousine was waiting. Next to the limousine, a hooker was waiting to see who the limousine belonged to. Dangerfield said something to her. "Forget it," she said, and walked away. He got into the limo and was driven away alone.

Jerry Lewis

You can always tell the dangerous ones by their eyes.

Cannes, 1983

"I had left," Jerry Lewis was explaining. "I was gone for about two minutes. The heart goes into what they call v-tach." He demonstrated, clenching his fist. "It gets half-way closed and it freezes. I was dead and this lovely black nurse came and hit me a Larry Holmes shot to the chest and brought me back. *Then* I went into a state of fear."

This was a strange conversation to be having on a lovely spring afternoon in the south of France, where down on the beachfront the carpenters were hammering together the billboards for the thirty-sixth annual Cannes Film Festival.

Up here in his corner suite at the Carlton Hotel, Jerry Lewis was chewing on little blue candies that had, he said, only seven calories each. He'd suck one for a minute or two and then feed it to the small dog that was attentively begging at his feet. Lewis looked tanned and fit, with that jet-black hair still slicked back like some kid from the class of 1956 going out on his first date. We were talking about his open-heart surgery last December.

"Here's where it started," he said, showing me his right leg, bare all the way up to his tennis shorts. "See this incision? That's a vein. The scar goes all the way up the leg, all the way up the chest, all the way up the shoulder, and over the shoulder and halfway up the guy in the next room. After the operation you have a five-year-old heart. I hope so. I was working twenty hours a day. I felt great. I have been smoking three and a half packs of cigarettes a day for forty-three years. I felt great, and then ...

"The irony is, Michael De Bakey is a good friend of mine. But he couldn't get to Las Vegas in time to do the operation because, frankly, I didn't have five minutes to spare. And I've seen the operation. I've *scrubbed* with De Bakey. In Vegas, the doctor was leaning over me and I knew everything he was going to tell me about. The Black and Decker electric saw I knew about—*varroom*, to cut you open; the retractor they screw to open up your sternum, I knew all about that."

I asked if he'd had one of those beyond-and-back experiences while he was dead. One of those deals you read about in the *National Enquirer* where everything is bright light and your relatives are greeting you to the great beyond.

He popped a blue candy and squinted, remembering. "I only know there was a feeling of nodding off, that's all. And then, coming back, a feeling of waking up, but *oddly* ... waking up but feeling much better the other way."

The big aftereffect of the surgery, he said, is a feeling of forgetfulness: "I'm not as sharp as I should be. Things I should know perfectly well will elude me for a few seconds. That's one. Second, I have the tearies. Say the slightest nice thing about me and I'll break down in tears. Third, depression and terrible nightmares. De Bakey says it's all part of the recovery process and will be over at the end of six months."

Or maybe sooner. Jerry Lewis was back again in a nation whose very soil should act as a tonic for him. For the French, he is one of the greatest living artists, a master of the cinema, an immortal clown and a great director. It is safe to say he is less exalted in America. This year at Cannes, he was to co-star with Robert De Niro in the opening night film, Martin Scorsese's *The King of Comedy*.

"This is my country," he said. "I only *live* in America." He looked out the window at the palm trees waving along the beach. "The difference is, in France, I have critical *and* audience success. In America, only the audience loves me. My last film *(Hardly Working)*, received the worst American reviews ever written in the history of mankind. But it made a fortune. Why do the French love me? According to the American critics, because the French are morons. But look at this."

He pointed to a foot-high stack of magazines. "This is just one week. Every magazine in France is writing about me. Here's a picture of me at the airport with my luggage. Here's *Cahiers du Cinema,* the film magazine; you think they've already written everything there is to say about me? Look at this: eighteen pages."

Isn't it sort of strange, I asked, that you're here in a film about a star who is kidnapped and almost killed by his fans? And now here you are in Cannes, where the photographers and TV crews and fans are going to be rioting when you walk up the steps of the Festival Palace.

"The adulation," he said. "I love it in France. Over here, they get only this close, and no closer." He held his hand out at arm's length.

"In America, they get closer. They come up on top of you and over your back. They want to touch you. The scary ones are the ones who want to *be* you."

Lewis looked down at the coffee table between us, where a tape recorder was quietly recording our conversation. It was his tape recorder. It had been on since I entered the room.

"Why don't you use a tape recorder?" he asked.

I guess I just never have, I said.

"The reason I'm asking," he said, "is that if you use the tape recorder, you could look in the other person's eyes. And the eyes tell the story. In a threatening crowd, you can always tell the dangerous ones by their eyes.

"To the fanatics—and they're out there—he wants to get inside of you and spend some time there, looking through your eyes. You can spot those raving cuckoo birds, and you've gotta watch out for them. They love you so much they can kill you. That's what *King of*

Comedy is about.

"I'll give you an example. Years ago, I was playing the Chicago Theater. Dean Martin and I were doing our act. Backstage after the show, I saw this woman. She had eyes that looked like Michael Landon's eyes when he did *Teenage Werewolf.* I saw her, and I forgot her.

"The next night, Dean and I were doing a benefit for Kup's Harvest Moon Ball. There was this same woman. There were ten thousand people there, and Dean and I were protected by thirty or forty cops, but she got to me. She screamed, 'Jerry, I love you!' She grabbed me like this." Lewis grabbed me by the neck. "Twenty of those cops couldn't get her off of me. My face was the color of your jeans. I hit her a shot in the stomach as hard as I could. I hit her so hard that I swear the lady is *still* walking around Chicago with some kind of residue from that experience."

He leaned forward and took a stick of gum from the coffee table. He stopped his tape recorder, reversed it, and played back a few words: *The eyes tell the story.*

He started the recorder again. "So what I've learned about how to handle crowds," he said, "is always walk slow. What they want is a good look at you. If you walk fast, they're afraid they won't see, so they run to keep up, and mob psychology snowballs, and there's a riot.

"In a crowd, I always walk nice ... and ... slow." He stood up and began to walk through an imaginary crowd. *"Hello! Here I am! Hi! Look how slow I'm walking. Hi there, Buddy! How are you?"*

He sat back down. "You gotta make personal contact so they're not afraid you'll get away."

And yet, I mused, you say you don't mind the adulation. *The King of Comedy* paints a chilling portrait of fans who are fanatics, and here you are in Cannes to take the cheers for playing their victim. Strange.

"I love it when it's intended as a compliment," Lewis said. "Let's face it. There must be a lot of guys around who would love for all of this to be happening to them."

Sylvester Stallone

As soon as they touch me, my hand balls up into a fist.

Dubuque, Iowa 1977

This is not a good day for Sylvester Stallone. His best friend has died the day before. A fan has walked up to him in the street and hit him in the jaw. A sex film he made when he was twenty-one has surfaced in California and is being offered for rental at private parties. He sits in a darkened dressing room in burly work clothes and smokes a cigar and listens to a record of Caruso singing *Rigoletto.*

Outside in the street, behind the police barricades, three or four hundred people are waiting patiently in the sun for a glimpse of him. Most of them are young girls. *F.I.S.T.,* the first movie Stallone has made since *Rocky,* has been shooting on location in Dubuque for seven weeks now, but the crowds never go away.

Veteran movie people who have worked on dozens of locations with all the biggest stars say they've never seen anything like it, the way Stallone generates such yearning and such magnetism. Once in a while the girls get up a chant: *Rocky! Rocky!*

"I have this photograph that is the strangest thing," Stallone muses in the darkened room. "I'm signing autographs, and this young girl is reaching out to touch me, and she has the most frightening look on her face, as if this instant is transcendent for her. She isn't touching me, she's touching Rocky, an unreal person. I look dumbfounded.

"At first, the crowds were fun. I signed a lot of autographs, although I've never understood what people want with autographs. But now the insults start. One girl called me a name. Then another one *hit* me! Hard, on the jaw. I asked her why she'd done a thing like that. *Because you got what I want,* she says.

"People want more than you can give them. At first they want to touch. Then they want to grab. I'm not a person anymore. I'm someone to be challenged and taunted and stripped of my own identity. At last I understand about McQueen, Streisand and Newman ... how they become reclusive."

He draws on the cigar. Caruso fills the silence.

"This is my finale to public life," he says at last. "I've had it. I enjoyed the attention for a long time, but now I'm getting paranoid. As soon as they touch me, my hand balls up into a fist. It's no longer a five-fingered object. One of these days some nutso is gonna have a knife. So I stay in my hotel room and paint. I love it there. I would have been a great Trappist monk."

The last time we talked, I said, was in Chicago, before *Rocky* had opened. You were right on the edge of all this success and you were saying it was a good thing it didn't come any earlier in your life ...

"Right, because if I'd done *Rocky* when I was twenty-one, today I'd no doubt be a disc jockey in Omaha. I couldn't have handled it. All the years of failure sort of prepared me. Even now, I find myself being talked into situations that are bad for me. There are so many bad people in this business. The maggots in three-piece suits. A movie like *F.I.S.T.* is an exception.

"This is ... this is ..." He searches for the word. "The first *sophisticated* film I've ever done. I'll probably never again be in a film this big, with a nine million dollar budget. Most of the films I was in before *Rocky* were shot by Freaky Films Inc. from the back of a pickup truck with somebody looking out for the gendarmes and the script girl in the hospital for penicillin shots.

"I remember my first film, when I was twenty-one. I was literally starving in New York. I lived for five days in the Port Authority Bus Terminal and didn't eat for most of that time, and I was cold and sick and broke. I was on the very brink of committing a criminal act, and I got this offer to be in a movie called *Party at Kitty and Studs.* They wanted to know if I'd take off my clothes. *Why not?* I said. I take them off for free at home every night.

"I don't think the movie was ever released. And yet you know what they're doing today? They're marketing that piece of scum in Hollywood. They want $100,000 rental to show it at private parties, the parasitical scumbags." He laughed bitterly. "Hell, for $100,000, forget the film, I'll be there myself. But at the time I made the film, it was the solution to a problem, which was that I was starving and broke."

There was a knock on the door; Stallone would be needed for the next scene and should go to the makeup department. He got up, stubbed out his cigar, turned off the stereo. He picked up the album jacket and looked idly at Caruso. He had something on his mind.

"The Oscar will never again mean what it would have meant this year," he said at last. "Not for me, and all the people who believed in me. Justice was not served."

He was talking about his Oscar nomination for best screenplay, although he was also nominated as best actor, and *Rocky* itself, of course, won as the year's best picture.

"You know," he said, "I wanted a duplicate of that statue, the one for best picture. I wrote it, I acted in it, but they wouldn't give me one. They gave statues to the producer and director. That bothered me. A *copy* was all I wanted, for Christ's sake. Even without any writing on it. I feel a little bitter about that now. I identify with the guys who were nominated five, six times, and the first time they had a ten-minute speech ready but by the time they finally won the goddamned thing they were like Gable: *Thanks.*

"I didn't even want the statue for myself. I wanted it for Jane Oliver. She was in the hospital and I wanted to take it to her. She died of cancer yesterday. Frigging cancer. She had it last December, when we were touring to promote *Rocky,* but she didn't tell me. She was my mentor, my psychiatrist, my mother, the most important friend in my life."

He braced himself and walked out of the room, heading for makeup and for the next scene, and for the crowds of girls behind the police lines.

He had one more thing to say.

"Now that she's gone, I can't trust anybody anymore now. There's such a void that she left. Now I can only trust people from the past."

Tony Curtis

I'm developing an insular relationship with myself.

Cannes, 1983

Tony Curtis was trying to think up a better title for his new movie. The current title was *Othello, the Black Commando.* "What do you think about *The Othello Conspiracy?*" he asked. "How about *Othello File? The Othello Connection?*"

His eyes drifted restlessly out the window of his third-floor room in the Carlton Hotel. Suddenly he jumped to his feet and pressed his nose against the glass.

"Will ya look at the build on that lady!" he shouted. He pushed the curtain aside. "There ... the one with the blonde hair and the leopard-skin leotard! See her?" I did not. "Standing in the middle of the intersection, chewing the hell out of that guy?"

I saw her. But from the third floor, I could not see so easily what Tony Curtis saw in her. "Jesus, I got great eyes!" he said. "She's really mad at that guy. Menachem, take a look!"

Menachem Golan, whose Cannon Group will distribute *Othello* once it is named, glanced out the window and shrugged. "Women like that are a dime a dozen at Cannes," he said. He turned his attention to a gigantic wall chart with colored pins stuck in it to record the sales of his twenty-seven current productions in fifty-six different world marketing territories.

"She's turning this way!" Tony Curtis said. "Look at those tits! She's really mad at that guy!"

He turned to move to another window. An overstuffed chair was in his way. He stepped on the seat cushion and hurdled the chair. He opened the French doors leading to the balcony and shouted, *"Mon petit! Mon petit!* Yoo hoo! Up here! Look up here!"

Incredibly, the blonde in the leotard heard him above the tumult of the Carlton Terrace, which on the last Sunday of the Cannes Film Festival was shoulder-to-shoulder with distributors, exhibitors and movie stars ranging from James Keach to Harry Reems. She shielded her eyes against the sun and looked up at the balcony where the tanned middle-age guy with the thinning hair was waving at her.

"Mon petit!" Tony Curtis shouted. "Don't be so angry! It's all right!"

Does she know who you are? I asked.

Curtis hardly glanced back over his shoulder. "She knows exactly who I am," he said. He shouted again: "Come up here, *mon petit.* Up here. Room 241! Two ... four ... one!"

She waved and turned to walk back toward the hotel entrance. She was followed by another blonde woman and by the small man she had been shouting at.

Curtis turned back from the window with a triumphant grin on his face. "And what were you asking?" he asked.

Well, about this new film ... I said.

"We're here selling the film. You call this a festival? I call it a marketplace. I'm in my element. This is my heritage. Some people criticize this festival for being too crass. Ha! What do they sell at the Fulton Fish Market? Fish! What does the Fulton Fish Market smell like? Fish! Case closed."

He sat down again in his chair by the window, put on a gray top hat, and picked up a silver-headed cane. He was otherwise dressed in a T-shirt and jeans.

"I've never sold a movie here before," he said. "I've acted, I've produced ... Now I've got a new job! Salesman. I sold the film to Australia this morning. The guy said would I come to Australia to promote it? I said sure. He said a lot of people make promises they don't live up to. I said he hadn't done business with me before. Besides, this picture, I got a piece of the action, so to speak. In fact, not just a piece. Let's put it this way. If your shirt is this film, my piece is a sleeve. I wonder where those girls are?"

He leaned back in his chair and let the sun fall through the window onto his face. He does not have, in middle age, the stunning handsomeness that first made him a movie star in the late forties and early fifties, but he has something that is perhaps more rare, boundless energy and optimism. Here he was, promoting a film that frankly sounded like B-grade exploitation, and his eyes shone with enthusiasm.

"This is a modern version of Shakespeare's great tragedy, *Othello,"* he explained. "Max Boulois plays Othello. He's a black general with two or three hundred mercenaries working for him. Just a small army, you know. He gets hired by minor league Arab oil sheiks who are fighting over a valley of land.

"I play his aide. My name is Colonel Iagovich. Get it? Then this white chick comes along. Her name is Dede, which is short for Desdemona, and she's worried about all the starving children, and wants to hire Othello's soldiers to fight for right. She is disturbed, to put it another way, by the inequalities of world leverage." He paused for a moment to listen to how that sounded. "Or call it what you will. Anyway, you can easily imagine what happens next."

He stood up and struck a pose with his cane. "Shakespeare," he said, "when he wrote this story, he got it from somewhere—and we got it from Shakespeare. What goes around, comes around. Only *our* version is a lot more human than Shakespeare, and the human condition is examined much more fiercely in our film than in Shakespeare. There will be no posturing! Next case."

How is life going for you right now? I asked.

"Terrific! I've just been granted a divorce, and in the settlement, I keep the house. I've had fourteen houses and three wives so far. Not necessarily in that order. This is the first time I've had any peace. I'm learning to sleep alone in a bed. I'm developing an insular relationship with myself. I'm so privileged to be with me, everywhere I go. I hope I don't screw it all up."

Where do you get your energy?

"I'm so driven, I don't understand it! I've been up since six this morning, and I'm *burning,* pal, *burning!* No drugs, no drinks ... I could no more sit out there on the terrace, I'd be so bored ... I'll tell you one thing." His voice dropped. "The privilege of living is a great privilege."

The reason I wanted to interview you at Cannes, I said, is that you're a legendary movie star and this is a legendary film festival, and I wanted to see how you went together.

"We suit each other perfectly," he said. "Cannes audiences and I embrace each other. I adore it! Cannes is an entity, and I reach out to it and say, *Give me five!*" He slapped his open hand against his palm. "I love it! I look out the window, and some chickie tears her shirt off and the photographers shoot her big tits, and she's selling a movie called *Tits Galore,* and that's show business, pal! That's where it's at! Case closed!"

He looked around impatiently. "I wonder where those ladies are?"

Menachem Golan looked in at the door.

"When those ladies get up here," Curtis said, "I want them shown right in."

"You have an interview with Australian television," Golan said. "They're setting up their cameras right now."

"Great! I love it!" said Tony Curtis. "You know some people actually knock this place? They were knocking Harry Reems to me. He's the porno star? I say so what! His movies are movies, too. They will be seen in perpetuity. They may change their titles, they may forget who made them, but they will last forever!"

Speaking of immortality, I said, I wanted to ask you about your children. Especially your daughter Jamie Lee Curtis, who is a movie star herself now.

"I have six children, all very devoted to their father, very loving," he said. "I have no truck whatsoever with my ex-wives. But I love the children. I don't see that much of them, but when I get a shade older, perhaps, God willing, I can have a house for all of us. Meanwhile, at this glorious time of my life, I am surrounded by so much unique success, I don't even know how I maneuvered it all. I could make ten to twelve million off my share of *Othello!* Do I take that lightly? No way, MacVay! But I'm not doing it for the money—I don't want to leave a lot of money to my children. I do it because I like the action! I don't know where it's going to take me, but, my dear friend, I want to go!"

Do you like the attention, the crowds, the flashbulbs?

"It's an occupational hazard, which I love. The young actors who say they don't want to give autographs, they don't want to be turned down, so they turn you down first. I know I'm not gonna be turned down, and I love it when beautiful young women look at me with sensual eyes, and part their lips in love and admiration."

Have you gotten lucky this trip? I asked.

"Lucky!" Tony Curtis put back his head and laughed. "Have I ever! I get lucky without even trying! I love it! I'm like a con man. They sail me around on a yacht, they drive me in a Rolls-Royce, I get a first-class ticket, and I don't even have to come up with seven and a half cents! I've been laughing for thirty years, pal!"

Someone said the Australian TV crew was ready. As Curtis walked into the hallway, the ladies from downstairs entered. They were statuesque and incredibly buxom, wearing Wonder Woman-style silver headbands, armbands, legbands, ankle bracelets and metal belts. They looked armored.

"The fourth Mrs. Curtis!" Tony shouted. The little man came in and introduced himself as their official translator.

"Enchanted!" Curtis said. "This is the *real* Cannes! Next case!"

He sat down in front of the Australian TV cameras with a blonde on each knee, his face framed by their bulging bosoms. The interviewer, a diffident BBC type with a cultured accent, cleared his throat nervously and began.

"Mr. Curtis, ah, we'd like to ask you first of all about some of your great co-stars, like Marilyn Monroe, for example."

"But she's dead," Curtis said. "I do not speak of the dead."

The inteviewer plowed ahead with questions about Othello and Shakespeare, and then signed off. Curtis got up and patted the two women on the back.

"How'd you like my autograph?" he said. They squealed with delight, and he signed autographs for them. Then he apologized that he would have to excuse himself to do another interview, and they departed down the hotel hallway.

As he headed for the next interview, Tony Curtis paused for a second, took my arm, winked, and said, "Can you believe this?"

Chapter Two

Rodney Dangerfield

What good would it do, if I got so much love I killed myself?

New York, 1983

Hey, folks! Folks! There's a guy up here tellin' jokes!

I will not soon forget my first sight of Rodney Dangerfield. He was standing on a table in his undershorts, shouting, "Don't worry! They sewed them shut!" Sweat was pouring off his face and neck. As fast as an assistant could throw him towels, he was mopping his brow. His hair was the color of old dishwater, his knees knocked, his eyes bulged out of his face, his hands and his elbows shook in different rhythms, and he was wearing black wing tip dress shoes and socks held up with a garter belt.

When I was a kid, I was so ugly, you'll never believe how ugly I was. I was so ugly, they wanted me to be the Poster Child for birth control.

"All right now, everybody, quiet down, please," said Jim Signorelli, who was directing Dangerfield's new movie. "Are you ready, Rodney?"

"Ready? I'm dyin' up here. This is the weirdest thing I ever heard of. I'm about to start bein' funny and so you tell everybody to shut up. *No laughs, everybody—he's being funny now!* I'll tell you what it is. It's a comic's nightmare, that's what it is!"

"Right," said Signorelli. *"Action!"*

Dangerfield, standing on the tabletop in his underwear and wing tips, began to vibrate. His elbows knocked against his rib cage, his hands were palsied, his neck jerked back and forth. A platoon of three tailors descended on him, measuring everything at once: his arms, legs, biceps, hat size, wrists, ankles and other parts not often measured by even the most meticulous tailors.

"Cut! Print!" said Signorelli. Dangerfield's vibrations slowed somewhat.

"Mr. Dangerfield?" a photographer said. "Could you turn this way, please?"

"Hey, take it easy, honey, will ya? I ain't got no good side!"

I'm so ugly, when I was a kid, my father bought a new billfold, and instead of my picture, he carried the picture of the kid who came with the wallet.

This was an old movie studio up in Harlem, where movies were made in the early days and are now being made again. The name of the movie is *Easy Money,* and Dangerfield plays a Rodneyesque character, an Italian-American family man who is given a chance to inherit the family firm if only he will swear off drinking, smoking, gambling and all other vices for one year.

Dangerfield clambered down from the table and pulled a dressing gown around his shoulders. He was still dripping sweat. "I like it cold," he said. "You know: semi-warm." His longtime agent and personal manager, Estelle Endler, a dark-haired woman with a great smile, ushered him off the set and into a dressing room. I crowded in after him, and we were joined by his nephew from Miami and his nephew's wife and children, who sat somewhat solemnly through our interview and seemed just a little unsure of exactly what the public role of a Rodney Dangerfield relative ought to be.

"This movie, it's killin' me," Dangerfield said. "I'm a nightclub comic. I can't go to sleep until 3:30 in the morning. On this picture, they get me up at 4:30. I'm dying. It's supposed to be flattering to be the star. I don't want to be the star no more. I want to maybe write a movie and appear in a few of the scenes. You know, *just* enough scenes so I'm in the goddamn thing, but not enough so I'm busting my ass every day."

But when you're a star, I said, the people love you. They want to see you in every scene.

Dangerfield thought about that. "You got the wrong guy," he said. "I'm not a true artist. I'm a comic. I know nightclubs. That's where I grew up. A true artist, he wants to give of himself for his public. He makes sacrifices for his image. It's all very flattering, but you can kill yourself. We all need love. Don't get me wrong. What the world needs now is love. But not to put your life in jeopardy. What good would it do me, if I got so much love I killed myself?"

He mopped his sweating neck with a towel.

"Plus," he said, "I quit smoking eight days ago."

And in this movie you give up everything?

"Almost everything. Smoking, drinking, gambling. It is coincidental that I gave up smoking for real while I am playing a man who gave up smoking. I gave up smoking because of my voice. My voice was getting hoarse. I needed it for the opera scene. I may never smoke again. I'm serious about this. There are still other vices you can do. I tried marijuana once. Once was enough. I play the slot machines occasionally. I like a couple of cocktails before dinner. Nice dinner, a couple of drinks."

My wife and I, we have a perfect plan to save our marriage. A nice little French restaurant, candlelight, a nice bottle of wine. I go on Tuesday, she goes on Thursday.

Dangerfield will be sixty this year. He is at the top of his game. He recently made his sixty-eighth appearance on the "Tonight" show. His last album, *No Respect,* won a Grammy. His cameo appearance in the 1980 movie *Caddyshack* was credited in the industry with helping to boost that movie's performance at the box office. He runs Dangerfield's nightclub in New York, and appears there occasionally. He has another album in the works.

It is not so much that he is peaking late, but that he started late. The Rodney Dangerfield story is an inspiration for anyone who ever wondered if it was possible, at the age of forty-four, to leave a career as a salesman and become a standup nightclub comedian. That's what Dangerfield did. In his youth, between the ages of eighteen and thirty, he had his first career, as a comedian named Jack Roy. Then he married, left show business, and settled down. Fourteen years later, still yearning for audiences, he made a second stab at a career, and when he was hired for the "Ed Sullivan Show" after a blind audition, he was reborn as Rodney Dangerfield.

Life on the road was murder. I played one date, it was so far out in the sticks, I was reviewed by Field and Stream.

Somewhere in the distant past of this strange and complicated man, there is even a real name. I was thinking that the nephew from Miami would probably be in a position to supply me with it, but I never got a chance to ask him.

"Now they want me to make another movie," Dangerfield was saying. "They want me to do a remake of *My Little Chickadee,* with W.C. Fields and Mae West."

Who are you getting, I asked, to play the W.C. Fields role?

"That's *one,"* he said. "I'm counting."

"We'll make the movie this summer," Estelle Endler said.

"That's what *she* says," Dangerfield said. "I don't want to work this hard. Who needs it? I hear about movies, I never get a chance to see them. Everybody talks about *My Favorite Year.* The movie starts at eight o'clock. I get off here at seven. By the time I get the makeup off and wash this gray dye outta my hair, already I'm late for the movie."

You've got to be the first person in history, I said, to dye your hair to *make* it that color.

"That's *two."*

"Tell about the character you play," Endler said.

"This guy?" said Rodney. "He's an Italian from Staten Island. That's a borough of Manhattan. I *know* you got Italians in Chicago. Maybe not from Staten Island. I know this guy that I play because I grew up with guys like this guy. In a way, he's like me. In another way, he's a character. No matter who I play, in some ways I'm playing myself, only a little off, you know? This guy is a nicer guy than the guy in *Caddyshack.* He's a wise-cracking guy, only more humble."

In a way, I said, that's like you. You play a guy who's loud and yet somehow humble ...

"Yeah," said Dangerfield. "I don't get no respect. Not to be too modest, but when I met Jack Benny for the first time, he told me his gimmick was, he was thirty-nine and a cheapskate. But my gimmick was, I don't get no respect—which he said everybody could identify with."

What makes you so popular? I asked. You're a hero on college campuses. You were asked to be the speaker at Class Day at Harvard. Why do kids forty years younger than you identify with you? You've got to be the only sixty-year-old standup comic who's a hero on the campus.

"Because I never grew up," said Dangerfield. "And, plus, it's a combination of things." He counted them off on his fingers. "One, I don't get no respect. Everyone thinks they're a loser in life, particularly some kid in college. Two, I got a young head, because I never grew up, or else I wouldn't be in this business, killin' myself. Third, I work quite hard at making everything I do funny. When I go on Carson, I always got all new stuff. Number four, which is, maybe I'm funny."

My wife likes to talk while she's making love. Last night, she called me up from the Holiday Inn.

"Work and sleep," he said. "That's all that's in the cards for me. I'm killing myself. I need love, but this is ridiculous."

An assistant director poked his head into the dressing room to inform us that Mr. Dangerfield was required for the next scene. He got up, toweled himself, and left the dressing room. Then he stuck his head back in the door.

"Excuse me, I gotta go and make a small fortune," he said.

He left. Then he came back. "Don't put that in about the small fortune," he said. "It might sound bad."

He left. Then he returned again. "*Plus,* another reason why I'm so popular," he said, "is that I'm just too much."

He left.

Guy goes into a bar with a duck under his arm. Bartender says, "Where'd you get the pig?" Guy says, "This is a duck." Bartender says, "I was talking to the duck."

three

Woman needs man, and man must have his mate

These are eyewitness accounts of some time in the histories of the two great Hollywood palimony cases, Groucho and Erin and Lee and Michelle, with a postscript about Marvin's eventual happy domestication.

Nobody asked me during all of those court trials, but I would have testified that as nearly as I could see, both Erin Fleming and Michelle Triola were warm and helpful companions to their men.

Not long after the Groucho piece ran in Esquire, *I met Groucho and Erin at the Cannes Film Festival, where Groucho was decorated by the French government. Late that evening, upstairs in his suite at the Carlton, Groucho held court and his admirers sat in a circle at his feet, and Erin brought him tea and held his hand and smiled at his double entendres, of which there were many. I had the feeling that Groucho might have stayed at home, if Erin hadn't acted as, essentially, the producer of the last act of his life.*

Lee Marvin, on the other hand, was not one to vegetate, and did not need Triola to keep him in the public eye. I have only the insights that can be gathered from the pieces. He is just as much a character now as he was then, but calmer and clearly happier. Getting off the booze probably has a lot to do with that.

Groucho Marx

The only great party is a boy and a girl and a whole cheesecake.

Beverly Hills, 1972

I. Tuesday afternoon at Le Bistro, a restaurant in Beverly Hills

Groucho Marx was wearing blue jeans, Hush Puppies, a brown sport shirt buttoned at the neck, an ancient tweed sport jacket, a cap and a pepper-and-salt overcoat. He peered into the gloom of Le Bistro, seeking out familiar faces, while a young lady introduced herself to me: "My name is Erin Fleming. I'm Mr. Marx's secretary."

"A likely story," Groucho said. He led the way up the stairs to the second floor. "I always eat on the second floor here," he said. "It's closer to the men's room. *Esquire* isn't my favorite magazine, you know. Interviews are really murder. They keep asking you questions. I could be brought up on a rape charge. I don't mind a hatchet job, if it's truthful ... *could* you pin a rape charge on me? Could you try? I'd appreciate it. You don't do any dental work, do you? I have to go to the dentist before I go to France."

The sun fell brightly into the upper room, which was less crowded than the fashionable downstairs. There was a Paris motif of brass and mirrors and plush maroon opulence. The tables were occupied mostly by ladies, in twos and threes and fours.

"Look at that, will you?" Groucho said. "Broads on alimony. It's disgusting the money they're probably spending."

We sat at a wall table opposite the bar.

"They have the world's finest cheesecake in this place," Groucho announced. "Believe me, I've had cheesecake all over, and this is the best cheesecake I've had. You know Miss Fleming here? She's an actress. She's done Shaw. She's even done Shakespeare. She's in the new Woody Allen movie. They say Allen got something from the Marx Brothers. He got nothing. Maybe twenty years ago, he might have been inspired. Today he's an original. The best, the funniest. Waiter?"

The waiter approached.

"How would you apprise the cheesecake situation?" Groucho asked.

"Very nice, sir," the waiter said.

"Don't change the subject. And bring pumpernickel, I want a lot of pumpernickel. Not toasted. This place has the greatest pumpernickel. And cheesecake. This picture is rated R that she's in, the Allen picture. I think it's very dirty. It might even be filthy. But that's only to me. I'm really a prude. I don't like dirty comedy. She showed me some of the script, and I was horrified just reading it. She does things in it I've never been able to persuade her to do in the privacy of my own home."

"Grouch!" Erin said.

"So anyway, as I was already saying, I'm going to the Cannes Film Festival. I'm going to be honored by the French government, they're going to make me a Cannes-man. For a while I thought it was canceled. I hoped so."

"Grouch, you know they've planned the whole festival around you," Erin said.

"No, they're showing films from all over the world," Groucho said. "It's an international event."

"But you're the big one, baby."

"A cup of lentil soup and the steak tarter," Groucho told the waiter.

"Very good, sir. The steak *tartare*."

"That's right, the steak tarter. And three cheesecakes. Lindy's, in New York, they used to talk about the cheesecake there. If they don't have it here today I'll kill myself. If you take one bite, I'll kill *you*. A piece of cheesecake here should cost a hundred bucks. What we should really do is order it now."

"I'll wrap mine up and you can eat it for dinner tonight," Erin said.

"It's worth taking home more than any broad in this place is worth taking home. This is going on the cover of *Esquire?* I was on the cover of *Harper's* once, all by myself. And I was on the cover of *Newsweek*. I was on the cover of *Time* twice—once by myself and once with my brothers. Christ, is it cold in here. I shoulda ordered chili."

"I'll get your coat and your cap, darling," Erin said. She fetched them from the cloakroom and Groucho got up and put on his overcoat and his Irish tweed cap. Then he sat back down at the table.

"First I'm going to Iowa," he said. "I'm going to be honored by the University of Iowa. Then I'm doing Carnegie Hall. It's the first time I've done New York in years. Then I sail to France. After I get back, I want to play Washington, Philly, Boston, probably Chicago. I'm glad that critic isn't there anymore, that Claudia Cassidy. She was the most vicious, with the possible exception of Percy Hammond. I guess this table is condemned. Where's my steak tarter? They put us here and left us to our own resources. Reserve three orders of cheesecake."

Erin got up to reserve us three orders of cheesecake.

"Percy Hammond reviewed us at the Majestic Theater in Chicago," Groucho said. "He said the Marx Brothers and several relatives ran around the stage for about an hour, why he'd never understand. That was one of his *good* reviews. Later, he came to New York and went to work for the *Herald Tribune*. He had a drinking problem. I wrote one of his reviews for him once. He reviewed Evelyn Thaw ... Harry Thaw's wife? He shot Stanford White. You never heard of *him*, for Christ's sake? He shot *Stanford White!* That's the trouble with being interviewed by a kid. Then the war came."

"What war, darling?" Erin asked, returning to the table.

"Second. They had a meeting at the *Trib*, six or eight of the big factotums. Ring Lardner was working there at the time. The editor suggested sending Percy Hammond to Europe to cover the war. *For Christ's sake!* Lardner says, *you can't do that! Supposing he doesn't like it?*"

Groucho allowed himself a smile.

"I'm gonna work onstage at Carnegie Hall," he said. "Talk, sing a few songs that nobody remembers anymore ... It's freezing in here!" He wrapped his coat around himself. "Everything I have is frozen ...

I'm not going to have a script, just a few notes to remind myself what I want to talk about. They're paying me ten thousand dollars for the night's work. Not bad. I'm eighty-one years old, and I'm proud of it. Usually it's the reverse, people lie about their age.

"I'm still alive, I'm still functioning ... intellectually ... my brain is still working, that is. I read that piece in *Esquire* about Teddy Kennedy. Is he serious about not running for the presidency? It said he hits the bottle. I have a couple of brothers who are dead—I'm not a drunk.

"Gummo and Zeppo live at the Springs, where there is abundant golf and tennis. I don't go down much, but I miss them. They come in whenever the weather gets too hot. I think we were the only group that never fought. Four-a-day, on edge, tired, fighting the audience, we never fought ... That was a great time, that was the time of the Algonquin crowd."

"You could tell the one about Woollcott," Erin said.

"*You* could tell the one about Woollcott," Groucho said. "You seem to remember it so well. I want to tell the one about Benchley. This was at the Garden of Allah. One night they were all drinking. *One* night! *Ha!* And ... will you look at that steak tarter?"

He examined it with appreciation, even lust.

"So Benchley takes a mattress and cuts it open, takes out the feathers, and glues them all over Charlie Butterworth's ass. Then they send for the doctor. The doctor asks Charlie to take his pants down."

Groucho rocked with silent laughter.

"The world is so serious now," he said after a moment. "Nothing used to be past Harpo. In those days, people used to joke more, they weren't so serious. I knew Fields well. He used to sit in the bushes in front of his house with a BB gun and shoot at people. Today, he'd probably be arrested.

"He invited me over to his house, he had his girlfriend there. I think her name was Carlotta Monti. Car-lot-ta *MON*-ti! That's the kind of name a girl of Fields would have. He had a ladder leading up to his attic. Without exaggeration, there was fifty thousand dollars in liquor up there. Crated up like a wharf. I'm standing there and Fields is standing there, and nobody says anything. The silence is oppressive. Finally, he speaks: *This will carry me twenty-five years.*"

Groucho scrutinized his steak tartare. "I'll try it and if I don't like it," he told me, "throw yours away."

"You know those magazines like *Playboy?*" Erin said. "They could learn a lot from Grouch. How to dress, how to enjoy life ..."

"It's very good steak tarter," Groucho said. "I only eat steak tarter at places I trust. Otherwise, I might get feathers on my ass."

"I'll have a taste," Erin said, extending her fork in the direction of Groucho's plate.

"Why don't you have a taste of *his?*" Groucho said. He leaned toward me. "She gets a sexual kick out of eating my food. The only kick she's getting, by the way."

"The subject of sex is incredibly complicated," Erin said. "*Playboy* printed some of the findings of Masters and Johnson ..."

"They were printed there *first?*" Groucho said.

"They subsidized some of their *research,*" Erin said. "Sweetheart, I told you this *before.*"

"Masters and Johnson, they're going to tell me I'm doing everything wrong. I *am* doing everything wrong, but I'm not worrying about it—*she* is."

"Ummm, this whitefish is delicious," Erin said.

"You see why she loves me?" Groucho said. "Not for what she can get at night, but for what she can get at lunch." He sang under his breath: "*Sometimes I love you, sometimes I hate you* ... that's a very accurate statement. Don't get married! Stay in love! Marriage kills love ... unless you're after five or six kids, and if you are the police will catch you. Look at what happened to Mussolini. What a *schmuck,* to die upside down. He wanted to see if his girl was wearing underwear. What a *schlemiel.*"

"But you do like McGovern, don't you baby?" Erin asked.

"Warren Beatty is organizing some stuff," Groucho said. "I think I like McGovern the best. But out at Iowa, I might not talk about politics. Maybe I might. I might if I feel like it. I won't if I don't. I spent my honeymoon in an upper berth going through Iowa. My wife was up there with me."

"Which wife?" Erin said.

"Ruth," Groucho said.

"Groucho was married to Ruth for twenty years," Erin said. "She was a wonderful woman. She died last week ... two weeks ago ...."

"She was a nice woman," Groucho said. "She went on to become what most women do, a big drinker. I had three wives and they all liked it. They used it as an escape. What *she* does, she runs and locks the bedroom door."

"I don't live in your house, Groucho," Erin said, making sure I got that down.

"Wait'll you get to Paris," Groucho said.

"Wait till I get into the *shops* in Paris," Erin said.

"Wait till I get into *you* in Paris," Groucho said.

He got up from his seat. "A good thing, this second floor," he said. "Close to the men's room. *Do you want the bridal chamber?* the fellow asks. *No, I always use the window.*"

He walked through the sunny room in overcoat and cap, nodding to the ladies as he passed their tables.

"He had this operation, very serious, after his divorce from Eden," Erin said. "A doctor named Joe Kaufman at UCLA saved his life. When I met him, he was spending all day in bed, he didn't care if he got up or not. Now he's filled with plans again ... and if you're going to mention me, do you have my name right? Erin Fleming? I was a stage actress in New York for nine years, off-Broadway. I got tired of playing in places where somebody who'd been on 'Mannix' got two hundred dollars more. I came out here, and several people wanted to introduce me to Groucho. He offered me a job working for him. I'm really only his secretary."

Groucho approached across the room, already talking: "I've had cheesecake in Paris, London, Mexico City. This is the best cheesecake in the world."

The waiter, just arrived from the kitchen, placed the cheesecake reverently upon the table.

"Send out the chef!" Groucho said. "My compliments! It's probably frozen, you know ...."

"Grouch, do you remember how you met me?" Erin asked.

"In my bedroom, five minutes ago. The only great party is a boy and a girl and a whole cheesecake. Where's the chef? Only goes to prove that Jews make bad waiters. *See this cheesecake? There's a fly in it! Quiet! Everybody will want one!*"

He inspected his cheesecake for the imaginary fly. "This is like an interview with Milton Berle," he said. "I got twenty-five dollars from *Reader's Digest* last week for something I never said. I get credit all the time for things I never said. You know that line in 'You Bet Your Life'? The guy says he has seventeen kids and I say: *I smoke a cigar, but I take it out of my mouth occasionally?* I never said that."

Erin wrapped her cheesecake in a paper napkin, for Groucho to have after his dinner.

"Now her," he said, "I keep throwing her out, she keeps coming back."

"You told me you didn't *mean* it, baby," Erin said playfully.

"She always comes back on Tuesdays. Tuesday is payday. Don't worry, sweetest. Your check is at home."

"I know, Grouch."

"She's so sentimental."

"Why don't you tell your story about Woollcott at the Algonquin, sweetheart?"

"I think I will." He took a big bite of cheesecake and chased it with black Sanka. "Woollcott was sitting at the Round Table, and ... that's a good idea, I'm glad you reminded me. When I play Carnegie Hall, I think I'll stay at the Algonquin."

"But that's so far from Bloomingdale's. Why can't you stay at the Carlton? Like you were going to?"

"No, no, I think I'll stay at the Algonquin."

"But babe," Erin said, "if you stay at the Carlton and I stay at my *apartment* ..."

"Who said anything about anybody staying at your apartment?" Groucho said. "I'll get you a room at the Algonquin. The guy who owns it is a very close friend of Gummo's. They'll be happy to have me there. And the whole theatre district is between Forty-third and Forty-fifth streets. It's a *wonderful* idea. I think I'll call them this afternoon."

"We'll talk about it later," Erin said firmly.

"You know," said Groucho, "I *can* always get a broad in New York, you know."

He reached inside his coat and came out with a cigar. "You want a cheap cigar?"

I don't smoke, I said.

"Don't change the subject."

Silence at the table. Groucho lit up while casting an appraiser's eye around the room.

"Maybe one of *these* ladies ... one of *these* muffs ... that's a lovely word, muff ... I hate that other word. Muff is a lovely word. I can't insult anyone. They all think I'm kidding."

Silence again. I hear you're keeping a diary, I said at last.

"I'm not keeping a diary. *She* is." He studied the end of his cigar.

"I am really," Erin said. "I hope to sell it to the *New Yorker.* I write one page a night. I start at ten and write until three, doing it over and over until every word is right."

"It'll be filthy," Groucho said. "Why don't you title it *My Free Trip to Cannes and Other Assorted Schweinerei."*

"Schweinerei?" Erin said.

"It's what you find in the bottom of a garbage can."

"I thought I'd call it *Groucho—The Living Legend."*

"I like Benchley's *The Life of Christ and Other Short Stories,"* Groucho said. He finished his Sanka. "I try to exercise a little every day," he said. "I like to take a walk. And I do try to sing a little every day. The throat is a muscle and if you don't use it, like any other muscle it goes to hell."

The luncheon was over and as we walked toward the door Groucho passed the time of day with the ladies at the tables: "Which way to Beverly Hills? Are you on alimony? How much do you get? Never mind—it's not enough. I'm very expensive."

Late that afternoon, the telephone rang in my hotel room. It was Erin, with the name and number of the person to contact in Ames, in case I could get out to the State University of Iowa.

"We spent some time this afternoon with Warren Cowan," she said. "From Rogers, Cowan and Brenner? Groucho has hired them to do his public relations, with this big thing at Carnegie Hall and Cannes coming up. I think there might be a move underfoot to give Grouch an honorary Academy Award, like they're doing for Chaplin."

That would be a great idea, I said.

"The Marx Brothers were funnier than Chaplin," she said. "And besides, they weren't leftists. And there's this feeling, you know, that he might as well get it before he croaks, et cetera. Before I came along, he never got out of bed. It gives him a goal to aim for. He's *so* funny. And so American, too. But in the article, just call me his secretary, okay? Instead of he's eighty-one and I'm some young chick. He's really been taken by a lot of sharp chicks. But we would *never* get married. Just call me his secretary, or his constant companion, or something. I do go with someone else, really."

II. Le Bistro, Saturday evening, eleven days later

The upstairs room had been reserved for a private party. Marshall Field, the publisher, and Bailey K. Howard, the former chairman of Field Enterprises, were throwing their annual pre-Academy Awards bash, and the cool alimony ladies at their sunny tables were nowhere to be found.

The party had been planned along Hawaiian lines, and waiters with Polynesian *hors d'oeuvres* pressed through a crush of the most incredibly diverse types: Alfred Hitchcock and Willie Shoemaker, Helen Gurley Brown and William Friedkin, Hugh Hefner and Ann Miller and Sig Sakowicz and King Vidor and Rhonda Fleming and Mike Frankovich. In the inner room a four-piece group played "Sweet Leilani."

Groucho and Erin arrived a few minutes before nine, and Erin staked out the first table inside the door of the inner room. Several chairs were tilted against the table to reserve them in anticipation of the Warren Cowan party, expected to arrive momentarily. Warren had a lot of ideas about what to do with Groucho's account, Erin said.

Groucho, meanwhile, was paying no attention to the chairs or to Erin, either. He was looking around the room with a mildly lecherous eye, and he perked up when Edy Williams walked in. She was wearing a floor-length white gown that was ... you couldn't be sure ... from certain angles ... see-through.

"Wanna dance?" he asked, softly.

"Aren't you Groucho Marx, the living legend?" Edy breathed, running a finger under his chin.

"It's not my fault all the others are dead," Groucho said.

Edy floated on through the room, Groucho following her progress closely.

"Want me to get you your food, darling?" Erin asked.

"I don't know what they have, baby. If it's this Hawaiian dreck, forget it."

Erin went to see what they had.

"I'm looking forward to this college date," Groucho said. "In vaudeville, we did all those little cities in Iowa, Illinois, the Midwest. I was brought up in small-time vaudeville. These days, there's no chance to try out your act in front of an audience. Television isn't much. I watch the political programs. Otherwise it's all junk except for a few shows. The two schvartzes, I watch them, and 'All in the Family.' That's it."

Edy Williams drifted up on Groucho's other side and whispered: "What do you think about birth control?"

"I didn't get the name."

"Birth control."

"Who in the hell is that? Are you in code?"

"*Birth* control, Groucho ... what's your opinion on it?"

"What do I—*Jesus Christ!* You broke my toe!"

Erin, who was trying to place Groucho's plate in front of him, jumped: "I'm sorry, honey, I was just trying to give you your ...."

"You stepped right on my toe. Watch where you're stepping next time." He turned back to Williams. "Birth control? I don't have to use it. I believe in it, though. I hate kids. They're a nuisance. They always want money."

He poked at the shrimp on his plate.

"What about women's lib?" asked Edy. "Should I burn my bra?"

"You'd sag," Groucho said. "After a while, you'd sag. You'd have to get them lifted. A lot of them are doing that, but not enough. Women look awful after they're forty or fifty. Nobody wants to lay them. Not even the milkman. I think that's why they don't *have* milkmen anymore. Women that age should be sent off to fight the war."

"Come with me to my water bed," Edy said, tweaking Groucho's right earlobe between her thumb and finger.

"I'm willing," Groucho said. "I don't know how many devices you have."

"I have two pretty good devices right here," she said, thrusting out her chest.

Groucho manipulated his eyebrows and reached for a cigar, enjoying himself. In a loud aside, he said: "She's talking dirty—I'm not. I don't mind. We could go home and whip the bishop together."

Edy Williams smiled. "That's the biggest cigar I've ever seen," she said.

"It's a Cuban cigar. A Monte Cristo. I happen to be a smuggler. It *is* rather phallic. I hope it excites you."

On the other side of the table, John Russell Taylor, the film critic of the *Times* in London, had settled in with two friends. They had all big plates of food and the waiter was pouring wine for them. From behind me, I heard Erin's voice in an urgent whisper: *"Those places are saved!"*

But that's John Russell Taylor, from the *Times* of London, I said. And he's with ....

"Those are saved for Warren Cowan! He'll be furious!"

Well, you can't ask them to leave, I said. They were here first and they have a right to ....

"Ohhhhh," said Erin, and left the room, possibly in search of Warren Cowan and his party.

A waitress approached Groucho with a tray of pineapple slices. He took one with his fingers.

"You want a fork?" she said.

"Your place or mine?" Groucho said.

Edy Williams moved in and snuggled on his shoulder. "Isn't the music wonderful?" she said. "Don't you just sort of want to lay on the beach and ...."

"That music has kept me out of Hawaii four different times," Groucho said. "They made it up in a day."

"What should a girl do if she's oversexed?" Edy asked.

"Put your lips real close to mine," Groucho said, moving the Monte Cristo to one side.

"How does it feel to be rich and famous?"

"Good. I like money. I support a lot of people I don't have to. I do exercises. I walk every day."

A voice in my right ear was saying, low and quickly, "Who are those people? It won't be any problem to have them moved. We can get rid of them in a minute." It was Warren Cowan, eyeing the film critic of the *Times* of London with a hungry vengeance. "I could clear them out," he said. "I could clear them out of those seats in no time ...."

John Russell Taylor and his friends, who had become aware of the situation, averted a crisis by saying that they were finished anyway. They left and Erin directed a platoon of waiters who moved in with fresh tableware. Warren Cowan and his party sat down.

"They're running a series of Marx Brothers pictures on the BBC and they want to interview me," Groucho told Cowan. "They had the effrontery to offer me two thousand dollars for a day's work. I answered them that it's been some years since I worked for that kind of money. For one night at Carnegie Hall I'll get ten thousand."

Groucho turned back to Edy. "I'm crazy about money," he told her. "You can buy good shoes, shirts, go to good restaurants, and smoke heavy, good cigars."

"Groucho was photographed in sunglasses for *Esquire,"* Warren Cowan said. "Groucho? Did you keep the sunglasses after they took your picture, I hope?"

"He gave them to the maid," Erin said.

"I *sold* them to the maid," Groucho said.

"What do you think about jury trials?" Edy Williams said.

"Jesus, she's dumber than I thought she was," Groucho said.

"Should I *really* burn my bra?"

"Why not? I love tits. I'm a leg man, but I love tits. For saying that, I certainly hope I get a cheap feel before I go home tonight."

"What about the rest of a girl?"

"I love hair, I love teeth, waists ...."

"If she has a mustache?"

He sang: *Oh, give me something to remember you by, when I'm far away and gone.* Warren Cowan conducted an imaginary orchestra.

"Is there a prosthetic doctor in the vicinity?" Groucho asked.

"What kind is that?" Edy said.

"I have a doctor, the best urologist in the U.S.A."

"Should he examine me?"

"He'd love to. Tomorrow he's gonna give me a shot, put me out ... maybe he wants to fool around with my netherlands. I'm making a long journey and he wants me to be in topflight condition."

During all of this Erin had been sitting sideways in her chair, looking around the room. Now she tapped Groucho's elbow. "Groucho ... you see that man over there? Right over there? With the velvet shirt and the pipe? I've always wanted to meet him *so badly.* He's Hugh Hefner, and if you could just sort of say you've always wanted to meet him, and then introduce me ..."

"Why don't you say *you* wanted to meet him, and introduce *me?"* Groucho said. He leaned toward me and said, "Are you with that girl? The starlet?"

No, I said, I'm not.

Groucho drew on his cigar. "If I were alone tonight," he told Edy, "I'd attack you. But I'm not alone." He ate a shrimp.

"This girl back here," he said, indicating Erin, "she loves me, and I don't blame her. I'm witty, I'm charming ... I live in a beautiful home, filled with oil paintings—expensive ones. I have a lot of money. I own a piece of the good pictures. *Room Service, A Night at the Opera, A Day at the Races, Duck Soup* ... they're playing more now than they did then. We're the biggest thing in the movie industry. And I live a good life. My idea of a good evening is to be at home, alone, listening to good political arguments on the television, reading .... I put on my pajamas, fill a pipe with very good tobacco, and I soliloquize while the world slides by."

Groucho rolled his Havana between his fingers. "I only want to live as long as I have my wits about me," he said. "When that goes, I quit. Chaplin said to me one day, *I wish I could talk on the screen the way you do.* I told him, *What are you worrying about? You got fifty million.*

"They're giving him an award at the Academy Awards, and he deserves it. I'm getting one at Cannes, and I deserve it. I'm as good a comedian as Chaplin. Better, because I can talk and he can't Sound ruined him. He made a couple of talking pictures and they were clinkers."

He looked at his cigar, and he looked around the room. He looked at his watch, and he said it was time to go. "You really ought to learn to enjoy a good cigar," he said. "When Maugham was ninety-one he still smoked fifty or sixty cigarettes a day. The doctors warned him to quit. *I'll quit,* he said, *when you give me something to replace it.* It's not easy to be a homo. Woollcott was *almost* a homo. He was accused of it, but he never made the grade. He was a very close friend of Harpo, and he never made a pass at Harpo. He never made a pass at me, either."

Groucho and Erin got up, and Groucho gave Edy Williams a peck on the cheek. Erin led Groucho over to the Hefner table, where Groucho gravely shook Hefner's hand. And then while Erin talked to Hefner, Groucho released her hand and bent to kiss the hand of Barbi Benton, Hefner's girl friend. He said something and she smiled.

At the checkroom, he let the girl help him on with his coat.

"You're a great broad," he said. "I hope you own this place sometime." He paused on the stairs, Erin a few steps below him, and then walked back up to the landing.

"You know," he said, "I'm going to Iowa. The students are going to honor me there. Then I'm appearing at Carnegie Hall, it's sold out. Then I'm sailing to France to be honored by the French government."

He let that hang in the air.

"I'd give it all up for one erection," he said.

He paused again.

"Sex isn't that important, you know. It's a very transient thing. It's a fleeting pleasure, elusive and temporary. Sex is very overrated."

And yet you'd trade in all those awards for one erection?

"They could give me the awards next year."

Lee Marvin I

Who takes the Pill for us now?

Malibu, 1970

The door flew open from inside, revealing Lee Marvin in a torrid embrace, bent over Michelle Triola, a fond hand on her rump. "Love!" he said. "It's all love in this house. Nothing but love. *All you need is love ....*"

Michelle smiled as if to say, well ....

"What's this?" Marvin cried. He snatched the *Los Angeles Times* from his doormat and threw it at the front gate. LaBoo went careening after it, barking crazily.

"You bring that paper back here and I'll kill you," Marvin told LaBoo. He snarled at LaBoo and walked down the hallway and into the living room. LaBoo charged past him and jumped onto a chair. "LaBoo, you son of a bitch, I'm gonna kill you," Marvin said.

"Hello, LaBoo," Michelle said tenderly.

LaBoo wagged his tail.

"I need a beer," Marvin said. "Who's gonna get me a beer? *I'm* gonna get me a beer? I feel like a beer. Hell, I *need* a beer. Where are my glasses?" He peered around him. "Ever read this book? I got it for Christmas or some goddamn thing. A history of the West. Look here. All these cowboys are wearing chaps. Workingmen, see. Look here. Bronco Billy dressed up in the East's conception of the Western hero. See. From a dime novel. That's how authentic a Western we made when we made *Monte Walsh.* Where's that beer? That author, he knows what it was *really* like. Get me a beer."

"Finish your coffee," Michelle said.

"I said get me a *beer."* Marvin paged through the book of Western lore, stopping to inspect an occasional page. When he stopped, he would pause for a moment and then whistle, moving on. Then silence. Only the pages turning. Now and again, a whistle.

"Where's that fucking beer, baby?" He dropped the book on the rug. "Look, if I want to develop an image, I'll do it my own fucking way."

Michelle went into the kitchen to get a beer.

"Anne ... she seemed to be a nice girl," Marvin said. "This was when I was in London for the Royal Command Performance of *Paint Your Wagon.* Nice-enough girl, Anne. Lord somebody or other kept pounding me on the back. I told him I'd already made other arrangements." Marvin whistled. "He kept poking me. Lord somebody or other, never did catch his name. I advised him to fuck off." A pause. A whistle. "If that's swinging, I'll bring them back to Malibu. Maybe to commit suicide ...."

A record, *Victory at Sea,* dropped on the stereo changer. *"Victory at Sea,"* Marvin said. "Well, thousands of ships went under, right? Tells you something."

Michelle returned with a bottle of Heineken. Marvin drank from the bottle, a long, deep drink, and then he smiled at her. "You gonna take off your clothes and jump on him now? Or later?" He smiled again. "Michelle, she's a good sport."

"Lee!" Michelle said.

"Where the hell are my glasses?" Marvin said. He took another drink from the bottle and looked on the floor around his chair.

"He took the lenses out of his glasses," Michelle said. "Last night. He said he didn't want to read any more scripts."

"Not another single goddamned script," Marvin said.

"So he took the lenses out of his glasses."

"I want simply to be the real Lee. The *real* Lee. The real Kirk Lee."

"You left the real Lee in London."

"Now I'm Kirk Lee. Not Lee Lee. Kirk Lee. I flew back from London with Sir Cary. I told him, I said, *Sir Cary, that's a nice watch you have."* Marvin pointed his finger like a gun and made a noise that began with a whistle and ended with a pop. *"A real nice watch, Sir Cary,* I said." Whistle-pop. On the pop, his thumb came down.

"Cary has the same watch you have," Michelle said.

"No," Marvin said, *"he* has the same watch *I* have. If I saw his watch in a photograph, I could identify it anywhere. But, who gives a shit?" Whistle-pop. "Going back to the old neighborhood. This was London. What was it? Bulgaria? No, *Belgravia.* Well it was only seven-thirty in the morning. *Don't you want to stay up and watch the junkies jet in?"* Whistle. "Fuck you, pal, I'm getting some *sleep."*

A moment's silence for symbolic sleep. Marvin closed his eyes and threw his head back against his chair. There was a door at the other end of the living room, opening onto a porch that overlooked the beach. Through the door you could hear the waves hitting the beach, *crush, crush,* and at this moment, while Marvin pretended to sleep, the morning resolved itself as a melancholy foggy Saturday.

"Have another anchovy, sweetheart," Marvin said, rousing himself at last. He drained the Heineken.

"I love them," Michelle said.

"She's been eating nothing but anchovies for the past day and a half," Marvin said. "You know why you like anchovies so much all of a sudden? You're knocked up. You're gonna have a little Lee Marvin."

"Lee!" Michelle said. "You can't say that."

"Why not?" he said. "Put it down: Michelle's knocked up. If you make it good enough, they'll never print it. And if they *do* print it, and come around and ask me, *did you really say that?,* I'll say, *sure, I said it.* I need another beer."

Michelle got up and went into the kitchen.

"She's not *really* knocked up," Marvin said.

He threw a leg over the arm of the chair. "I got a haircut before I went to London," he said. "I mean, it got a little ridiculous there after a while. I didn't get my hair cut for two movies, and it got a little long. I'm going back to a ... not a crew cut. Back to, oh, about a Presbyterian length. I'm tired of all this horseshit about hair."

Marvin sighed, got up, and walked out to the porch. The air was heavy with fog.

"That goddamn buoy," he said. Just down from his stretch of beach, a buoy stood in the sand. "It floated in one morning and they stuck it up there. It's on their property. Christ, I hate the sight of it, but I can't do anything about it. It looks like a phallic symbol. Hell, it *is* a phallic symbol. You get up in the morning and come out here and there's that goddamn *buoy* staring you in the face."

He yawned. Down on the beach, a setter ran howling at a flock of birds. There was a chill this Saturday morning, and sounds were curiously muffled. Marvin peered out to sea. "Is that Jennifer Jones coming in on the surf?" he said. "No? Good."

Michelle came up behind him with a Heineken. "Thanks, sweetheart." He walked back into the living room and sat down. "What was that we saw? Bob and Carol and Bill and Ted? What a piece of shit that was. Good performances, but what a piece of shit."

"I loved it," Michelle said.

"You go for all that touch-me-feel-me bullshit anyway," Marvin said. "Esalen. They take your money and teach you to put one hand on two nipples. Big fucking deal, baby."

"It's about *love,*" Michelle said. "It's *looking* at people. Look at me with love, Lee."

"Take off your clothes, baby." Whistle. "Who takes the Pill for us now?" Pop! "LaBoo, come in here, you mean black prince." LaBoo came in from the porch and settled down on the rug with resignation and a sigh. "And *still* she wants to marry me," Marvin said. "It used to be, we'd check into a hotel, it was Mr. Marvin and Miss Triola. So she changed her name to Marvin, to save all that embarrassment. Now it's Mr. Marvin and Miss Marvin ...."

He yawned and took a pull of Heineken. Michelle excused herself and wandered down the hallway. Silence. The waves. "I never did read that interview in *Playboy,*" Marvin said. "I read excerpts. It was all a lot of shit. They sent some guy to interview me. I sucked him in *so bad.* I even gave him the garbage-man story. *How do you feel about violence in films,* he says. *I'll throw you the fuck out of here if you ask me that again,* I say."

Michelle wandered back into the room. "You took some pills?" Marvin said. "How many did you take? Should I call the doctor?"

Michelle smiled. LaBoo, on the carpet, sighed deeply.

"LaBoo," Michelle said, "you're supposed to stand around and pose in a movie star's home. That's what a poodle is for."

"He stands around and shits, that's what kind of star I am," Marvin said. "It's not everybody gets a Jap lighter from Hugh Hefner. *Gee, thanks, Hef.*" Whistle. Pop. "Well, the royal family *seemed* to like the movie, anyway. Lord somebody said he liked Jean Seberg. That was something."

"Jean has good insides."

"What?"

"I said Jean Seberg has good insides," Michelle said.

"Jesus Christ, I'm living with a dyke!" Marvin said. Whistle! Pop! "My ex-wife had something about *Playboy* when I read it."

"Playboy exploits women," Michelle said. "Women's liberation is against *Playboy."*

"Against *Playboy?"* Marvin said. "Whyever more?"

"It exploits women," Michelle said. "It presents women as sex objects."

"Why not?" Marvin said. "Take a snatch away from a broad and what's she got left?" Marvin spread his legs and breathed deeply. *"Oh me oh my, why must I be a sex symbol? Why won't they let me act?"*

LaBoo snorted in his sleep, waking himself. He stood up, made a circle, lay down again and closed his eyes.

The telephone rang. LaBoo growled with his eyes closed. Michelle went to answer it.

"Who's calling?" Marvin said.

"Meyer Mishkin."

"Tell him nothing for you today, Meyer, but call back tomorrow." Marvin finished his Heineken, turned it upside down, watched a single drop fall out. "My agent," he said. "He keeps wanting to know if I've read any more scripts. Fuck scripts. You spend the first forty years of your life trying to get in this fucking business, and the next forty years trying to get out. And then when you're making the bread, who needs it?

"Newman has it all worked out. I get a million. He gets a million two, but that includes $200,000 expenses. So, if that's the game ..." Marvin shrugged. "I never talked to Newman in my life. No, I talked to him on Park Avenue once. Only to give him a piece of advice. This fifteen-year-old girl wanted his autograph. He told her he didn't give autographs, but he'd buy her a beer. *Paul,* I said, *she's only fifteen. I don't give a shit,* he said." Marvin whistled. "I think it shows," he said. "With Newman, it shows. Cut to an old broad in Miami Beach looking at his picture in *Life* magazine: *A Gary Cooper he ain't.*"

Marvin took another beer from Michelle. "I'm waiting for some young guy to come along and knock me off so I can go to the old actor's home and talk about how great we were in nineteen-you-know. Am I waiting for him? I'd hire guys to knock *him* off. Something the other day really brought it home ...."

He rummaged in a stack of magazines and papers next to his chair.

"I lost it."

Michelle held up a book.

"No," he said, "the other one. Yeah, here it is. *The United States Marine Corps in World War II.* Wake Island. Let's see."

He produced a pair of glasses and put them on. "This cat in command. Let's see here ..." He paged through the book, looking for something. "This cat—yeah, here it is. He was defending the island. When the brass asked the defender of the island if there was anything to be done for them, the cat wired back: *Yes. Send us more Japs.*"

Marvin whistled and squinted down at the page in wonder.

"*Send us more Japs.* Well, Japs were the last thing we needed at the time. Cut to John Wayne: *Yes, send us more Japs!* The bitch of it is, not until years later did it come out that it's the decoder's job to pad messages at the beginning and the end. So all the world was applauding this bastard's nerve, and what the world took as a gesture of defiant heroism was merely padding."

Marvin got up and went into the kitchen. "Something good about Duke, I gotta admit," he called back over his shoulder. "When he's on, he's on. *Send us more Japs.*"

There was a rattle of bottles from the kitchen. "You stole all the beer! Michelle? You drank it all?"

"We're out," Michelle said.

"Make the call," Marvin said, coming back into the living room.

"It'll take them two hours to get here," Michelle said.

"Make the call. Make the call, or I may have to switch to the big stuff."

"I have other plans for you this afternoon."

"No—not that!" Marvin fell back in his chair. "Anything but that!" Horrified.

"It's such a foggy, gray old day," Michelle said. "We ought to just sit in front of the fire and drink Pernod. I like foggy, gray days ...."

"Can the dog drink Pernod?" Marvin asked. "Now why the hell did I ask that? The dog gets no Pernod in this house." He stood up and looked through the window at the surf, his hands in his pockets. "I mean she really could have hurt herself, Jennifer. Came floating in on a wave .... What's the number of the liquor store, honey?"

"Oh, nine four six six something. *You* ought to know."

Marvin went into the kitchen to make the call. "Yeah, hi. Listen, this is Lee Marvin down at 21404." Pause. "Heh, heh. You did, huh? Yeah, well this is me again." Pause. "Heh, heh. Yeah, pal, get anything cold down here. Beer. Yeah. What? Whatdaya mean, light or dark? The green one." He hung up.

"Didn't you order any anchovies?" Michelle said. "It goes back to my Sicilian grandmother."

Another record dropped on the turntable: faint, ghostly harp music. Marvin whirled wildly, looking up into the shadows of the far corners of the room. "Jesus, mother," he said, "will you *please* stay out of the room? I asked you to come only at night." He hit the reject button. "I studied violin when I was very young," he said. "You think I'm a dummy, right? I'm only *in* dummies. *The Dirty Dozen* was a dummy money-maker, and baby, if you want a money-maker, get a dummy."

By now he was rummaging around in the bedroom.

"Lee," Michelle said, "you're not going to put it on and parade around in it again? Are you?"

"Where is it?" Marvin said.

"I think it's in your second drawer," Michelle said. "His cap and gown. He got an honorary degree."

Marvin came out of the bedroom with a pair of binoculars. "Look what I found," he said. He went out on the porch and peered into the mist at a thin line of birds floating beyond the surf. "What are they? Coots, or ... are they ducks?"

Marvin's son, Chris, walked into the living room. "Hi, Chris," Marvin said. "Are these coots, or ... ducks?" Chris went out onto the porch and had a look through the binoculars. "Hard to say," Chris said. He put a leash on LaBoo and took him down to the beach for a walk. Marvin fell back into his chair. The grayness of the day settled down again. On the stereo, Johnny Cash was singing "Greensleeves." The beautiful music of "Greensleeves."

"Do you realize," Marvin said, "that he gets three million a year for singing that shit? *I walk the line, I keep my eyes wide open all the time.* I met him in Nashville. He said, *You haven't heard my other stuff? No,* I said, *I haven't.* He sent us his complete twenty-seven fucking albums. Jesus, Johnny, I like your stuff, but for Christ's sake ..."

Marvin got down on his knees and pulled twenty-seven Johnny Cash albums off a shelf.

"He's embarrassed," Marvin said, "I'm embarrassed. We have

nothing to say, really. So he sends me all his albums. I tried to listen to all of them. It took me two weeks."

"How old is Cher?" Michelle said.

"Cher?"

"Yeah."

"We don't know yet," Marvin said. "These glasses are no goddamned good. Where are my glasses?"

"He went out on the porch and stepped on his other glasses," Michelle said. "They didn't break, and he said it was an act of God, telling him not to read any more scripts. So he took the lenses and scaled them into the ocean. Now he can't see."

"Why," Marvin said, "does it take sixty-seven percent of my income to pay the publicist? He says I should take some broad to lunch, right? It costs me thirty-seven dollars to get out of the joint, and then she knocks me. You know what I asked her? *I'll bet you've never had an orgasm, have you,* I asked her."

"Lee, you didn't say that? Really?"

"I never said anything like that in my life."

Another record dropped on the stereo. "When it comes to 'Clair de Lune,'" he said, "I have to go pass water. Tinkle, is the expression. Oh, sweetheart, do you think this day will soon be o'er? I have a hangover. We had fun last night. Went up to the corner, had a few drinks, told a few lies."

He disappeared down the hallway. Chris, a good-looking kid of sixteen or seventeen, came back with LaBoo, who was banished to the porch to dry out. LaBoo squinted in through the window, wet and forlorn. "Poor LaBoo," Michelle said. "It's the second time he's been rejected today."

Marvin returned. "So what have you decided on?" he asked Chris.

"I was looking at a four-door 1956 Mercedes," Chris said.

"Hitler's car?" Marvin said. Whistle. Pop! "Kid, you deserve the best because you're the son of a star. Why don't you get a job?"

"Chris is working at a record store," Michelle said. "He's working for free right now, until the owner of the store makes enough money to pay his employees."

"Jesus Christ," Marvin said.

"I was looking at a BMW," Chris said. "It's $2,100. New, it would be three thousand."

"Why not get new?" Marvin said.

"I don't have three thousand."

"But big daddy does."

"Let's order pizza," Michelle said. She picked up the phone and ordered three pizzas, one with anchovies.

"You're pregnant," Marvin said. "She's got to be. Christopher, you're going to be a grandfather."

LaBoo, who had edged into the house through a crack in the door, walked out of the bedroom now with a pair of women's panties in his mouth.

"Christ, LaBoo, keep those *pants* out of sight." Marvin said. "Last night, she says, *where'd you get these pants? I dunno,* I say. She says, *well they're not mine.* I say, *honey, I sure as hell didn't wear them home.*" Marvin sighed and held his hands palms up in resignation. "The only way to solve a situation with a girl," he said, "is just jump on her and things will work out."

He took the pants from LaBoo and threw them back into the bedroom. "So what do you think?" he asked Chris.

"The BMW has fantastic cornering, Dad," Chris said. "It has really fantastic quality."

Marvin paused at the door to look out at the surf. "Don't be deceived by quality," he said. "Get something you like now, and trade it in later. The car may turn out to have such fantastic quality you'll puke seeing it around so long."

He sighed and sat down in his chair again.

LaBoo jumped into his lap.

"LaBoo, you mean black prince," Marvin said, rubbing the dog's head carelessly.

Lee Marvin II

You don't want two doors on a hideaway.

Tucson, 1983

"Yo! Up here on the roof!"

Lee Marvin came striding to the edge of the roof, a hammer in his hand. He waved. "Be right down!"

He disappeared from view. The cabdriver offered to come back later and pick me up, on the grounds that nobody else would ever be able to find his way here, but I said I'd take my chances. The cab backed down the driveway in a cloud of dust and I looked around.

Marvin lives here in the desert outside Tucson in one of those rambling sand-colored Arizona homes that looks like a cross between an old Spanish bunkhouse and an *Architectural Digest* cover. It was surrounded by desert scrub and tumbleweed—except, of course, where nature had been driven back to make room for a manicured green lawn and a swimming pool. A weathered pickup truck and an old Chrysler Imperial were parked in the driveway.

"Over here," Marvin said. He was at ground level now, leading the way through construction debris. "This is my hideaway." We walked into a large, tall room that was completely empty, except for two large fish.

"That's my 607½-pound blue marlin, there on the wall," he said. "World's record for five years. And this is a 1,234-pound black marlin from Australia that my wife caught."

That's the largest fish I've ever seen, I said.

"I wouldn't be surprised."

We stood regarding the fish.

"Later," he said, "there'll be a wet bar, a big leather couch here in front of the fireplace, a couple of chairs ... it's a hideaway. It only has one door. That's very important. You don't want two doors on a hideaway."

He stepped over some lumber on the ground and entered the older part of the house through a kitchen door. His wife, Pam, was in the kitchen with one of their grandchildren.

"This is Trevor," Marvin said. He touched the child lightly and tenderly on the head.

Trevor solemnly extended a hand. I shook it.

"Between us," he said, "Pam and I have eight children. Four apiece. Two boys and six girls, four of whom are married, resulting in nine grandchildren, two of whom are staying with us now. It's a big house. It goes on and on. You can't see all of it from here. I couldn't get out of it what I put into it, but what the hell? I live here. That ought to be worth something."

"Let me know when you're ready for lunch," Pam said. "I'm going into town later."

We took some coffee into the living room.

I liked the movie, I said.

"I haven't seen it yet. I was going to fly up to Los Angeles and see it, but, what the hell, I like to stay out of that town as much as conveniently possible. I'll see it down here. You know, it's only my third movie in six years."

He seemed satisfied, as if that were an important accomplishment. The movie is *Gorky Park*, based on the best seller by Martin Cruz Smith, and Marvin plays the sinister American millionaire who is behind a scheme to smuggle out rare Russian sables. The movie also stars William Hurt, as a Moscow policeman, and Joanna Pacula, as a young Russian girl who holds the key to the mystery.

"I read the book when it first came out," Marvin said. "It fell apart at the end, but I liked the rest of it. Usually I never read a book when I think I might be in the movie, but then again, who knew I was going to be in this movie? The screenwriter was Dennis Potter. He agreed about the end. He said he would only write the screenplay if he didn't have to come to New York. That seemed sensible enough to me. Who the hell wants to go to New York? Then I realized he was talking about the *movie*, not *himself*. He didn't want to set any *scenes* in New York, because since we couldn't shoot in the real Moscow, it would look funny if we shot in the real New York. Once again, perfect sense."

The movie was shot mostly in Finland, which also doubled for

Moscow and the Soviet countryside. Marvin spent a lot of the winter over there, wearing perhaps the most expensive and elegantly tailored wardrobe he has ever worn in a movie, and playing a man who looks rich, intelligent and dangerous.

"I think the movie will break some new ground this season," he said. "It is about adults talking to adults, and trying to make sense out of what they're saying. I get *so* depressed going to the movies these days."

He sipped his coffee. "You say you've seen the film?"

That's right, I said.

Marvin leaned forward and his voice took on a conspiratorial edge.

"How was Bill?" he asked.

William Hurt? I thought he was very good, in a peculiar sort of way.

"Peculiar?"

Well, he gives an edge to the character, as if there's more there than meets the eye ...

"What do you mean, peculiar?" Marvin said. "He's a pain in the ass. That's not to say he isn't a good actor. That, I'll give him. But I knew I was in trouble on the first day I met him. I said, *How about joining us for dinner?* And Bill said, *How's your soul?* And I said to myself, *Oh, shit, one of them.*"

One of what?

"One of the profound. Bill is great when he has lines to say. Give him dialogue, and he does just fine. But on his own, you don't know what the hell he's talking about. What he needs in life is a script." Pause. "Also a director."

Marvin leaned back in his chair and stretched.

"Don't get me wrong. I like Bill. Once I found out he was full of shit, then it was easy. I can relate to that. For example, one night we're sitting around in the hotel in Helsinki. Bill says, *There it is again!* I say, *There WHAT is again?* He says, *That stuff in the bottom of the glass! They're trying to poison me!* I look in the glass. There's a little sediment from the wine. I told him I put it there. He didn't believe me. *The KGB! They're out to get me!* I told him, quite frankly, I'd love to meet the KGB. It might be interesting. We could go out for an evening and do Helsinki together."

Marvin looked at his watch and said it was time for lunch. In the big dining room, cold meats, shrimp and cheese were laid out on the table. He broke out a couple of cans of Diet Coke.

You're not drinking so much these days? I said.

"If I were," he said, "I'd be dead."

How do you like life here in the desert, sort of out of the mainstream?

"*Sort of* out of the mainstream? I'm as far away as I can get. I hate the Los Angeles scene. Beverly Hills isn't my style anymore, being that I'm not part of the party hierarchy. I was always down at the beach even when I did live there. Listening to the waves roar. Down here, I can hop a 7:30 flight, be in Los Angeles by nine, rent a car, do my business, fly back at five, and be home for supper. I read, I get involved in a lot of dumb projects, I'm helping this guy fix the roof... I don't think I've actually made three films in Los Angeles in fifteen years. Pam?"

His wife, who was just getting ready to leave, stuck her head in the door.

"How long have we lived here?" he asked her.

"Since you made *Shout at the Devil*," she said.

"Then came *The Big Red One*," he said, "right after *Avalanche Express*. See, that's the way we tell time out here in the desert. We'll say something was two years before I made *Death Hunt*."

That was the movie you made with Charles Bronson? I said. The one where you chased him all the way through Alaska?

Marvin submerged a cold shrimp in a basin of cocktail sauce.

"I like Charlie," he said.

Marvin and Bronson, I said. The two toughest guys in the movies.

"He has an image, and he's never let up on it," Marvin said. "He wants you to think he's *sooooo bad*. We did our first film together. It was called *You're in the Navy Now*. That was thirty-five years ago.

We've done five or six films over the years. We look at each other and shake our heads. Jesus. He's humorous, he's so bad. So mean. He wants to intimidate you, but there's a little gleam way back behind his eyes, if you can see it. We were sitting in London once in a very posh club, wearing black suits, talking to a girl. Charlie says, *Yeah, sweetheart, it's tough lying on your side in a coal mine.* I said, *Jesus, Charlie, you ain't been in a coal mine in thirty years.* He drives around in a Rolls-Royce and he's talking about hard times down in the mine."

We finished our lunch and pushed back from the table.

"The girl was very good," he said. "You know. The girl in the picture."

Joanna Pacula?

"Yeah. Fresh off the boat from Poland. She's about twenty-two years old. She was just plain old *nice.* She has all the best aspects of what you'd want in a daughter. For that matter, I looked pretty good in the picture, too. The character was a heavy, but he was a *suave* heavy. To play a suave heavy was an appealing thing to me, to conduct myself as my family would have liked me to conduct myself when I was younger. And ... now I'm older. I don't work as much. I work more than I want to, though. I'd rather just sit around here and do nothing. In my age bracket, I'm not exactly ready for *On Golden Pond* yet, but I don't see myself making teenager pictures.

"I'm happy here. I go to bed early. I get up to greet the dawn. Pam and I have a good time. I met her, you know, back in Woodstock, New York, when I got out of the Marines after the war. We went around together for the summer. I was in summer stock. I left to be an actor. She didn't want to go at that time. We met up again years later."

I toyed with the idea of asking Marvin some sort of obligatory question about the whole palimony controversy, but he looked so happy, rotating his can of Diet Coke, that I figured, what the hell.

We walked out onto the lawn and regarded the desert in silence and then it was time to drive to the airport. Marvin climbed in behind the wheel of his Imperial.

"This is a 440-cubic-inch Chrysler Imperial," he said, in the voice of a tour guide. "Cars like this have not been manufactured for years and years. It will do one hundred twenty-five miles an hour. It gets fifteen miles to the gallon. It has 137,900 miles on the speedometer."

We headed down the dusty road to town.

What was your best role? I asked.

"I dunno."

What about Hickey in the film of *The Iceman Cometh*?

"Oh, Hickey, yeah. Now that I've done *Iceman,* I don't ever want to see it again. O'Neill is so difficult on an actor. He forces you into it. Playing that drunk changed my life in a great way. It taught me the severity of great performances. I'd been lucking my way through for a long time, acting instinctively. *Iceman* forced me to want to be right. I think I went a bit mad, playing *Iceman.* I was stuck for so long in that one night in the gin mill."

We made the turn onto the highway.

Did you ever think about writing an autobiography? I asked.

"Years ago," he said, "there was a book about me. One of those as-told-to books. I said a lot of astounding things in that book. That was back when I was still in the image-building stage. I wasn't misquoted. I really did say all of those things."

We pulled over to the curb.

"But," he said, "whether they're true? Well, they might be true and they might not be true. What do I know?"

four

A fight for love and glory

Edy Williams, Lord Grade, John Wayne, Kirk Douglas and Sybil Danning are all in this chapter together not only because they are larger than life, but because they know it, glory in it, and carry it off with some style.

The other actor who moves through two of these pieces is an old buddy-boy of mine named Billy (Silver Dollar) Baxter. I call him my buddy-boy because with Baxter you are either his buddy-boy or you are "rapidly on the verge of becoming one of my ex-friends, and taking on all the possibilities of becoming a complete stranger." Baxter is the closest living equivalent to a character in a Damon Runyon story. For years he has attended the Cannes Film Festival, acted as the mayor of the bar at the Majestic Hotel, handed out silver dollar tips to the perplexed waiters, and bewildered the croupiers at the casino by winning one of their engraved, gaudy twenty thousand-franc chips and then assuring them of his plans to have it turned into a belt buckle.

Edy Williams

Irving! Brang 'em on!

Cannes, 1981

When they write the history of the movies in the dark days after the passing of Hollywood's Golden Age, there ought to be a mention of Edy Williams, the Last Starlet. When, and if, she attends her last Cannes Film Festival, an era will have ended.

All the Hollywood studios used to have half a dozen starlets under contract. Their duties were simple: They had to look gorgeous, attend acting classes, play bit parts in movies and, most importantly, pose for thousands of cheesecake photographs and be on call twenty-four hours a day for the opening of a supermarket, the christening of a boat or the dedication of a shopping center.

The primary duty of a starlet was to be photographed while in the act of being a starlet, and Edy Williams understands this in the innermost recesses of her ambition. She is so good at being a starlet, so tireless and dedicated, that she was, in fact, the last official starlet in Hollywood. She was under contract to Twentieth Century-Fox until 1971. Now she is the last starlet at Cannes.

To be sure, there are other girls who take off their bikinis on the beach or pose in motorcycle helmets and fishnet stockings. But they aren't trying to be discovered—they're just being exhibitionists. Edy Williams hopes again this year, as she has at Cannes almost every year since 1974, to be discovered.

In the dreams of the starlet, I suspect, there is always that scene where the cigar-chomping producer spots a lovely young woman on the terrace of the Carlton Hotel and shouts, "Who is that girl? I must have her for my next picture. Sign her up immediately."

That has not happened yet to Edy, but she was on the terrace of the Carlton again the other day, breathlessly saying hello to genial Sam Arkoff, a man who founded American-International Pictures in 1954 and has already produced 450 movies without finding it necessary to hire Edy Williams. Now Sam has sold AIP and is back in independent production. Maybe this year?

"I don't know what to do about my image," Edy said one night, thinking out loud and a little poignantly. We were having dinner at Felix, one of the in-spots along the Boulevard Croisette. Every waiter and busboy in the restaurant was making six trips a minute past our table to gaze in awe at her plunging neckline.

Across the table from her, Silver Dollar Billy Baxter shouted

"Irving, brang 'em on." The waiters, who have all been trained by Baxter to believe that their names are Irving, raced to his side with a glass of Scotch. This was a conference of war. Silver Dollar Baxter, who is the second-most visible American at Cannes (after Edy Williams), had agreed to counsel Edy on her image.

"Irving," said Baxter, "brang Miss Williams here some champagne. Good stuff. None of that cheap French crap. And Irving, do me a favor, huh? Clean ashtrays. And the menu. What do you recommend, apart from another restaurant?"

"Oh, Billy, you always know what to say," Edy said.

"Only thinking of you, sweetheart," said Silver Dollar Baxter. "Now what are you complaining about? Look at that dress you're wearing. It covers up so much I can hardly see everything."

"Do you think it's right for evening?" asked Edy Williams.

"What's the stuff all over your boobs?"

"Gold sparkle. It's my new makeup. Do you like it? But, Billy, I was thinking. You know, I'm not in my twenties anymore. I was thinking if maybe my bikini routine is getting a little dated."

"What bikini routine? You mean where you go down to the beach and take off your bikini?"

"You know what I was thinking? I brought along tapes of my nightclub act. I have a portable stereo that's real loud. I was thinking, what if I play my tapes and do my nightclub act on the terrace of the Carlton, huh?"

"What if you fall off the edge of the terrace and bust your ass?"

"I was thinking of a new image for my thirties. Maybe something a little more reserved."

"I can't believe my ears," Billy said. "More reserved? We're talking about the girl who jumped into the ring before the Ali-Spinks fight and took off her clothes in front of seventy thousand people in the Superdome."

"They were caught completely by surprise," Edy said.

"What did it feel like?" asked Silver Dollar Baxter. (As a public relations stunt he once had two starlets push a brass four-poster bed down the middle of Broadway.)

"What did what feel like?"

"Taking off your clothes in front of seventy thousand people. You know, I'm not sure ... I gotta check on this ... I'll bet you are the only person in history to take off her clothes in front of seventy thousand people. At once, anyway."

"It was real scary," Edy said. "The worst part was right before I did it. I was standing at ringside, and I was scared. What if they didn't like it? What if everybody booed? Or didn't pay any attention?"

"That's gotta be every girl's nightmare," said Silver Dollar Baxter. "There she is, she jumps in the ring, she whips off her clothes in front of seventy thousand people, and they shout, *Put 'em on!*"

"But it was the most unbelievable sensation, when I was in the ring and they were all cheering," she said. "I knew what Ali must feel like. Then they made me leave the Superdome. They wouldn't let me stay for the fight. And I had a ticket and everything."

"Irving," said Silver Dollar Baxter, "look at these flowers. It looks like you picked them up off the street."

"Somebody was telling me I was using too much makeup," Edy said. "But for the photographers, if you don't wear enough makeup, your eyes don't show up. And you never know when they're going to take your picture."

Two days later, in the daily English-language newspaper at Cannes, there was a photo of Edy posing in front of the James Bond poster that covers the front of the Carlton Hotel. The poster, two stories high, shows Bond framed by two long, lovely female legs. Edy was posing with her legs in the same position, and without her bikini top.

"Doesn't look like she made too-extensive revisions in her image yet," Silver Dollar Baxter said. "Wait a minute. What's this?" He was reading the daily gossip column by Peter Noble, editor of *Screen International*. "Says here Edy has a pilot for her new TV show. It's a physical exercise show called 'Keeping in Shape with Edy.' "

Baxter was sitting by the pool of the Majestic Hotel, watching the fleet of nine airplanes flying past with banners advertising *Super-*

man III. Just then, Edy appeared at poolside and planted a big kiss on Billy's cheek.

"What do you think about my pilot?" she asked him.

"Edy," said Billy, "if you ask me, you could bring it in on instruments."

Lord Grade

I have the biggest stars. Charles Bronson and Miss Piggy.

Cannes, 1979

"Dear Lord Lew," wrote Silver Dollar Billy Baxter. "Here is a list of the people you should invite to your yacht on Sunday. All good people. Signed, B.B." Baxter licked the flap on the envelope and sealed it. "Signed with the sign of the Double B," he said, "my personal voucher that his lordship is gonna enjoy their acquaintanceship."

Now it is probably the case with most of us that if we had a one hundred forty-foot yacht riding at anchor in the harbor at Antibes, we would have no difficulty in finding people to invite on board. But Lord Lew Grade had enlisted the cooperation of Silver Dollar Baxter in making up the guest list because he wanted just a small party—ten or twelve people at most—and Billy Baxter is known at the Cannes Film Festival for his ability to produce ten or twelve of the right people at the drop of an invitation.

"Rex Reed originally said he doesn't know if he could make it," Baxter was saying the next day, pacing nervously in front of the Hotel Majestic, scanning the boulevard for signs of Grade's Mercedes limousine. "He says he's gotta interview Monica Vitti, for chrissakes. I tell him he can interview her any year but this is his lordship's inaugural cruise."

Do you mean the yacht hasn't sailed before?

"Naw. It's twenty years old—back when they made real yachts. I mean Lord Lew bought it yesterday so he hasn't seen it yet. We're all gonna be walking up and down the harbor, looking for the right yacht, so at 9 A.M. today, my phone rings, and it's sexy Rexy wanting to know when we sail."

You don't have an inaugural cruise at the drop of a hat.

"Irving! Brang 'em on!"

Baxter is under the impression that every waiter everywhere in the world is named Irving. Because he tips with silver dollars, the waiters agree. One hurries to fill Baxter's hand with a vodka and grapefruit juice.

"Look at this place," Baxter said, surveying the veranda of the Majestic, one of the two most exclusive hotels in Cannes. "Last year it was crawling with Iranians fighting to spend their money. That was before the Allhetoldya Cockamamie. Here comes the limousine now."

We all piled in—film critics from the United States and London, hand-picked by Baxter for an audience with Grade, who began in show business as a tap dancer and operator of pony rides, and, at seventy-two, is the multimillionaire chairman of ITV, the British entertainment conglomerate that brought you "Voyage of the Damned," "Jesus of Nazareth" and "Love and Bullets."

We drove down the Croisette, the magnificent boulevard that separates the grand hotels from the Mediterranean. We drove along the coast. We drove past the Hotel Cap D'Antibes, which is so exclusive that the really big tycoons rent suites there, twenty miles outside of Cannes, and make deals involving the minor tycoons who are only staying at the Majestic.

Baxter explained: "In terms of the status order, first you got the guys in town in rooms costing merely two hundred fifty dollars a day. Then you got the guys out here, who are so big they don't even go into town—to come all the way to the Cannes Film Festival and never set foot in Cannes, that's class. Then what you got is the guys like Lord Lew, who buy a yacht for a couple of million and anchor it offshore in sight of the Hotel Cap, so the big shots out here are eating their hearts out. You get any bigger than that, you're Niarchos, you float in with your navy. Look at that! That used to be Jack Warner's villa! Now they're having picnics on his private beach! He'd kill 'em."

The limo pulled up to the Antibes yacht harbor, and there was no mistaking Grade's yacht—long and sleek and glistening with brass and varnish. The lord was pacing nervously by the gangplank. He had on gray flannel trousers, a blue blazer and a straw hat. In his hand was one of the twenty-five dollar cigars he fancies. Smaller objects have been used as Little League bats.

"I was growing nervous," Grade said. "I thought perhaps you hadn't been able to find the yacht."

"You kiddin'?" asked Baxter. "A yacht this size, you could fire off a machine gun."

Grade puzzled over that for a moment, and then extended the hospitality of the ship. The crew lined up to be introduced: captain, first and second mates, chief stewardess and her assistant. "Make yourself at home," said Grade. "You can sunbathe topside. There are drinks in here. We'll serve luncheon off the Cap. I thought perhaps something cold that we could eat on deck, instead of having to use the ship's dining room."

"Listen to the stereo," Baxter said. "Frank Sinatra. He's everywhere. Where's Irving?"

Alexander Walker, film critic of the *London Standard,* wandered through the yacht taking inventory, and returned with his report: "It sleeps eight, not counting the crew, which lives on board. Three full baths. Impeccable interior decoration, with original prints everywhere. And a large shaded deck. That would be Lord Grade's preference. He avoids the sun with a passion. He's never happier than when he's in the shade, watching other people in the sun. Cannes is a problem in logistics for him every year, unless it rains."

Lord Grade found himself at the rail with Richard Corliss, editor of *Film Comment,* who told Grade that the Muppets had been on the cover of a recent issue.

"That's my pet project right now," said Grade. *"The Muppet Movie.* I have the biggest stars. Charles Bronson and Miss Piggy."

Luncheon was announced. A table in the shade was spread with linen and covered with cold smoked salmon, rare roast beef, cold lobster tail, caviar, green salad, fresh strawberry tarts. The stewardesses urged glasses of chilled white wine upon us. Far away across the glistening blue waters of the Cote D'Azur, the hapless tenants of the Hotel Cap D'Antibes shaded their eyes on the verandas of their merely thousand-dollar suites and squinted enviously at Lord Lew at anchor.

"I have been thinking," Grade said, "of writing my autobiography. My life has been filled, for example, with coincidences. When I began in London, for example, I was in an office on Little Argyle Street, across from the Palladium. Now ITV's home offices are on Little Argyle Street." He arranged cold salmon on his fork. "And I own the Palladium."

"What an amazing coincidence," said Rex Reed.

"I began as a dancer," Grade said. "I did a double act with my brother, Lord Delfont. I was a natural at the Charleston, but the others I had to finesse. It was called eccentric dancing. Like this."

He stood up, clasped hands above his head and bumped to an imaginary rhythm. "We played Paris, Germany ... we were always broke. Those were the days. I remember I was in love with twins ... two lovely girls ... dancers ... I couldn't make up my mind between them."

He sighed at lost opportunities.

"One of the problems we face in this industry today," he said, "is the director who insists upon the final cut of his film. And the star who insists on a certain director. Where is the respect for the man who must find the money? The only director I have absolute faith in is Ingmar Bergman. He made *Autumn Sonata* for me. Now we hope to do a fifteen million dollar picture together, although I haven't yet told him so."

Luncheon drew to a civilized conclusion, punctuated by strawberry tarts. Grade passed around a box of his enormous Havanas. Billy Baxter said he would take one, but he was worried about overweight luggage charges.

"And yet," said Lord Grade, "television—television! What an impact! With one successful program, we reach ten times as many people as with a hit movie. My most successful television program was, of course, 'Jesus of Nazareth,' directed for me by Franco

Zeffirelli. What a great event!

"Do you know that a survey was taken of 6,525 people. Forty percent of them said they had learned most about Jesus from my program. Twenty-one percent named the Bible. Thirty percet named the church."

"Let's see," said Rex Reed. "That still leaves nine percent undecided."

Lord Grade sighted down his cigar at Reed. "The survey," he said, "was taken before the reruns."

John Wayne

I thought Injuns didn't show pain ... 'specially Comanche war chiefs!

Durango, Mexico, 1973

"You have three things here that make it a great place to shoot a Western," Jack Casey was explaining. "You have the tall pines, you have the high desert, and you don't have any jet trails."

What else is Durango known for? I asked.

"Not a whole hell of a lot else," he said. "There's a cotton mill and a mountain made out of iron that I know of. Otherwise, you might say we're twenty-five miles from everywhere. Duke put this place on the map."

The car from the airport passed the largest and most modern structure I was to see in Durango, the penitentiary, and reached the outskirts of town. "We're here," Jack said. "Campo Mexico Courts."

The Campo Mexico Courts was a giant semicircle of semi-detached cabins, each one with a carport leaning against it. There was a two-hole miniature golf course, a swing, a slide, and several large slabs of concrete. Each slab honored a Western that had been filmed by a cast staying at the Campo Mexico Courts.

There was a slab for *War Wagon,* with the handprints, footprints and signatures of John Wayne and Kirk Douglas. There were also slabs and autographs for Glenn Ford, Bruce Cabot, Ben Johnson, James Garner and Rock Hudson.

"Duke put this place on the map," Jack said. "His first picture in Durango was *The Sons of Katie Elder.* Since then he's shot so many shows here that his company owns a piece of one of the Western sets outside town."

What else did he shoot here?

"Well, he shot *The Undefeated* and *War Wagon* here, and *Chisum* —that was a big one. And *Big Jake*. And *Train Robbers*, which hasn't been released yet. And now this one. How many is that? Six? And now two Westerns are being shot here at the same time—Duke's picture, and Peckinpah's Billy the Kid thing. It's gotten to be a regular industry."

Later that evening, I was taking a drink of the bottled water in my room when I heard a duck next door. I walked to the door, saw no duck, and stepped out onto the porch. At that very moment, Dub Taylor stepped out onto the porch next door.

Dub Taylor is an actor whose name you may not remember, but you have seen him in a dozen movies. He played C.W. Moss' father in *Bonnie and Clyde*. He looked at me and quacked.

"Hell, I can do it with a call or without one," he said. He pulled a duck call from his pocket, hung it around his neck on a leather strap, and quacked some more.

"My pappy taught me," Dub said. "There's different calls for different times. You want them to land, you gotta *tell* them to land. You got to get your vocabulary straight. Ducks is smarter'n some people."

He came over and sat on my porch.

"Yes," he said, "been married for years. That's my son you see on 'Gunsmoke.' I been in the business more than thirty-five years. Frank Capra gave me my start in pictures. Before that, I was an entertainer. Vaudeville. I played the xylophone and the harmonica some.

"Hell, this here's a regular character actors' convention. Between the John Wayne movie and the Sam Peckinpah movie, every character actor in the world is staying at the Campo Mexico Courts right now."

As if to prove him right, Jack Elam walked past, wearing a ferocious beard.

"Jack," Dub said.

"Dub," Jack said.

"We see each other *all* the time," Dub said. "There's always work for a character actor. Lessee who we got down here right now. We got Slim Pickens—you ever see him in a movie? He's been in a thousand. We got Harry Carey, Jr., and L.Q. Jones, and Jackie Coogan. Marie Windsor is down here. Denver Pyle. Neville Brand. Strother Martin was supposed to be down here, but he couldn't make it—they even named his character for him just like they named Denver's character Denver."

He paused for a quack or two.

"The secret is," he said, "that I am ninety percent pig crap. Only ten percent intelligent. Ninety percent of the people is ninety percent pig crap, and so when they see me, they recognize themselves."

He nodded as if that settled it.

You must make a lot of money as a character actor, working all the time, I said.

"Hell, no. I got in hock to Seaboard Finance twenty years ago, and in all that time I never been able to get out from under. They know me by the sound of my voice now. I never sign nothing—I tell 'em I can't read, can't write. Just call up and say, *Seaboard, this is Dub again.*"

The next day, Wayne's picture was shooting in an old cotton warehouse next to the railroad tracks in Durango. The warehouse wasn't soundproof, so everything had to stop when a train went past.

Inside the warehouse, the prop men had constructed an outdoor clearing. The floor was covered with damp dirt and sawdust, and everyone was coughing and sneezing. It sounded like three in the morning on a bad night in the TB ward.

"There's no question about it, it's a dilemma," John Wayne said. "It's a question of wetting down the dirt and freezing our ass off all morning, or not wetting down the dirt and fighting the dust all afternoon."

He took a paper cup of hot chili soup from a tray and drank it down.

"Haven't you got that horse steadied yet?" he said.

Two wranglers were trying to position a horse in the clearing. The shot called for the horse to be facing west, and the horse wasn't having any. The horse wanted to face east.

The scene they were preparing to film was a basic one. John Wayne and Neville Brand, who plays a Comanche war chief, are riding on the same horse when they're swept off by a rope strung across the clearing by treacherous enemies. Brand breaks his leg, and Wayne sets it.

"Christ," Wayne said, "isn't there *anyone* on this set who can handle a horse? We might as well just move the camera and shoot the way the damn horse wants us to."

The wranglers tugged and pulled, and the horse braced its legs like a mule.

"Get one of those fellows on the horse's head and the other fellow on the other end," Wayne said. "Have them push at the same time."

Andrew V. McLaglen, the director, nodded morosely. He was wearing a surgical face mask—whether to avoid catching cold, or to avoid spreading a cold of his own, it was difficult to say. The wranglers pushed and pulled, and the horse came around. Wayne, doing most of his own direction in this scene, ran through his lines with Neville Brand. In the event you have not seen a John Wayne movie in the past thirty years, they may sound unfamiliar:

Wayne (picking himself up off ground): *Holy Christmas!*

Brand (sprawled against tree): *Like takin' candy from a baby, huh? Ha, ha, ha!*

Wayne: *Very funny.*

Brand: *I'll tell ya somethin' else that's funny. My leg's broke.*

Wayne: *Let's see.*

He kicks Brand's leg.

Brand: *Aaaaaaiiiiiiieeeeeee!*

Wayne: *Well, I guess you're right.* (He kneels down beside Brand.) *I'll have to straighten and splint it.* (He pulls a cigar from his pocket.)

Here's somethin' to bite down on. This is gonna hurt.

Brand: *Thanks. I ... Aaaaaaiiiiiiieeeeeee!*

Wayne: *I thought Injuns didn't show pain ... 'specially Comanche war chiefs!*

Wayne and Brand ran through this dialogue a couple of times, getting it more or less right but not quite *exactly* right, and Wayne finally called for silence: "What does a guy have to do to get a little damn quiet around here? This scene isn't easy."

Silence. Wayne and Brand got it right. Wayne walked over to his chair—with "Duke" stitched across the back—to talk to an interviewer from the *London Sunday Express.*

"Would you say you are a conservative?" the Englishman asked him.

"Hell," Wayne said, "I always *thought* I was a liberal. Listening to both sides before you make up your mind—doesn't that make you a liberal? Not in the terms of today, it doesn't. These days, you have to be a fucking left-wing radical to be a liberal."

"I see," said the man from London.

"My favorite man was Taft," Wayne said.

"Yes, yes," the man from London said. "Very good president, wasn't he? Yes."

"Not *that* Taft, you dumb asshole," Wayne said. "*Robert* Taft."

"Yes, yes, I see," the reporter said.

"All the things the liberals were for, he was for, but in a quiet way," Wayne said. "And he didn't only tell people of their rights, he told them their *responsibilities.*"

"Of course."

"But I guess you're right," Wayne said. "Politically, I *have* mellowed. I don't give a good god damn."

Outside the cotton warehouse, a dog began to bark.

"Somebody quiet that dog," Wayne said. "BANG! Thank you."

Laughter.

"It's funnier with a baby," Wayne said, smiling. "Wasn't that Fields who did that? *Quiet that baby! BANG! Thank you.*"

"Very funny," the man from London said.

"Belittling our president, that's what they're doing," Wayne said. "He's a man with power, and the decency to *use* that power fairly. When he mined Haiphong harbor, all the cute boys, the Severeids and the Cronkites and those other assholes, said that would end the Russian trip. Well, they were wrong. The Russians know who's boss."

"Yes, of course," the London reporter said.

"Nixon acted with *honor*," Wayne said.

"Yes, yes."

"You know the only thing that's better than honor?" Wayne said.

"No, what's that?"

"In her."

He laughed, and after a moment the man from London laughed, too.

"You play chess?" John Wayne said.

Yes, I do, I said.

"Those Russians were through Chicago, weren't they," he said.

A couple of weeks ago, I said.

"They pretty good?"

That's what I read.

"They're just about the best. Except for Fischer, they are. Christ, that fellow can play chess!"

What'd you think about his tactics?

"He won, didn't he? In chess, that's all that counts. It's not a game of luck, it's a game of logic. Fischer had the better logic."

We left the big warehouse and walked to Wayne's trailer, which was parked outside. He pulled down his battered old chess board and set up the pieces. Chess has been John Wayne's game for more than forty years.

The Duke drew white and opened with his queen's pawn. I tried the Nimzo-Indian defense and the game moved along fairly conventional lines, or so I thought until we arrived at the middle game and the Duke was a bishop and a knight up on me. Wayne's photographer, David Sutton, sat on the edge of the couch and kibitzed. Wayne smoked small cigars and said nothing.

Well, how would you have felt, playing chess with John Wayne? The first time I ever saw him in person, he was directing *The Green Berets* at an Air Force base down in Georgia, and he looked so intimidating and authoritative in uniform with his battle helmet on, that I could hardly think of a thing to say and was barely able to prevent myself from saluting.

I've interviewed him a couple of times since then, but the feeling has never quite gone away ... the feeling that John Wayne is in some measure larger than the rest of us. There is something in his bearing and manner, and something in our memories of the dozens of Saturday afternoon matinees we spent in his shadow, that will always impart this quality about John Wayne to the people who grew up and went to the movies in the 1940s and 1950s.

Sitting across the chess board from him, I felt, perhaps, something like poor Spassky must have felt. I knew I was a decent chess player, as strong as Wayne, anyway; and Spassky knew that *he* was the world champion, and Fischer just a callow boy from Brooklyn. Still, there was something ... some ... aura, some ultimate confidence, that ...

As it happened, Wayne grew overconfident and absentmindedly allowed me to pin his rook and knight. I took the rook, and maneuvered into a situation where I had mating chances. We exchanged moves, and then I sat looking at the board and realizing that all I had to do was move my queen and he would be mated.

"God ... damn!" Wayne said.

I mated him.

"God *damn!*" Wayne said.

Well ... I said.

"You was robbed, Duke," said the photographer.

"God damn," Wayne said, staring at the board. "If I hadn't a said *god damn*, you wouldn't a never seen that."

Back in the cotton warehouse, shooting began on the scene in the clearing. Wayne handed Neville Brand the cigar, Brand bit down, and Wayne rotated the broken leg.

"Aaaaaaiiiiiieeeeee!"

"Good. Cut." McLaglen, the director said. "Let's get one more."

"He's a natural," the British journalist told me.

Yep, I said.

"He's made so many Westerns, he acts by instinct, without thinking."

Well, I said, if anybody knows how to make a Western, John Wayne does.

"Look at this," the British journalist said, as Wayne stooped down to twist Neville Brand's leg again. "Watch. He stoops down, he says his lines, and without even thinking he just instinctively knows not to goose himself with his spurs."

It was indeed so. Wayne stood up and ambled over.

"What was the greatest Western ever made, Duke?" the British journalist asked.

"Hell, I dunno," Wayne said. "Whatever it was, it was probably directed by Jack Ford."

"What'd you think about *High Noon*?" asked the man from London.

Wayne looked pained. "What a piece of you-know-what *that* was," he said. "I think it was popular because of the music. Think about it this way. Here's a town full of people who have ridden in covered wagons all the way across the plains, fightin' off Indians and drought and wild animals in order to settle down and make themselves a homestead. And then when three no-good bad guys walk into town and the marshal asks for a little *help,* everybody in town gets shy."

John Wayne studied the end of his cigar.

"You know what I would have done, if I'd been the marshal?" he said at last.

"No, what?"

"I would have been so god-damned disgusted with those chicken-livered yellow sons of bitches that I would have just taken my wife and saddled up and rode out of there."

Chapter Four

Kirk Douglas

If I were really sophisticated, how could I, a grown-up man, carry a gun in a movie?

Los Angeles, 1969

This was a restless man. He rocked on the balls of his feet. He looked, turned, looked back to where he'd turned from. Demons were gaining. He peered out the window. Opened the door. Closed the door. Peered out the window. Evoked a pastoral image.

"There was a lovely little picket fence," Kirk Douglas said. "And a mailbox with my name on it, and a soft little carpet of green grass out there in the middle of the desert. It got to be a joke. But I've spent so much of my life on locations that after a while ... well, we had that goddamn trailer fixed up like a garden spot. The crew members used to compete to see who could think of something new to add."

And that was on ...

"That was on this one. *There Was a Crooked Man.* The last of my current trilogy and my fiftieth picture. *Jesus!*"

Douglas took a seat on the very edge of a sofa. He leaned forward, his elbows braced on his knees. Then he slammed his hands together, looked down at the carpet and shook his head.

"Fifty pictures." His voice caressed the words. "That's what it all amounts to, you know. Staying power. I was a star before I even *heard* of Julie Andrews."

He smiled the Kirk Douglas smile, half nostalgic, half rueful, half ferocious.

"I remember meeting Tito once. The English ambassador had been waiting six months to present *his* credentials. Tito sent his private plane to pick me up, and we talked for three hours. Turned out he'd seen just about every one of my movies. He sees one or two movies a night. He said they take his mind off his problems.

"And that's where it's at. That's what movies do. Take *Lonely Are the Brave.* There was a movie that communicated on all levels. Maybe it was anti-Establishment, or maybe it was about a kooky cowboy. A movie like that is so much better than some foreign horseshit about an actor chewing for twenty minutes.

"But you never know. I made a movie two years ago, *A Lovely Way to Die.* They pushed me into it. *Kirk,* they said, *you oughta make a cop picture.* It was a bomb. Well, why was *Bullitt* a success? Nobody understood *Bullitt.* It had two good elements in it: the chase, and the killing in the bedroom. Otherwise, it was as hard to understand as *Last Year at Marienbad.* I didn't know what *that* was about either. The foreign directors are always fumbling about in obscurity, and the critics are always writing about the juxtaposition of black and white and the existential dilemma and all that shit, to disguise the fact that *they* don't understand the first damn thing about it either ...."

Douglas wore frayed denims, no shirt, boots. Hair long and combed back like Ratso in *Midnight Cowboy.* He'd just come from the set. Now he went into the bedroom of his bungalow on the Warner Brothers lot and came back wearing a blue terry-cloth robe.

"But now, yes, I've made a trilogy I'm proud of. My forty-eighth, forty-ninth and fiftieth pictures. *The Brotherhood, The Arrangement,* and *There Was a Crooked Man.* It gives me a certain measure of pride to look back at these three pictures and realize I've come this far and remained intact."

He backed into a corner of the room, and stood looking up at the ceiling.

"*The Brotherhood.* I got a lot of indirect messages from the boys on that one. They wanted to meet me."

The Mafia?

Silence.

He was gently tapping his head against the wall.

You weren't ... uneasy?

A sharp laugh. He advanced from the corner, sat in a chair. "I know Italians and I like them. A lot of my father's best friends were Italians. I responded to that in making the picture. I put a lot of warmth into that character. Those immigrants were tough, more *intensive* than people are these days. I'd love to discuss the picture with ... the boys. I'm not interested in movies, anyway; I'm interested in people. I love talking to interesting people, people like O.J. Simpson, Andretti ... I love champions. A champion has something *special* about him."

Douglas was filled with nervous energy, raw vitality. He couldn't remain still. It was in a sense actually wearying to be caged in a room with so much restlessness. Douglas walked halfway across the room and then whirled, fixing me on the quivering tip of a rhetorical point.

"I preceded a lot of this youthful revolution," he said. "And Thoreau did too, back in 1825. Compared to Thoreau, Saint Francis of Assisi was peanuts. And don't get me wrong. There's nothing the matter with building castles in the air. It wasn't so much Thoreau as his philosophy. It's like, you ever hear that song? *It's gotta be me, just gotta be me ....*"

Douglas sat again on the couch, as the last notes lingered. He was quieter now, subdued, called back to the present.

"Too often," he said slowly, "I have not been what I wanted to be. I've succumbed to pressures. Yes, I have. The things I've done that I liked, I've always done against advice. The bad films everybody was high on. The good films, they advised me against. But ... by ... God! From now on, *it's gotta be me!*

"*Champion,* for example. I had a chance to be in a picture with Gregory Peck and Ava Gardner over at Metro. I said, no, I want to make this picture *Champion.* The agents thought I was nuts. On the other hand, I let myself be pushed into *A Lovely Way to Die,* and what a load of shit that was. And *War Wagon.* Well, *War Wagon* wasn't bad. It was entertainment. I rather enjoyed it. But that woman, Pauline Kael—did you see that piece she wrote about it, about *War Wagon?* If Pauline Kael were sitting here right now," he said, indicating an empty chair, "I'd tell her, you're a bright dame, but you're full of shit."

He stood up, continuing to address Miss Kael.

"Don't crucify *me* because of what your idea of a movie star is," he said, pointing a finger at the chair. "I didn't start out to be a movie star. I started out to be an *actor*. You people out in the East have no idea what goes on out here." He punctuated his speech with short thrusts of the finger. "No awareness or knowledge whatsoever. You lose track of the human being behind the image of the movie star."

Leaving Pauline Kael speechless, Douglas turned back to me.

"You know," he said, "sometimes an interviewer will look at me and say—you're bright! They're actually surprised I might be bright. Well, I say, what if I wanted to be a writer? I just might be better at it than you are! Ever think of that? There are a lot of journalists who are just plain dumb.

"And I understand what's going on here, for example. The subtleties of the situation. An interviewer is not simply reporting what somebody said. It's a point of view toward that person. It incorporates the point of view of the interviewer."

He jerked his thumb over his shoulder toward the chair where Pauline Kael was not sitting.

"I don't need a critic to tell me I'm an actor," he said. "I make my own way. Nobody's my boss. Nobody's *ever* been my boss. Your only security is in your talent. I didn't get into this business as a pretty boy. I've made good pictures, bad pictures, I've been a maverick, I've never been under contract, except for one year at Warner's after *Champion*—I've made my own way!

"You know what it makes me think of sometimes? That picture *Young Man with a Horn*. Bix Beiderbecke in his lonely personal quest to hit that unattainable note. I like to play that role. The rebel. The guy fighting against society. The champion!"

Douglas lay down flat on the floor and braced his feet on top of the coffee table. He rested his head on his hands, and looked up to the ceiling. He talked in a faraway, thoughtful, pensive, reflective, philosophical voice.

"In all dramatic stories," he said, "death is the inevitable end. There aren't many songs you have to sing. They're all variations on a theme. I'm attracted and fascinated by how difficult it is to be an individual. The thing of being a so-called movie star works *against* you. Sure, you can always make exciting pictures, adventure pictures, but when you try something different they dump on you because you're a star. And yet that theme of the individual, fighting against society ... it's always obsessed me. *Lonely Are the Brave ... Spartacus ... Champion ...* it doesn't matter if you're a nice guy or you're a bastard. What matters is—you won't bend!"

He swung his legs off the coffee table and rolled over onto his stomach, resting his chin on his hands, sighting along the hallway toward the kitchen, where lunch was being prepared.

"Somebody who *won't bend.* That's what *The Brotherhood* was about. But a star's image is determined by what the public wants. They want me to be tough. A loved enemy. Neither the public nor the critics want you to do something they don't want you to do."

He sat up now, cross-legged on the floor.

"That's why the perfect movie star is John Wayne. I was in a lousy picture with him once, *In Harm's Way.* I used to think about John Wayne that he brings so much authority to a role he can pronounce literally any line in a script and get away with it. But I figured *In Harm's Way* had a line even John Wayne couldn't get away with. It was: *I need a fast ship because I mean to be in harm's way.* I thought, oh, shit, I've gotta hear him say *this* line. But you know what? He said it, and he got away with it. Now *that's* John Wayne ..."

Lunch was served: vegetable soup with herbs, relish plate, rolls and butter, cold cuts if you wanted some but nobody did.

"And there's nothing wrong with a John Wayne movie," he said. "I hate arty-farty pictures. What you always hope to make is a good, honest picture with balls. We did that with *Spartacus.* That was the best big spectacle ever made. *Ben-Hur* made almost three times as much money and didn't even compare. In our spectacle, the characters dominated the setting. It was a picture about men, not production values. Well, it made money. But my best pictures have seldom been my most successful. *Lust for Life* wasn't a big moneymaker. *Paths of Glory* has now finally broken even. *Lonely Are the Brave* ... boy, the non-artists really balled *that* one up. Instead of putting it in a little theatre and waiting for the reviews, they shoveled it into saturation bookings before anybody heard about it.

"That's what I mean, *it's gotta be me!* You got to fight!" He clenched his fist and shook it, and clenched his teeth, too. "In *The Brotherhood,* that great scene in the bedroom with Irene Papas, where I'm drunk and we both have all our clothes on and, Jesus, that scene was erotic! It could have easily fallen on its ass, and Martin Ritt wanted to cut it out of the script, but, no, you got to *fight* for those things.

"But then you make the money on the others. I was offered a million and a half to star in *The Fall of the Roman Empire.* And you know something? Now that I look back, I was a fool not to take it."

Douglas wasn't hungry. Too wound up. He dabbed at his soup with a roll and finally stood up and paced back and forth, chewing celery sticks.

"I have a sixteen-millimeter print of every movie I ever made," he said. "It was a fight to get them! But I can look at those prints, fifty prints after this one, and I know there's good stuff there, great things in those pictures, and they can't take that away from me. Like in this forty-ninth picture, *The Arrangement.* A-ha!" He smacked his fist into his palm. "Working with Kazan was a real experience. An actor's director. He relates to the actors. He'll do anything short of committing a homosexual act to get the best out of his actors."

Smack! "But you've got to fight for what you believe in. I remember in *War Wagon,* I fought with them for the nude scene. Remember, where I was walking away from the camera bare-ass? I said that's the only honest way to shoot it. I'm in the sack, see, and John Wayne's knocking at the door, and we've already established that I wear a gun at all times. So we play the whole scene at the door, me with my gun on, and when I walk back to bed you see the gun is the only thing I'm wearing! Great! You put pants on the guy, the scene isn't honest anymore.

"I'm not surprised, though, they wanted to destroy the scene. Dealing with Universal is always ... well, they were the aces who got me where I lived on *Lonely Are the Brave.* I wanted to call it *The Last*

Cowboy. It had a simplicity to it. But the aces put it through a computer and came up with a nothing title. And things like that ... and *A Lovely Way to Die* ... I hated that one ... I said, from now on I'm only doing what I want to do. And now, after fifty pictures and the last three damn good ones, it's time to take inventory."

Douglas collapsed on the couch, legs outstretched, heels digging into the carpet, arms crucified on the sofa's back. He sighed.

"I'm getting to be a tired warrior," he said. "I've killed so many Romans, and so many Vikings, and so many Indians."

He sighed again.

"The killing must stop."

A pause. A silence. It became a long silence.

"What I need," he said again, "is a pause to take inventory."

He twisted to lie flat on the sofa, head braced against one arm, feet propped up on the other. "You know what I did the other day?" he said. "I did a crazy thing. I took a walk out there on the back lot of Warner's. Back there behind Stage 19. And it was like it was haunted ...."

Very slowly, he lifted his feet and swung them around to rest them on the carpet again. And then he rested his elbows on his knees and his chin on his hands and it was like he was looking back in time, remembering other days, other rooms ...

"There were staircases," he said. "Dozens of staircases. You've never *seen* so many staircases. And you could imagine ghosts on them. Cagney. Flynn." He chuckled nostalgically. "Bogey." His voice took on a wondering quality. "And you couldn't help thinking, one day these staircases were seething with activity. And as you walked among them, that line of poetry came to your mind. You know, the one about *what town or peaceful hamlet* or something or other. Well, I can't remember how it goes ... 'Ode to a Grecian Urn,' that's the one. And you can't help thinking, Jesus! The ghosts that walk here at night. Because movies are filled with the stuff of everyone's dreams, and you know what a studio is? A dream factory. Staircases ... barrooms ... barbershops ..."

Another silence. Douglas stood up, put his hands in his pockets, looked out the window. His voice came back over his shoulder.

"And then it occurred to me, hell, I'm a star, too. And the final test is staying power. After forty-seven pictures, I was still in there, working in interesting movies. I was glad I had those sixteen-millimeter prints. It's a rough business. You lose that freshness. It's a struggle to stay alive in every picture ... and, hell, I don't know.

"I turned down *Stalag 17,* Holden won an Oscar. I turned down *Cat Ballou,* Marvin won the Oscar. But, hell, you never know. Decision making ... I'll tell you one thing. Five pictures in a row like *Paths of Glory,* and I'd have been out of business. And then when you *try* something ambitious, like when I went back to Broadway in Kesey's *One Flew Over the Cuckoo's Nest.* Van Heflin warned me. He said, *they hate actors who've made it. They'll kick you in the ass if they can.* But, hell, I was just like any other regular fellow making a couple of million a year." He laughed at that. "I knew Kesey early on, and then I met him again later. I did the play because I believed in it. But Kesey ... Christ, I don't give a shit what anybody does. But to destroy a talent is wholly unjustified. God, Kesey looked bad when I saw him again.

"There is something sad and dramatic about the disintegration of a talent. At the start, Brando was the best. And now ... well, it was a damn shame he had to miss with Kazan. Kazan, of course, wanted Brando to play the lead in *The Arrangement.* The two of them, together again. But after Kazan talked with Brando, he felt Brando wasn't quite with it ... didn't have the old enthusiasm ... but, hell I don't want to get into that. And yet, you know something?"

Douglas turned away from the window now and sat on the floor. His knees were pulled up and he bridged them with his arms.

"Being a star doesn't really change you. If you become a star, *you* don't change—everybody else does. Personally, I keep forgetting I'm a star. And then people look at me and I'm reminded. But you just have to remember one thing: the best eventually go to the top. I think I'm in the best category, and I'll stay at the top or I'll do something else. I'm not for the bush leagues. I remember as a kid of twenty, on Broadway, I had a chance to take a good role with a road company, or stay in New York playing a walk-on and an offstage echo. I stayed. I wanted that association with champions."

Douglas looked up almost fiercely.

"*Champions!*"

* * *

The next morning, the door to his Beverly Hills home was opened by a maid who hadn't been informed that anyone had an appointment with Mr. Douglas. The housekeeper also looked suspicious. They thought perhaps a mistake had been made. A misunderstanding. Perhaps if ...

"Hi, I know who you are," Peter Douglas said. "He's okay," Peter told the servants. "Come on in here and have a seat. I knew you were coming. I like to keep in touch around here ..."

Peter was perhaps twelve, sandy-haired, personable, looked like his father. He wore tennis shoes and a T-shirt.

"Dad'll be down after a while," he said. "You want some pretzels? No? I'd offer you something else, but at the moment" (he sighed dramatically) "it's pretzels and that's it."

Peter shrugged his shoulders stoically. "Know the one I'd like to make a movie out of? *Fail-Safe.* I'm Peter, by the way. I'm just a slave here."

Peter headed toward the pool. The room he left was a sort of den and library, half open to the living room and the bar. There were several animal skins on the floor, and a two-year run of *Time* laid flat on a shelf with the spines overlapped. And there were a lot of books on the shelves, and a display of primitive carvings and statues, and ...

"How about a cup of coffee?" Kirk Douglas said. He had entered silently on bare feet. "It'll be here in a minute." He grinned in anticipation. "That first cup ... ah!"

He touched one of the skins with a bare toe. "How do you like that leopard skin?" he said. "Isn't it a beauty?" He sat down and his voice became serious. "What a terrible thing it is to kill. I impulsively went on one safari. I thought, Jesus, I can't shoot an animal. But once we left Nairobi, I discovered the real me. A killer. I shot about thirty animals. I was shocked and embarrassed. I was confused. I asked myself, *Do I really want to kill?* The philosophers say, know thyself. But what really counts is how honest and how brave you are. You ask of a man, where is he strong? Where is he weak? The bully with the low voice may be secretly frightened ...."

The coffee came, and with it a plate of chocolate-chip cookies. Douglas picked up his saucer in his hand, sipped, considered his cup. "The home of the brave," he said finally. "What a violent nation we are! A violent people. *That's* why there's so much violence in the movies. The Greeks had a word for it. It's catharsis. Audiences love gangsters. Virtue is not photogenic. Christ, even Disney bakes people into cookies."

He paused to nibble a chocolate-chip, and then held it up. "Great? The best! They have to be. They were made by my cook. But the West ... there was a certain simplicity and directness there."

He leaped to his feet, balanced the coffee cup in his left hand, adopted a shoot-out stance (legs wide, right hand poised) and snarled: "Smile when you say that!" Then he shook his head in resignation. "It's childlike," he said. "No one can be an artist without a childlike quality. If I were really sophisticated, how could I, a grown-up man, carry a gun in a movie?"

He put down his cup and picked up one of the primitive statues in the room. "Take this," he said. "Childlike in its innocence. Look here. On this side, you can see it's a woman. And then you turn it around and, well, on this side, it's pretty obviously a man. It has an innocent bisexuality. It comes from a society where all things mix naturally together.

"Reminds me." He sat down again, still considering the statue in his hands. "Kubrick once had this great idea. We'd make the world's greatest pornographic film. Spend millions on it. And then maybe only show it in one country, like Switzerland, and fly people in to see it. Kubrick. A great director. I thank him for so much that is good in *Paths of Glory* and *Spartacus*. You know, at one time with *Paths of Glory*, even Kubrick wanted to cop out. He wanted to rewrite the script, make it a sort of B picture, a commercial thing.

But I'm glad we stood by our guns. There's a picture that will always be good, years from now. I don't have to wait fifty years to know that; I know it *now.* Certain pictures have a universality of theme. *Champion* did. Audiences are all the same. They love the guy who's up there on top. And yet, you know, in real life ...." He sighed and finished his coffee.

"Somebody asked me not long ago if I was going to write an autobiography. Well, I have one good enough reason. I'd write it for my four sons. But nobody else would be interested. My life's too corny and typical to make a good autobiography. I wouldn't even do it as a movie. My life's a B script. My life. The violins playing ... the kid who didn't have enough to eat ... the parents who were Russian immigrants ....

"I taught my mother to write her name. It's like my parents came out of the middle ages, and in one generation I jumped to here." He indicated the room with a sweep of his hand. "My parents did the one essential thing. They didn't miss the boat. I grew up in Amsterdam, New York. My parents never did understand my success. I'd say, *Ma! I just signed a million-dollar contract! But son,* she'd say, *You look so thin ....*"

He leaned forward intensely. "And yet my mother was a great woman," he said. "She had little formal knowledge, but she knew much about life. They used to come to her with sores, with boils. She'd take out an old, moldy loaf of bread and apply it to the sore, as a poultice. And this was years before penicillin."

He gave a wry twist to his mouth. "My life," he said. "A B picture. And yet my life is an American life. Because the real American life, the typical one, *is* a B picture. Like mine—the kid who worked up from abject poverty to become the champion. But you got to fight! Our forefathers set the bar so high we keep trying to go under it, instead of over ...."

He stood up again now, and looked out the window to where two of his sons were swimming in the backyard pool.

"Look at those kids,' he said. "Olympic material."

He smiled, watching as Peter did a racing dive off the edge of the pool. Then he spoke again, slowly. "At this period of my life," he said, "I look at this trilogy, these last three pictures, and I must admit I feel I'm functioning well. You have to set your own standards. I was nominated for *Champion*. Broderick Crawford won that year. I was nominated for *Lust for Life*, but Yul Brynner won. You set your own standards. You have to. And then these arty-farty foreign movies come along, and ...."

He whirled and strode away from the window, his fist slamming into his palm. The softness was gone from his voice; he was angry.

"You know why they criticize me?" he said. "I'm criticized because I can jump over two horses! And they sneer. *Hollywood,* they say. Hollywood. Well I for one am plenty proud of Hollywood. They go over there to Europe and they forget their roots and they lose the nourishment of Hollywood. I say if you want to grow a plant, put it where there's some good horseshit to grow in!"

He walked rapidly toward the bookcase, and indicated a set of matched volumes. "See those?" he said. "It's a rare edition: *150 Years of Boxing*. It's all in there, and it's all the same. Acting is like prizefighting. The downtown gyms are smelly, but that's where the champions are."

Sybil Danning

It started out as Conan Meets Body Heat
and ended up as Superman Meets the Hulk.
Chicago, 1983

When she heard about the gladiator's cloak, Sybil Danning knew that things were not going to be great between her and Lou Ferrigno. This was on the set of *Hercules,* in Rome, where Sybil was co-starring with the onetime Incredible Hulk.

The tension had been building. Ferrigno had already insisted that Sybil give up the role of Circe, the good sorceress, and play Adriana, the evil Greek princess. Now he wanted her to wear a cloak.

"None of the *other* gladiators wore cloaks," Danning said. "I was the only female gladiator. Why did I have to wear a cloak? It wasn't fair. Also, all the gladiators rode in together on horseback, except me. Lou wanted me to ride at least five feet behind him."

She seemed amused by his presumption. How could a cloak possibly add to the appeal of Sybil Danning? This evening in Chicago, for example, she was wearing a blazer and pants. There was nothing under the blazer. The regulars in the bar at Riccardo's took turns walking past the table at a snail's pace.

"There was another thing," Danning said. "Ferrigno insisted that the movie be rated PG. It started out as *Conan Meets Body Heat* and ended up as *Superman Meets the Hulk.* There could be nothing R-rated in the film. He didn't want to disappoint all the little kids who loved him as the Incredible Hulk."

She sipped her Bloody Mary.

"Well," she said, "this is definitely a *Hercules* for kids, all right. For the little, little, young, *young* kids."

When you are known as the Queen of the Bs, you do not develop a lot of false illusions. Sybil Danning has probably been in more different movies in the last fifteen years than any other actress in the free world, and they can't all be *Citizen Kane.*

"I think the costumes deserved more credit than some people gave them," she said. "One review said they looked like Frederick's of Hollywood. I had one leather costume that was a cross between Late Greek and Early Egyptian. Very authentic. Some things you do for the roles, some things you do for the money."

Before *Hercules,* for example, she made *Gladiators,* also with Ferrigno. That was where the tension between them started to build. At about the same time, she made *Chained Heat,* in which Danning plays the leader of a prison gang. In a few days she was to start filming *Playing with Fire,* a teenage sex comedy co-starring Eric Brown, of *Private Lessons.* Then it was off to Brazil to film *Jungle Heat* ("a female *Deliverance,* with me in the Burt Reynolds role") and then back to Hollywood for *Cops,* with Danning on the homicide squad.

Sybil Danning? If the name does not immediately ring a bell, try to think back to the cover of the August 1983 *Playboy.* That was Sybil on the cover in a chain mail swimming suit, right next to the line *Queen of the Action Flicks Heats Up a Ten-Page Pictorial.*

I noticed, I said, a lot of leather and chains in the ten-page pictorial. Was that your idea?

"Leather and chains?" Danning said. "Not really. Well, there was a shot of me in the thigh-high leather boots, wearing the sort of chain harness. Is that the one you were thinking of?"

That was the one I was thinking of, I said.

"The whole thing with *Playboy* has been a long drawn-out affair with a happy ending," she said. "I was first photographed for *Playboy* back in 1979. At that time I was not ready for total nudity. I told them they could photograph half of me."

The right or left half? I asked.

"Funny. Then the Bo Derek issue came out. Remember? Where you could see everything except her chromosomes? And so my photos were not daring enough. *Playboy* kept after me, though, and finally, this year, I felt emotionally and physically ready to do a totally nude layout. Also, we made a good arrangement involving display on the cover for both the American and foreign editions. If you're going to do something like that, you want people to know, don't you?"

She unrolled a large poster showing her posing on the cover of *Playboy.*

"This was a good photo," she said, "but in the Japanese edition they used a more aggressive pose, with my arm up in the air, and you could see *everything*—I mean I had a little rash under my arm, and you could even see that. They're supposed to airbrush their photos to make them look better, but they airbrushed nothing on me. Sometimes a little airbrushing doesn't hurt. Remember that cover of Raquel Welch leaning over with the *incredible* behind? That wasn't all her. She wanted a little more, and they airbrushed it in. And for their thirtieth anniversary edition, they're going to have to give Joan Collins a waist."

How do you know all this stuff? I asked.

"Little birds."

She ordered another Bloody Mary. I asked her where she was staying.

"The Whitehall," she said. "I wonder if Richard Burton is staying there, too. He's in town for *Private Lives.* They keep their guest list very hush-hush, you know. They won't even tell you if *you're* staying there."

What would happen if Richard Burton *did* happen to be at the Whitehall? I asked.

"Nothing. He's happily married. I had my chance."

You did?

"When I was making *Blackbeard* with him in Budapest. That was the one where I was chandeliered to death."

Let me be sure I get this down correctly, I said. You were chandeliered to death?

"Afterwards, Richard asked me to come into his dressing room. I was such a fan of his. I was so scared! He was so sweet, romantic, sexy and tender. There were so many women on the picture. There were eight women in the film, and each one worked one week. I shouldn't be telling all of this. Richard is in town and he might read it."

Just tell the parts he'd be interested to read, I said. He's not crazy about giving interviews. Maybe he'll demand a retraction and I can get an interview that way.

"Well, we were drinking vodka. The next thing I knew, I was swept up in his arms and out into his Rolls-Royce, and there we were, going across the river from Pest to Buda. And he put his arm around me and said, *Here I am, a poor coal miner's son, sitting in my Rclls with a beautiful blonde. I'm going to spend the night with you.*"

And what did you say to that? I asked.

"My answer was no."

And what did he say then?

"He said, *All right, then, I'll only spend five hours."*

And then what?

"We got to my hotel, and I didn't even look back, I went right up to my room, alone. And when I got the door closed, I thought to myself, *What an idiot!*"

He was?

"No. I was."

five

It's still the same old story

Martin Scorsese's first feature was the student film he started while he was still at New York University. It was originally titled I Call First, *later retitled* Who's That Knocking at My Door, *and it starred Harvey Keitel. When it had its world premiere in the Chicago Film Festival, I had been a movie critic for about fifteen minutes. I predicted in my review that within ten years Scorsese would be the American Fellini. He telephoned me from New York: "Do you think it will take that long?"*

Werner Herzog speaks of the "voodoo of location" and must shoot his jungle pictures in the real jungle with real whirlpools, poison arrows, snakes and quagmires. The stone faces on Easter Island were made by people like him because movies had not yet been invented. He is the only living ancient astronaut.

Ingmar Bergman is the only director who may be a saint, and like saints he is not always worldly. For several years, he and Charles Bronson had the same press agent, a man named Ernie Anderson. When Bergman made his famous trip to Hollywood in the late 1970s, he telephoned Anderson and discovered that Ernie was working on a Bronson picture.

"Can I come over to the set?" Bergman asked.

"Well ... yeah, I guess so," Anderson said, not sure how his

macho star would receive the great man.

On the set, Bergman asked Bronson to explain what they were doing in that day's scene.

"Well," said Bronson, "this is the scene where they use the special effects of the machine-gun blast. All these little capsules of blood under the costume are fired by little electrical charges ... the guy over there has a rheostat ... and ... uh ... but wait a minute. Why am I explaining this to you? After all, you're a director, aren't you?"

"Please continue," Bergman said. "It's fascinating to learn about these things."

"You mean," said Bronson, "you don't use machine guns in your pictures?"

Werner Herzog

Frogs do not apparently need images, and cows do not need them either. But we do.

Cannes, 1982

On the day after *Fitzcarraldo* had its world premiere at the Cannes Film Festival, I sat and had tea with Werner Herzog, the West German who directed it. Werner Herzog is a strange, deep, visionary man. With other directors, I have an interview. With Herzog, I have an audience.

He does not speak of small matters. He would not say so, but he obviously sees himself as one of the most important artists of his time—and so, to tell the truth, do I. He makes films that exist outside the usual categories. He takes enormous risks to make them. In a widely discussed article in the *New Republic,* Stanley Kauffmann wondered if it is an item of Herzog's faith that he must risk his life with every movie he makes.

It is a logical question. Herzog makes movies about people who have larger dreams and take greater risks than ordinary men. Herzog does the same. He once went with a small crew to an island where a volcano was about to explode. He wanted to interview a man who had decided to stay behind and die. Herzog has also made movies in the middle of the Sahara, and twice he has risked his life and the lives of his associates on risky film projects in the Amazon rain jungles.

His *Aguirre, the Wrath of God* (1973) told the story of one of Pizarro's mad followers who pressed on relentlessly into the jungle in a doomed quest for El Dorado. Now there is *Fitzcarraldo,* based on the true story of an Irishman who tried to haul a whole steamship over dry land from one Amazonian river system to another.

As nearly everybody must know by now, Werner Herzog did the same thing in filming *Fitzcarraldo.* But Herzog's historical inspiration (who was named Fitzgerald) had the good sense to disassemble *his* steamship before hauling it overland; Herzog used winches and pulleys to haul an entire boat overland *intact.* And that afternoon over tea at Cannes, he was not modest about his feat: "*Apocalypse Now* was only a kindergarten compared to what we went through," he said.

At forty, he is a thin, strongly built man of average height, with hair swept back from a broad forehead. He usually wears a neat mustache. He spent an undergraduate year at a university in Pennsylvania and speaks excellent English; he once made a movie, *Stroszek,* on location in northern Wisconsin, and it included a striking image of the lost American Dream, as his hero, Bruno, looked in despair as the bank repossessed his mobile home and left him contemplating the frozen prairie.

I had seen *Fitzcarraldo* the day before. I also had seen Les Blank's *Burden of Dreams,* an unblinking, unsentimental documentary about the making of *Fitzcarraldo.* It is good to see the two films together, because Blank's documentary paints a portrait of Herzog seemingly going mad under the strain of making his impossible movie. I asked Herzog about that: Did he really crack up during his months in the rain jungle and his legendary problems with civil wars, disease, Indian attacks and defecting cast and crew members?

"Sanity?" he said. "For that you don't have to fear. I am quite sane." He somehow sounded like the vampire hero of his *Nosferatu.* He sipped tea. "I make sense. I don't push myself to the edge."

Having said that, he proceeded to contradict it: "It is only the project that counts. If the nature of the project makes it necessary for me to go very far, I would go anywhere. How much you have to suffer, how little sleep you get .... I am the last one to look for a situation like that, but the last one to back out if it is necessary."

He looked out over the veranda of the hotel, at the palm trees in the spring sunshine.

"I would go down in hell and wrestle a film away from the devil if it was necessary," said the man who had just told me he didn't push himself to the edge.

Do you feel you have a personal mission to fulfill? I asked. Other directors sign up Goldie Hawn and shoot in Los Angeles. You sign up Klaus Kinski and disappear into the rain forest.

"If you say *mission,* it sounds a little heavy," he said. "I would say 'duty' or 'purpose.' When I start a new film, I am a good soldier. I do not complain, I will hold the outpost even if it is already given up. Of course I want to win the battle. I see each film more like a high duty that I have."

Is your duty to the film, I asked, or does the film itself fulfill a duty to mankind? Even as I asked the question, I realized that it sounded grandiose, but Herzog nodded solemnly. He said his duty was to help mankind find new images, and, indeed, in his films there are many great and vivid images: a man standing on a drifting raft, surrounded by gibbering monkeys; a ski-jumper so good that he overjumps a landing area; men deaf and blind from birth, feeling the mystery of a tree; a man asleep on the side of a volcano; midgets chasing runaway automobiles; a man standing on an outcropping rock in the middle of a barren sea; a man hauling a ship up the side of a mountain.

"We do not have adequate images for our kind of civilization," Herzog said. "What are we to look at? The ads at the travel agent's of the Grand Canyon? We are surrounded by images that are worn out, and I believe that unless we discover new images, we will die out. Die like the dinosaurs. And I mean it physically."

He leaned forward, speaking intensely, as if time were running out. "Frogs do not apparently need images, and cows do not need them, either. But we do. Michelangelo in the Sistine Chapel for the first time articulated human pathos in a new way that was adequate to the understanding of his time. I am not looking to make films in which actors stand around and say words that some screenwriter has thought were clever. That is why I use midgets, and a man who spent twenty-four years in prisons and asylums (Bruno S., the hero of *Stroszek*) and the deaf and blind, and why I shoot with actors who are under hypnosis, for example. I am trying to make something that has not been made before."

I said *Fitzcarraldo* almost seemed to be about itself: a film about a man who hauled a ship up a hill, made by a man who hauled a real ship up a real hill to make a film.

"It was not planned like that," Herzog said. "It was not planned to be as difficult as it was. It came to a point where the purpose of the film, the making of the film, the goals of the film and how to make the film all became one and the same thing: to get that ship up the hill. When Jason Robards fell ill and returned to America, before I replaced him with Klaus Kinski, I thought about playing Fitzcarraldo myself. I came very close."

Why did you have to use a real boat?

"There was never any question in my mind about that. All those trashy special effects and miniatures that you see in Hollywood movies have caused audiences to lose trust in their eyes. Here, in my film, they are given back trust in their own eyes. When the boat goes up the mountain, people look at the screen, looking for some thing to tell them it's a trick, but it's no trick. Instinctively, they sense it. An image like that gives you courage for your own dreams."

He smiled, a little grimly. "It's a film," he said, "that will not have a remake. That man who is going to make this film again has to be born first." He paused for thought. "The mad King Ludwig II of Bavaria," he said, "could have made this film."

I observed that in *Burden of Dreams* there seemed to be some controversy over the safety and practicality of hauling the ship up the hill.

"I had engineers," Herzog said, "and I disposed of them. I had the basic idea of winches and pulleys, of a chain of combined winches. In pre-history, you can see that perhaps man did that same thing. In Brittany, there are huge boulders of rock that may have been moved two miles up ramps, with an artificial hill and a crater at the end. Whether that is how they moved those rocks or not, I fantasized about it. I saw them on a long walk I took across France and Germany. If *Fitzcarraldo* has a passport and we must list its place of birth, I would list Carnac, in Brittany, where those boulders are one of the miracles of the world. That ass Erich von Daniken, who writes of the ancient astronauts, cannot believe man is capable of such a feat, but I say give me two years and two thousand men and I will do it all over again for you."

But when you were pulling that ship up the hill, I asked, did you ever question your purpose? Did you wonder if it was all just a little ludicrous?

"There were always low points and lower, and points below the lowest," he said. "I did not allow myself private feelings. I had not the privilege of despair, anxiety, pain. I never paused, I never lost faith, and I have faith enough for fifteen more films."

Fifteen more films like this one?

"I doubt if I or anyone else can make a film like this again," he said. "Film history has shown that this profession of filmmaker has destroyed almost everyone. You can be a cello player until the age of ninety-five. You can be a poet until you die, but the life-span of a filmmaker is fifteen years, of making good things. Then they crumble into ashes. I am more than twenty years already. Of course, it has to do with physical strength. For my next project, instead of a film project, I will set out after this film festival is over and walk twenty five hundred miles on foot."

Where will you go?

He shrugged.

Chapter Five

Clint Eastwood

You have to make a choice.
Are you gonna showboat to the fourth wall, or get with the program?
Carmel, Calif., 1984

For a man who got his start by striking matches on a hunchback and shooting three men with one bullet, Clint Eastwood has inspired an amazing amount of serious analysis. I was looking at some of the literature out on the patio behind the Hog's Breath Inn, the restaurant he owns here on a side street not far from the ocean. There was the Norman Mailer essay ("He is living proof of the maxim that the best way to get through life is cool") and the *New York Review of Books* article ("What's most distinctive about Eastwood is how effectively he struggles against absorption into mere genre, mere style"), and the *Los Angeles Times* piece on the strong women in his movies ("Eastwood may be the most important and influential feminist filmmaker working in America today").

Clint Eastwood, the Man With No Name, Dirty Harry, Joe Kidd—a *feminist filmmaker?* I put the articles aside and studied the menu. It was going to be either the Eiger Sandwich or the Dirty Harry Burger, and I'd almost made up my mind when Clint Eastwood materialized at the table and sprawled in a chair. He is very low key. He sat in a corner with his back to the patio, to give himself some small measure of privacy, but before he could tell the waitress he would have an iced tea, two little girls had come up, smiling and giggling, for his autograph.

He has a system. He signs *Clint Eastwood,* and *while* he is signing it, he asks, "Who's it to?" Then they say something like "It's to my brother Billy," and he writes *To Billy* above his signature. By asking the question while he's signing his name, he saves a few seconds every time. He has been around long enough to realize that no one ever wants an autograph for themselves. They always want it for their girlfriend or their brother Billy.

"This early hour isn't so bad," he said. "I've been in here times when the autograph hounds got so thick I was driven out. I'd have to tell people I'd meet them down the street."

How does it make you feel, all the requests for autographs?

"Like the Chinese water torture. One autograph is no big deal. But they keep coming all day long, day after day, and each one is a little tug at your patience, until you feel like screaming."

He all but scowled at his iced tea. Then he thought of something funny. "Once in the desert, Bob Daley and I were scouting for locations. We ran out of gas. Bob got out and tried to thumb a lift, but in half an hour he got nowhere. Then I uncoiled myself and decided it was time for the old high profile. So I stuck out my thumb. Nothing. Finally some kids gave us a lift to Vegas. Once we were into Vegas, they were all over me like a cheap suit. Where the hell were all these people when I needed them?"

Our plan today was to do a couple of interviews, one for print, one for television, and the idea was to do TV first, while the light was good. Eastwood's publicist had rented a hospitality suite at a motel as a possible location for the TV interview, but Eastwood said there was nothing more boring for a TV backdrop than motel wallpaper. I told him he was, after all, a movie director. *He* should direct the interview. He liked the idea. He began to talk about beaches and cliffs and promontories, and the problem of light reflecting off the white Monterey sand, and finally he said he would get his car and lead us to a place he knew.

Eastwood was not driving just any car. He had to jackknife himself behind the wheel of a Morris Mini Countryman, the tiniest station wagon ever built "It has a Mini Cooper 8 engine," he said. "Overpowered. It handles like a go-kart." Inside, everything was customized; a vehicle that had once been the bottom of the line in the British auto market now had power windows, tinted glass, a mighty stereo system, and, behind the wheel, the most important movie star in the world.

Eastwood pulled the car into the local Shell station. "It goes six months on nine gallons," he explained. He has lived in Carmel for twenty years and knows all the locals, and introduced me to the station owner, Dick Lugo, while a crowd materialized for his autograph. A little gas spilled on the finish of the Countryman, and Eastwood frowned and got a water hose and splashed it off. Then we drove down toward the beach.

"I filmed a lot of *Play Misty for Me* down here," he said. "You could point your camera in any direction, and it looked good. Carmel doesn't allow any street lights or neon signs." He led a little parade across the sand to the shade of some low-slung cypress trees. Now he was functioning as a director: "How about a shot of the two of us walking across the dune and settling down under these trees, and then a closeup of us sitting down, and then come in for the over-the-shoulder? I think the relative shade here will look good on videotape."

Outside of the movie industry itself, few people even think of Clint Eastwood as a director, and yet he has directed ten films—*Play Misty for Me, Breezy, High Plains Drifter, The Eiger Sanction, The Outlaw Josey Wales, The Gauntlet, Firefox, Bronco Billy, Honky Tonk Man* and *Sudden Impact.* He is known for always finishing on time and on budget, and has arguably been responsible for more box office dollars as a director than any other active filmmaker in the category below superstars like Spielberg and Lucas. Eastwood is also not often thought of as a producer, although he takes great pride in controlling his budgets, and scornfully compares the inflated thirty-million-dollar costs of *Rhinestone* and *The Natural* with the three and a half million dollars for his own *Sudden Impact.*

No, Clint Eastwood isn't thought of as a director or as a producer, but as an actor. And then not so much an actor as a character: As the tall, thin, crag-faced man of violence who tightens his jaw and narrows his eye and kills with a series of exotic weapons like the .44 Magnum, "the most deadly handgun in the world," and adds a little refrain like *Do you feel lucky?* or *Come on. Make my day.* To an unusual degree in these days when actors cheerfully abandon their mystique and unveil intimate details to *People* magazine, Clint Eastwood retains the privacy of the great male stars of the 1930s and 1940s.

We sat under the cypress tree Eastwood had selected, and began to talk. He told a chilling story, of how the manufacturers of Magnum revolvers had planned to issue a limited edition of the Automag model he used in *Sudden Impact,* and wanted Eastwood to allow his name to be engraved on the barrel.

"I turned them down. That'd be all I need, for one of those guns to turn up in the wrong place at the wrong time."

How do you feel about your identification with violence?

"I think the Dirty Harry pictures exist in an old Hollywood tradition of the tough cop, the law-enforcer. I try to make the kinds of action pictures I think people want to see. I'm concerned about the guy with a few bucks in his pocket who wants to go out and have a good time, and see a movie that delivers."

How does that fit in with the image Eastwood has been gaining lately from the experts on popular culture, who claim him as the most important feminist director in the world? Their argument is based on a pattern in most of Eastwood's movies, where there are strong women to balance the strong men, and cops have female partners, men have iron-willed mothers, macho lovers find that their women have ideas of their own, and killers incur the wrath of avenging females ready to settle the score.

In the recent Eastwood movie, *Sudden Impact,* for example, Sondra Locke plays a woman who single-mindedly tracks down and kills the men responsible for the rape and insanity of her sister, and when Dirty Harry discovers the motive for her behavior, he has nothing but understanding.

In the latest Eastwood movie, *Tightrope,* Eastwood plays a New Orleans cop who gets his sexual kicks by handcuffing women before having sex with them. Then he gets assigned to a case where a man slasher is killing prostitutes—including some of the women Eastwood has handcuffed. Will the cop find the killer before he becomes a suspect himself? The Eastwood touch: In the course of his investigation, he meets a woman karate instructor (Genevieve Bujold) who teaches women how to fight off rapists, and whose strength allows Eastwood to learn how to let a woman touch him freely.

"It's very simple," Eastwood said. "I've always been interested in strong women. When I was growing up, the female roles were equal to the men, and the actresses were just as strong as the actors. Now, in a lot of movies, you seem to have half a cast. The guy will be a big macho star. The woman will be a wimp. Women in the audience don't like to see that, and I believe men don't, either. Isn't it going to be twice as interesting to have two strong characters?"

How did weak women find their way into so many recent movies?

"Men do the casting, and they cast for looks. They cast an interesting man, and then for the woman they go for a model, a centerfold girl. That's taking the acting profession lightly. I resent producers who have good female roles and hire inexperienced women. They're sinking their own ships."

Eastwood, on the other hand, has been responsible for launching a few careers. Tyne Daly played Dirty Harry's partner in *The Enforcer,* and her role in that movie was spun off fairly directly into the TV show, "Cagney and Lacey." He has also been responsible for redefining certain ideas about sexiness. In *Tightrope,* for example, the Eastwood character is surrounded by glamorous, bizarre hookers, and in a more routine movie one of them would doubtless become the romantic interest.

Not here. The Genevieve Bujold character is deliberately presented without glamour ("I asked her to play the role without any makeup, and she jumped at the chance.") She is often seen covered with sweat and grime. She is clearly in her late thirties. And yet the final moment, when the man allows the woman to touch him, is more romantic and erotic than any linkage with a sweet young centerfold could have possibly been.

"Bujold has that thing a lot of actresses don't have," Eastwood said: "Vulnerability, combined with great strength. Sondra Locke has it, too. I think the feminist training of the 1970s sidetracked a lot of actesses into thinking they weren't allowed to be vulnerable. Feminism doesn't mean the female John Wayne."

In *Tightrope,* Eastwood allows himself to play a character with sexual hangups. He is not always a nice man. Why, I asked him, wasn't he more concerned with his "image"? Why didn't he have any hesitation about playing a perverted character?

He grinned. "Just too dumb, I guess."

After every one of the four Dirty Harry movies, Eastwood has announced that this one is the last one—that Callahan is hanging up his Magnum. Yet he keeps making them, and *Sudden Impact* will be one of the year's top box office winners. Will there be another one?

"Not as of now. The way we made this one was curious. They were taking a marketing survey to see whether the public was interested in seeing Sean Connery in another James Bond movie. So to disguise the question, they surrounded it with other questions about other actors and other characters. They threw in Dirty Harry, and to their amazement he placed first. So they came to me and said I had to make another one. They were ready to start that Friday. But there has to be a good story, and those are hard to come by. Finally, we got one."

What makes a good story?

"I'll tell you one thing I insist on. The single weakest point of most modern thrillers is at the end, where they usually have a chase. And the chase hasn't developed since the days of cowboy pictures, where you had two riders out there on the range. They seem to think the chase itself is enough. But people have seen too many chases. They're bored by one more car crash. In *Tightrope,* I took out the cars in the script and we did the chase on foot. But the key question you have to ask is, *What is this chase doing to the characters?* What's going on in addition to the chase? Unless you can answer that question with something interesting, the end of your movie is going to be routine no matter how much you spent on it."

Where do you get Dirty Harry's catch-phrases, like *make my day.* Do you try to come up with a good one for every movie?

He shrugged. "They just seem to emerge from the scripts. They seem like good ideas at the time."

We talked some more, there under the cypress, with Eastwood

occasionally sticking a spear of beach grass into his mouth, or lobbing a pebble into the distance. Both, I reflected, were cinematic activities that brought visual interest to his answers. This man was a consummate actor. Finally we stood up, shook the sand from our shoes, and returned to our back table on the patio of the Hog's Breath.

Right away, it was clear that the customers in his restaurant weren't going to give Clint Eastwood a pass. There was a slow but steady parade to his side, until it was obvious that everyone in the room was going to ask for an autograph. Frequently, the autograph seekers would interrupt Eastwood in the middle of a sentence, and when they used the standard rituals ("I hate to bother you, but ..."), he frowned, but the frown was always down at the piece of paper he was signing. He was distant, but courteous. Autographs are a fame tax the public exacts from celebrities.

"Do you mind if I take your picture?"

"Snap it."

"And now if you would sign these napkins ..."

"I'm thinking of passing a rule: Either a Polaroid *or* an autograph, not both."

Eastwood ordered a glass of white wine. The sun was sinking, and it was chilly in the outdoors. Gas flames were lighted in the patio fireplaces. I told Eastwood that since he was the most popular movie star in the world (an assessment nobody in the movie industry would argue with), I would like him to talk about what he did on the screen, and how he did it. Ignoring the question of whether he was, indeed, the world's top star (how do you respond to a statement like that, anyway?) he said the single most important thing for him, in any scene, is to be able to believe it.

"I try not to think too much about my acting, maybe out of fear of losing whatever it is that I do. But I think I know what it is that people respond to. I believe the situation. I've played some outrageous things. In *A Few Dollars More,* I shot people without looking at them, and hit them without knowing where they were. If I had done that tongue-in-cheek, it wouldn't have worked. A lot of my best-known scenes have not involved difficult acting choices, but let somebody else try acting in them, and see how they play.

"Another thing, I don't play to the fourth wall—to the audience. I don't beg audiences to come to me. If they don't like what I'm doing, they can take a hike. Sometimes with actors you have the feeling they're reaching out and begging to be liked, and audiences don't go for that. You have to make your choice: Are you gonna showboat to the fourth wall, or get with the program?

"I'll give you an example of the kind of acting I admire: Bill Murray in *Ghostbusters*. He's in a totally ridiculous series of situations in that movie, but he plays every scene as if he really believes it. He never feels rehearsed. He makes it interesting every time. That's the best compliment you can give an actor."

What other performances have you admired?

"Oskar Werner in *The Last Ten Days*. Albert Finney in *Saturday Night and Sunday Morning*. Maggie Smith in *The Prime of Miss Jean Brodie*. Montgomery Clift in *The Search*. The first half of *Sergeant York*, when Gary Cooper was in the back woods. On the other hand, the kind of acting I do *not* like is something like *Frances*, last year, with some of the most overt overacting known to mankind. They were out of control in that movie; it's the kind of thing you get nominated for. Emotional gymnastics. But will people look at it forty years from now? Yet actors like Gary Cooper and Henry Fonda have got to be eighty-five before we see how good they were."

As a director, what do you look for in an actor?

"I don't think most directors know anything about acting. The most they can do is create a comfortable environment. Actors know the most difficult problem in acting, which is to act in a scene with a person you don't know, while you're both playing characters who know each other very well. You have to break down your natural reserve in the presence of a stranger. As a director, I can help actors do that sometimes.

"Otherwise, as a director, what I do is come in on time and under budget. It's a job. I don't believe in standing around and shooting forty takes of everything. The director who shoots the same scene all day is probably stalling because he doesn't know what the next shot is going to be. A guy like John Ford would edit in the camera—only shoot what he knew he would need. I cover more than Ford did; I go in for more closeups than he used. But I have a similar approach. When you read that a little movie like *Rhinestone* cost thirty million, or that *The Natural* cost twenty-nine or thirty million, I look at my three-and-a-half-million budget for *Tightrope,* or *Sudden Impact,* which cost less than that, and I gotta ask myself if somebody skimmed $15 million off the top."

Does your budget include your salary?

"No, we're talking actual production costs. But all the same, I could make four pictures for what they spent on *The Natural.*"

It was almost dark out, now, and time to call it a day. The parade of autograph-seekers had never slowed, but now there was one more fan approaching the table, and he would bring a chill that was deeper than the night air.

This fan had been drinking. He had some story he wanted to tell Eastwood, but it was coming out in such a disjointed way that it was hard to follow. Something about having been at the Hog's Breath before, looking for Eastwood and not finding him, and coming back tonight, because of something about a police training program, and ...

From somewhere on his body, the man drew a .44 Magnum and held it in his hand.

There was an instant when everyone froze.

"I hope that's not loaded," Eastwood said.

"Naw," the fan said. He opened the empty chamber.

"What do you want?"

"For you to autograph the stock," the fan said, and pulled an awl from his pocket.

Eastwood looked very grim.

"I hate to autograph firearms," he said.

The guy said something about how all the boys on the force admired Eastwood so much. Eastwood frowned. But he took the awl and scratched his initials, C.E., into the wooden stock of the most powerful handgun in the world.

"Be careful where you leave that," he told the guy.

Martin Scorsese

Who the hell wants to make other pictures
if you can't have a relationship with a woman?
New York, 1983

Walking back to my hotel after dinner with Martin Scorsese, I asked myself how much longer he would go on driving himself up the wall with his obsession of finding happiness with a woman. For all of his adult life, Scorsese has been searching for love and serenity with a woman, and he has never found those comforts for very long.

Out of his pain, however, he has directed some of the best films ever made about loneliness and frustration. Pausing for a stoplight, looking up at the Manhattan canyons where lonely people sleep on shelves all the way to the stars, I reflected that Scorsese's hurt has at least inspired great films. If he stays miserable, I thought, he might make some more masterpieces like *Taxi Driver.* On the other hand, he might simply go off the deep end into bitterness and despair.

We had just talked for three hours about *The King of Comedy,* Scorsese's problematical new film—a movie the studio was ready to give up on, until some good reviews started coming in. For Scorsese, the making of the film coincided with a painful period of his life, a time when he fell in love with Ingrid Bergman's daughter, Isabella Rossellini, was married and was divorced. Although it is easy to see *The King of Comedy* as the most barren and unemotional of all Scorsese's films, that is not the way he sees it. Maybe that's because each scene is connected in his memory with a hurt in his life.

"The amount of rejection in this film is horrifying," Scorsese said. "There are scenes I almost can't look at. There's a scene where De Niro is told, *I hate you!* and he nods and responds, *Oh, I see, right, you don't want to see me again!* I made the movie during a very painful period in my life. I was going through the Poor Me routine. And I'm *still* very lonely. *Another* relationship has broken up."

Since Isabella?

"Since. I'm spending a lot of time by myself now. I go home and watch movies on video and stay up all night and sleep all day. If I didn't have to work I'd sleep all the time. I've never had such a long period when I've been alone."

Just the way he said that, quietly, without emphasis, much more softly than he usually speaks, places it in a special category. Perhaps it gives an additional dimension to *The King of Comedy,* a movie about a man so desperately isolated that even his *goals* do not include a relationship with another human being.

The character, Rupert Pupkin, played by Robert De Niro, has constructed a set for a talk show in his basement, and he sits down there night after night, holding chatty, condescending conversations with life-size cardboard cut-outs of Liza Minnelli and Jerry Lewis. Rupert Pupkin doesn't feel cut off from life—he feels cut off from talk shows. His life consists of waiting. He waits outside stage doors, outside office buildings, in waiting rooms and on telephones. He wants to be on television. He wants to be on first-name terms with Liza and Jerry and Tony and Joyce and the other members of America's amorphous extended family of television "personalities," who all seem to know each other so very well.

Rupert does not know how to have a conventional conversation, but he knows the form for talk shows; he has studied talk-show host "Jerry Langford" (Jerry Lewis) so carefully that he even knows how he dresses, and what his credo for beginning comics is: "Don't tell them it's the punch line, just tell them the punch line."

Scorsese says that both Rupert Pupkin and Jerry Langford remind him of himself. Pupkin is young Marty Scorsese, camped out in agents' offices, scrounging loans to finish his student film, hustling jobs as an editor in between directing assignments. Langford is Martin Scorsese at forty, famous, honored, admired, besieged by young would-be filmmakers asking him for a break.

"Last night," Scorsese said, "I went to the 10 P.M. show of *King of Comedy.* On the screen, the scene is playing where Rupert pushes into Jerry's limousine and says he's gotta talk to him. He's out of breath. *Take it easy, kid,* Jerry tells him. Meanwhile, in the back row of the theater, a kid grabs me by the arm and he's saying he's got to talk to me. He's out of breath. I tell him to take it easy. It's the *exact same scene* that's on the screen!"

Time. What that story is about is time. There was a time when Marty Scorsese was an intense, asthmatic, talented kid from New York University who wanted to make movies. He had a lot of self-confidence. Now time has passed and Scorsese has achieved all the things he dreamed of. There are those who believe he is the greatest of American directors, the most personal, the most obsessed. But if he once thought that success would bring him happiness, he now thinks again. Since famous film directors are supposed to be able to have whatever they want, the fact that Scorsese is famous and yet *still* unhappy must seem to him a terrible irony.

Scorsese at forty is bearded, slight and often cheerful, despite the burden of his unhappiness. He comes to dinner dressed like a successful undertaker, wearing an expensive dark-blue suit and a double-breasted navy-blue topcoat. Perhaps he looks like the well-dressed Mafioso who ran New York's Little Italy when he was growing up there. He was in Israel recently to scout locations for a project called *The Last Temptation of Christ,* and when they took him out in the desert in a helicopter, he wore the blue suit and the blue topcoat and the expensive black shoes. Most directors wear desert jackets to dinner. Scorsese wears a suit to the desert.

"The studio was ready to give up on *King of Comedy,*" he said. "They sneak-previewed it. The response was not great. Good, but not great. I told them this was not the kind of movie where preview audiences meant anything. If you are not prepared in your mind to see this movie, it can be a very strange experience. The way to sell this movie is, basically, on the track records of De Niro and myself, and on the story line. The studio was ready to put the movie on the shelf. It was dead and buried. Then some of the good reviews started coming in, and they reversed themselves. Now it looks like it might do all right."

One of the reasons the studio was afraid of the movie (Scorsese did not add) was that the subject matter is extremely touchy. In the movie, Rupert Pupkin kidnaps Jerry Langford and holds him for ransom. The ransom demand is a ten-minute slot for a standup comedy routine on the talk show. Since it is well known that Scorsese's *Taxi Driver* (about an alienated assassin) was seen by John Hinckley before he shot Reagan, *The King of Comedy* seemed in some circles almost like an invitation to trouble for someone like Johnny Carson.

Such fears were not alleviated by Paul Zimmerman, the onetime *Newsweek* film critic who wrote the movie, and who brashly told a New York press conference, "It is not the job of art to serve as a security system for celebrities."

For Scorsese, though, the movie does not precisely seem to be *about* kidnapping a celebrity. That is simply the plot line, in a screenplay that Zimmerman wrote twelve years ago and that Scorsese originally turned down six years ago. "It seemed like a one-joke movie at the time," he said. "But then I began to see that it wasn't about kidnapping, it was about rejection. It required a new visual style for me. I'm known for my moving camera. I'm usually all over the place. This film has very little camera movement, and when the camera moves, it means something. Look at the scene where the receptionist tells Pupkin that Jerry won't be back until Monday, and Pupkin says he'll wait. Look how the camera moves. It moves to show how solidly planted Rupert is. It's a nice move."

But it comes, I said, out of your sense of loneliness and rejection?

"Yes."

Simple as that?

"Simple as that."

Scorsese's first movie, *Who's Knocking at My Door?*, was about an Italian-American kid from New York who fell in love with a blonde on the Staten Island ferry, and wanted to marry her before he discovered that she was not a virgin. Angry and confused, he rejected her, and at the end of the movie they were both alone and we had the feeling that he would stay that way. Freud wrote about the "Madonna/whore complex," the hangup of men who have only two categories for women: First they idealize them, and then, when they discover that their perfect woman is only human after all, they rigidly reject them.

Without getting into your personal psychology, I said to Scorsese, are you still replaying the same scenario?

"I'm still stuck at the *Who's That Knocking* stage," he said. "Except ... it's not so much that I reject, as that something goes wrong. Maybe I'm impossible to be with."

The same pattern, of idealization and rejection, turns up in Scorsese's other movies, including *Mean Streets, Taxi Driver* and *Raging Bull* (where Robert De Niro, as Jake La Motta, marries a sixteen-year-old sexpot and then is driven mad with jealousy when other men look at her). I could only guess at the forms that Scorsese's own obsessions take, and I did not want to really press the subject, although he seemed willing to talk about it.

What eventually happened, toward the end of our dinner, was that I discovered by accident how deeply he was hurt. I mentioned a new film named *Exposed,* by James Toback, starring Nastassja Kinski. I said I thought Kinski possessed whatever rare magic Marilyn Monroe had; that whatever Kinski appears in, good or bad, she commands the screen.

"I can't bear to see Kinski in anything," Scorsese said. "She reminds me too much of Isabella. It tears me apart. I can't even go to see a film by the Taviani brothers, because Isabella and I had a little courtship on the set of one of their films. I can't ever go back to the island of Salina, where Visconti's *The Leopard* was shot, because we were there. In fact, I can hardly even *watch* a film by Visconti without growing depressed."

By memories of Isabella?

"By memories of a period when I thought I was happy. I'll put it that way. A period when I really thought I had the answers."

OK, then, I said, I've got a new movie that can't possibly depress you or bring up any old associations. It's called, *Say Amen, Somebody,* and it's this wonderful documentary about gospel music.

"Can't see it." Scorsese was grinning, but he was serious.

Why not?

"It's distributed by United Artists Classics." He sighed.

You mean you can't see a film that is distributed by a company that is connected to a woman you once loved?

He smiled. "I'd see the United Artists logo and it would ruin the movie for me."

Maybe you could come in after the logo had left the screen?

"I'd know."

With some directors, you fear that they will lose their early fire and obsession, and, in middle age, turn to directing safe and cheerful commercial projects. With Martin Scorsese, I don't think we have that to worry about.

Ingmar Bergman

If you've not slept well or you're suffering from lust —
I call those technical problems.

Stockholm, 1975

When he is in Stockholm, Ingmar Bergman lives in a new apartment complex called Karlapan. It's comfortable, not ostentatious; Bergman doesn't often have friends in because he considers it not a home but a dormitory to sleep in while he's making a film. His wife Ingrid prepares meals there, but if the Bergmans entertain it is more likely to be at his customary table in the Theater Grill, a stately restaurant directly across the street from the back door of the Royal Dramatic Theater. The table is not easily found, or seen; it is behind a large mirrored post, so that Bergman, who can see everyone in the room, is all but invisible.

During the eight or ten weeks it takes him to direct a film, Bergman awakens at a reasonable hour, around eight, and drives to Film House in a little maroon car. Film House is a large modern structure twenty-five minutes' walk from the center of Stockholm, and it houses not only film and television production facilities but also the theater, film and dance faculties of the University of Stockholm. The building is always filled with discussion and activity, much of it centered around the bar of the Laurel and Hardy Pub on the second level, but when Bergman is in residence to make a film, a certain self-consciousness seems to descend on Film House: It's the same, I was told, as when the Pope is in the Vatican.

Bergman parks in a reserved space near the side door of Film House and joins his actors and technicians for breakfast. It is served in a cluttered little room presided over by the hostess for this picture; for every film he makes, Bergman hires a hostess, and lists her in the credits. Her job is to make coffee and serve afternoon tea and fuss over people in a motherly sort of way. When you are making a picture about the silence of God, or metaphysical anguish, or suicide—as Bergman usually is—it helps if everyone feels right at home and there's a pot of coffee brewing.

The film he is working on today will be called *Face to Face,* and it is about an attempted suicide by a self-tormented psychiatrist, who will be played by Liv Ullmann. "For some time now," Bergman wrote in a letter to his cast and crew, just before production began, "I have been living with an anxiety which has had no tangible cause." His attempt to work it out led to the screenplay for *Face to Face,* in which the woman will face her terrible dread (common enough in Bergman), will attempt to surrender to it (also nothing new), but then will transcend it, will have a small victory over her darker nature (this hopefulness has only started to emerge in Bergman's work in the past three or four years, since *Cries and Whispers,* and is the cause of much speculation among his friends).

Face to Face will be Bergman's thirty-sixth film and it comes in his thirtieth year as a director. His career falls out into a certain pleasing symmetry: After early screenplays, he began directing in 1945 as a very provincial Swedish imitator of the Italian neorealists; he had his first international success in 1955, with *Smiles of a Summer Night;* in 1965 he began work on *Persona,* that most profound of modern films; today, he is considered one of the greatest living filmmakers. For *Face to Face,* he has gathered around him once again, as he does almost every spring and early summer, his basic crew and a group of actors he has used time and again. Only occasionally will there be a new face.

Now they join him for coffee. Liv Ullmann is dressed in an old cotton shirt and a full blue denim skirt; she wears no makeup and her hair is tossed back from her forehead as if to make the declaration that she's been asleep until fifteen minutes ago. Bergman first met her on a street corner talking to her friend Bibi Andersson, just at the moment he was casting *Persona*. He liked the way they fit together, and cast them together, on the spot. She has since become one of the most important actresses in the world, but here in Film House she is friendly and plain-spoken, more like a den mother than a star. This is her seventh film for Bergman.

Gunnar Bjornstrand, tall and stately in his seventies, gravely considers the room and leafs through his script. He was the squire in *The Seventh Seal* and the father in *Through a Glass Darkly*, and is one of the most familiar figures in Bergman's repertory company. He has been ill recently, but he came out of retirement to play Ullmann's grandfather in the new film, and has responded to the work so well that Bergman has expanded the role for him. This is his sixteenth film for Bergman.

Katinka Farago, a robust woman in her thirties, hardly has time for coffee; she wants a moment to speak with Bergman about the next week's production schedule, and he listens and nods as she explains, urgently, her problems. It is the duty of a production manager to have problems; no one has ever met one who did not. Katinka came to Stockholm from Hungary in 1956, a refugee, and got a job as Bergman's script girl. He made her production manager a few years ago, in charge of all the logistics of time, space and money. This is her seventeenth film with Bergman.

Sven Nykvist photographs Bergman's films. He is a tall, strong, fifty-one, with a beard and a quick smile. He is usually better-dressed than Bergman, but then almost everyone is; "Ingmar," a friend says, "does not spend a hundred dollars a year for personal haberdashery." Nykvist first worked for Bergman on *The Naked Night* in 1953, and has been with him steadily since *The Virgin Spring* in 1959. This will be his nineteenth title for Bergman, and the two of them together engineered Bergman's long-delayed transition from black and white to color, unhappily in *All These Women* and then triumphantly in *A Passion of Anna* and *Cries and Whispers.*

Nykvist is in demand all over the world, and commands one of the half-dozen highest salaries among cinematographers, but he always leaves his schedule open for Bergman. "We've already discussed the new film the year before," he says, "and then Ingmar goes to his island and writes the screenplay. The next year, we shoot—usually about the fifteenth of April. Usually we are the same eighteen people working with him, year after year, one film a year."

At the Cannes Film Festival one year, he said, Bergman was talking with David Lean, the director of *Lawrence of Arabia* and *Dr. Zhivago.* "What kind of crew do you use?" Lean asked. "I make my films with eighteen good friends," Bergman said. "That's interesting," said Lean. "I make mine with 150 enemies."

It is very rare for Bergman to invite visitors—the word "outsiders" almost seems to apply—to one of his sets. It is much more common, during a difficult scene, for him to send one technician after another out to wait in the hall, until the actors are alone with Bergman, Nykvist, a sound man, an electrician, and the demands of the scene.

"When we were making *Cries and Whispers,*" Liv Ullmann recalls, "none of the rest of us really knew what Harriet Andersson was doing in those scenes of suffering and death. Ingmar would send away everyone except just those few who *must* be there, and Harriet. When we saw the completed film, we were overwhelmed. It was almost as if those great scenes had been Harriet's secret—which, in a way, they were supposed to be, since in the film she died so much alone."

Liv is sitting in her dressing room, waiting to be called for the next scene. It will be a difficult one; she must explain to her child in the film why she tries to kill herself.

"They say Ingmar has changed," she says, "and he has. He doesn't look the same when he walks on the set. He's mellowed, in a nice way. He's sweeter. We've all been through some hard times with him—fights on the set—but he seems more tolerant now."

Perhaps, she said, Bergman has worked through the problem of death which haunted so many of his films. "He's faced it as a reality, and accepted it, and suddenly there's almost a sense of relief: In *Cries and Whispers* and *Scenes from a Marriage* there's a kind of acceptance at the end that wasn't there before. And in this film. He's been saying for years he's going to make a film of *The Merry Widow*. Well, now I really think he will. It may not be *The Merry Widow*, but it will be something warm and sunny. He is the most adult director in the world, making serious films for adults, but now if he could really let the child inside of him come out ... and I think he's reached the point where he can."

She lowers her voice. There is movement down the corridor, and it may be Bergman. She isn't supposed to be giving an interview; Bergman is very concerned about the scene coming up, and he wants her to think about nothing else. Ullmann smiles; it will help her, she says, to think of anything *but* the scene. Every actress approaches these things in her own way.

Elsewhere in Film House, people seem able to think and speak of nothing else but Bergman. He is the greatest Swedish artist, they agree—an artist of world importance. And yet he was not much loved until recently in his native land. His two best markets are the United States and France. In Sweden, he was accused of dealing only with the bourgeoisie, of not facing social problems, of being concerned only with himself and not with society. These are charges he more or less agrees with, but they do not bother him.

In the bar of Film House, drinking aquavit and a beer, the Finnish director Jorn Donner waits to talk to Bergman about a documentary he's making for television: "Three Scenes with Ingmar Bergman." Donner elaborates on Bergman's problem. "He is known all over the world, and yet he can't afford a single failure," he says. "Up until *Cries and Whispers*, each film was paying off the debts of the last. For *Cries and Whispers*, there was so little money that the actors were asked to work for three thousand dollars each and ten percent of the profits. He gave ten percent to Liv, Harriet, Sven, Ingrid Thulin, and thirty percent for himself—and this was a film he totally produced himself!

"Harriet asked me if she should work for three thousand dollars. I said, certainly, to work for Ingmar—and if that's all the money there is. After the film was made, it was turned down by every major distributor. And then look what an enormous success it was! And followed by a bigger success, *Scenes from a Marriage.* And now *The Magic Flute.* But no one suspects how close he came to not being able to raise the money for *Cries and Whispers.*"

It's true; until *Cries and Whispers* in 1973, Bergman hadn't had a financial success since *Persona,* released in 1966. There were great pictures—*A Passion of Anna* and *Shame*—and interesting failures like *Hour of the Wolf* and a movie that no one liked much, *The Touch,* with Elliott Gould, but they all lost money.

Then the tide turned. Not since the days of *Smiles of a Summer Night, Wild Strawberries* and *The Seventh Seal,* in the late 1950s, has Bergman found more success with audiences than in the last few years. And *Scenes from a Marriage* found him an audience, at last, in Scandinavia, too: His neighbors on the Baltic island of Faro, where he lives as much of the year as possible, saw it on television and understood at last what it was that he did. Then Bergman's version of Mozart's *The Magic Flute* played on Swedish television on the first day of 1975, and one of every three Swedes saw it. "It's as if he's in harmony with himself," says Bengt Forslund, a Swedish producer. "All those years of films about suffering and death, and suddenly Ingmar's found all of this joy to draw on."

The red light is still on over the door to Bergman's sound stage. When it goes off, that means Bergman is not actually shooting—but entry is still forbidden except to the favored, like his wife, Ingrid. She slips through the door with some letters that need to be answered. And then it's time for the afternoon tea break. The hostess has set up tea and cakes and Bergman at last acknowledges the interviewer.

He has a little room, long, dim and cool, like a monk's cell. It's across from the sound stage and down the way from the dressing rooms, and is furnished simply, with two chairs, a cot, and a table (on which rest two apples, a banana, a box of Danish chocolates and a copy of the script). When he is concerned about the direction a scene is taking, he will declare a break, come into this room, lock the door and lie down on the cot until the scene is clear in his head.

"So it is thirty years since I directed my first picture," he said. "It's strange, you know, because suddenly you have the feeling there was no time in between. The feeling when you wake up, go to the studio, see the rushes, is still exactly the same. Of course, in 1945, I was more scared, more insecure—but the tension and the passion, and the feeling of surprise every day—that's the same. I solved the problems, or didn't solve them in exactly the same way.

"The artistic problems are already solved when you write the script. But then there are the technical problems. The shooting schedule, the lab, a sick actor ... and it has to do with your *own* conditions, too. If you feel well, or depressed—you are not a machine. And yet you must be on top of things for nine or ten weeks—if you've not slept well, or you're suffering from lust ... I call those technical problems."

English is not his best language, but he speaks it well enough. Growing up before the Second World War, he was taught German, like all Swedish schoolchildren. As he speaks, he seems to have it all clear inside, what he wants to say. He accepts questions gravely but without a great deal of interest. It's less of an interview than an opportunity to share in his thought process. I asked him about the recent change in the direction of his work, away from despair and a little toward affirmation.

"Well," he said, "you mature. You grow up mentally, emotionally, and it's not a straight line, it's more like the growing of a tree. On the island where I live, the trees always have a strong wind from the northeast, blowing so hard that they grow almost flat against the ground. It's that way with people. You think you're in control, but really you're being changed every day by everything around you.

"Perhaps, someday, I'll stop growing. But I hope that I'll understand it myself, and, in that moment, stop making films. You know, filming and directing on the stage, are both the same in the sense that you try to get in touch with other human beings. There's always that hope. But if you have the feeling you have nothing more to tell, to say—it's wise to stop making pictures. You can still work in the theater, because there you're working with big men—Shakespeare, Strindberg, Molière—so if you're old and tired and sick, at least you still have your experience to share with other actors, you can help them put across the play. To make a film is something else. If you have nothing to say, it's time to stop, because the film is you."

You talk about getting in touch with other people, I said. In so many of your films, that seems to be the subject—people trying to make contact.

"That is exactly right. If I believe in anything, I believe in the sudden relationship, the sudden contact between two human beings. When we grow up, we suddenly feel we are completely alone. We find substitutes for loneliness—but this feeling of a certain contact, a certain instant understanding between two people, that's the best thing in life. It has nothing to do with sex, by the way."

And so, at the end of *Scenes from a Marriage,* when the man and woman have been divorced for years, you have them holding each other "in a cottage in the middle of the night somewhere in the world."

He nodded. "You know," he said, "I was very surprised by the success of that film, because I wrote it only from my own experience. It took three months to make, but a lifetime to experience. Very strange.

"I was on my island with my wife, and I was preparing a stage production, and just for fun I started to write some dialogues about marriage. I started with the scene where he tells her he will go away. Well, I always write by hand, and I asked my wife, who is the only person in the world who can read my handwriting, to type it up. She found it amusing. Then I wrote the fifth scene—even more amusing!—and then the first. I could have written twenty-four more.

"But I had no idea of what would happen. No feeling of what to do with these scenes. Perhaps I could make some sort of program for television. I asked my friends Liv and Erland Josephson to read it, and they were interested. Well, everything happened just like that. It was the biggest success in the history of Swedish television—and all over Scandinavia. At last, my neighbors on the island had seen something of mine they could relate to."

Scenes from a Marriage was shot in sixteen-millimeter, unlike his previous work, which had all been in the standard thirty-five-millimeter. That was fine for television, but now Sven Nykvist was telling him that the new sixteen-millimeter Kodak color film was so good that features could be shot in it, too, with little difference in quality, a great advance in flexibility, and for a lot less money. Bergman was dubious, but agreed to shoot Mozart's *The Magic Flute* in sixteen-millimeter.

It was a project commissioned by Swedish television, and he decided to film it as it might have been performed in a little eighteenth century theater like the Drottningholm Court Theater, perfectly preserved for two hundred years in a royal park outside Stockholm. The theater's interiors and its ingenious stage machinery—good for making thunder and lightning and waves—were duplicated in Film House, and the opera was shot in sixteen-millimeter.

After its Swedish television premiere, Nykvist and Bergman screened a thirty-five-millimeter theatrical print blown up from sixteen-millimeter, and were happy with the quality; Bergman agreed with Nykvist that the image was clear and subtle even by their demanding standards, and they decided to shoot in sixteen-millimeter from then on. *Face to Face* was being shot in sixteen-millimeter—although that was one of the few things regarding it Bergman seemed to be absolutely sure of.

"It's a little difficult to talk about right now," he said, "because we're in the middle of things and often it's not until I take the film back to my island and begin to edit it that it becomes clear to me. Of course I can say, yes, it's about a woman who tries to commit suicide, and the picture is sort of an investigation of why she does that, but—honestly, I don't know. I wrote it, but when I shoot a film I never think of it as my own script, because then I couldn't shoot a single scene. It's very personal, and yet I have to be cold, analytical, about it. Sometimes I read what I've written—dialogue that was written with emotion, and then I try to understand intellectually what a character means, and sometimes I make very strange mistakes.

"The problem is that film is the best way to the emotional center of human beings, but it's very hard to be intellectual about it. There's some sort of strange emotional logic in film that has nothing to do with the meaning. If you're the director, you have to be very careful about what you reach for, because the emotions may make you find something else altogether. But, even then, that's all right, if it makes others feel something ... what makes me unhappy is when the audience is indifferent."

I asked him about *Persona*, the story of an actress who one day decides to stop talking, and about her relationship with the naive young nurse who's assigned to spend the summer in the country with her. The film created a great deal of critical confusion and debate in 1966, and has continued to reveal levels of emotion; it has the ability to make audiences feel it when they don't really understand it.

"Now there's an example of what I mean," he said. "I have no theories about it. If you asked me to explain it, I couldn't. But I know that *Persona* literally saved my life at the time I was writing it. I was very ill. I hadn't lost my mental balance, but I'd lost my physical balance. I had an ear disease ... I couldn't stand up or even move my head without nausea. So I started to write down some lines every day, just a few lines, just for the discipline of going from the bed to the table without falling over. As a filmmaker, I could not work if I could not move. Now here was a story about an actress who stopped working one day, surrendered her ability to talk, and the young nurse who admired her, who wanted to understand her, but was treated badly by her ... there's something there, but I can't explain it."

Persona contains one of Bergman's most famous shots, the faces of Liv Ullmann and Bibi Andersson photographed in such a way that the features of the two women seem to blend. They seem about to become one another, which, in a way, is what happens in the film. They seem capable of exchanging or sharing personalities. I asked Bergman about this shot, and also about his frequent use of two-shots to show characters who are in the same frame but not looking at each other or communicating.

"The two-shot, and the closeup, too, are marvelous, because ... well, you don't have them in the theater. They give you the eyes, the skin, the mouth, and that's fascinating. And when you cut it, rehearse it, edit it, two people talking, now in closeup, now brought together into the two-shot, you can work out a wonderful rhythm, a sort of breathing, and it's beautiful.

"And the most beautiful of all is that you're close to the human face, which is the most fascinating subject possible for the camera. On TV a few days ago, I saw a little of Antonioni's new picture, *The Passenger*. And, you know, I am an admirer of Antonioni, I've learned so much from him, but I was struck by the moment they cut from his film to a closeup of Antonioni himself, for the interview.

"And as he was sitting there, here was his face, so normal, so beautiful and so human—and I didn't hear a word of what he was saying, because I was looking so closely at his face, at his eyes." Bergman held out his hands as if to compose the memory for the camera. "The ten minutes he was on the screen were more fascinating than any of his, or my, work. It told you a novel about his whole life. With my actors, with their faces ... that is what we can sometimes do."

Now it was time to go back onto the sound stage and finish the day's shooting. People were waiting for him in the hallway: A secretary said he had been chosen to receive the Donatello Award of the Italian Republic; could he come to Florence if a private jet were sent? Bibi Andersson had stopped by for a visit, she was accompanying the Swedish Prime Minister, Olaf Palme, on a state visit to South America, and then she'd go to Warsaw in Bergman's production of *Twelfth Night*.

Bergman was quiet, friendly, dictating a reply to Rome and another one to his producer, Dino De Laurentiis, explaining why he could not oblige Dino's old friend, the countess in charge of the Donatello Award. He kissed Bibi and said he would come to see her in Warsaw if he could. And then he went back behind the big soundproof doors and the red light blinked on. Some tourists being taken through Film House had not recognized the ordinary-looking man of fifty-seven, with his thinning brown hair, his frayed blue jacket, his carpet slippers.

The rhythm of the seasons has been set for seven or eight years now, ever since Bergman moved to Faro, which close inspection of the map reveals as a tiny unnamed blue dot north of the island of Gutland, in the Baltic Sea. It is the last speck of Sweden, a wild bird preserve inhabited by nine hundred shepherds and fishermen, and foreigners are not allowed there because of a nineteenth century military agreement with Russia. Bergman found his island by accident, as a ferry-stop north of Gutland, while looking for a place to shoot *Through a Glass Darkly*.

He built a house there, sturdy and spacious, and after waiting for three years for the permit he built an editing facility and the simple studio in which he did the interiors for *A Passion of Anna* and parts of *Shame*. He would return to Faro in a month or so, and spend the autumn editing *Face to Face*. This winter, he will direct something for the Royal Dramatic Theater—he thinks perhaps something by Shaw this year. When the production has opened, he'll return to Faro, finish with *Face to Face*, and begin work on next year's screenplay.

Copies will go out soon to Sven and Katinka and the others of the eighteen friends, and to the actors he has chosen to use this time. The female lead will probably be played by Liv, although Bibi was in *The Touch* and Ingrid and Harriet joined Liv in *Cries and Whispers*. The male lead may be Erland, although Max von Sydow, who has been in eleven of Bergman's films, is said to be eager to return to Stockholm again after several pictures overseas. Shooting will begin in the late spring and early summer, and editing will follow in the fall.

"I think I have ten years left," Bergman had said at the close of the interview.

"There's a deal, sort of," Katinka Farago had said, speaking of Bergman's relationship with the people he makes films with. "One may get offers to work on other pictures ... but one doesn't take another picture without asking Ingmar first. He pays what the others pay; it's not a question of money. But there is no one else like him."

Orson Welles

One of the great creature comforts!

Los Angeles, 1978

Orson Welles spoke to me on the radio as I took my morning shower. "Fedders Air Conditioners!" he said. "One of the great creature comforts."

I stepped out of the shower, soap in my eyes, and reached blindly for a towel. At such moments, my mind tends to stray. I consider questions of philosophy, of grammar.

When Welles mentions "great creature comforts," I found myself wondering, where does the emphasis fall? Does he mean "great *creature comforts,*" or "*great creature* comforts"? Welles is, of course, one of the great creatures of our time.

Questions like that often go without answers. Almost always, in fact. *But not today!* I reminded myself. After years as a movie critic, after hours and days spent interviewing every mope and would-be has-been who's stumbled into the spotlight of fame, *today I was going to interview Orson Welles!*

An interview with Orson Welles is not to be taken lightly. The president of the United States is easier to get to. Welles is an inhabitant of two continents, and his presence is coveted on both. In the world of celebrities, he stands apart. He is known everywhere. His voice is as famous as his face.

He is one of the world's most prestigious dinner guests—so

awesome a presence, so rare a capture, that Marlene Dietrich once held a dinner party in his honor, and he neglected to come, and the other guests were thrilled to be at a party in his honor *even in his absence.*

Welles is also, of course, one of the gods of the world of cinema. All the lists agree: His *Citizen Kane* is the greatest movie ever made, and his *The Magnificent Ambersons* is close behind. When a British film magazine polled the world's movie critics, in fact, the only director who placed two films among the ten greatest ever made was Orson Welles.

And today, I told myself, chugging down orange juice and coffee, *today* I was going to interview, not only Orson Welles, but also Kermit the Frog.

Some days just have that little spark of magic other days lack.

Orson Welles had been flown to Hollywood for one day's work on *The Muppet Movie,* the first full-length feature starring TV's Muppets. He was a co-star in a scene with Kermit the Frog. He would play a movie tycoon, and Kermit would play a frog answering a classified ad:

WANTED!
Frog willing to become
superstar!

As I drove to the studio, I tried to think of questions for the great man. What do you ask Orson Welles, when you have half an hour and a week would not be long enough? Maybe, I thought, maybe I should just keep quiet and let Welles recite epigrams and solemn observations, interrupted by an occasional flash of dazzling wit.

Inside gigantic Sound Stage 15, there was an electric sense of purpose. Carpenters, painters, Muppeteers and assistant directors raced about on urgent missions, in the final countdown before Orson Welles met Kermit the Frog.

I reflected that it must have been much the same backstage when Kennedy met Khrushchev, Sadat met Begin, and Farrah Fawcett-Majors met Cheryl Ladd. People of a certain stature, you know, don't just run into one another. They *meet.* They create a stage.

Jim Henson, who created the Muppets, wandered over and said hello. He seemed almost as awestruck as I was: To think that his Kermit was going to play a scene with Orson Welles!

Kermit did not, of course, have his own private dressing room, just a plastic cover to keep the dust off. But over there ... there in the corner ... was the dressing room in which Orson Welles was even this very minute preparing himself for the morning's first shot. Was that a wisp of cigar smoke curling from inside?

The movie's press agent strolled over with hot coffee. And then the producer joined our little group and said there were doughnuts, too.

This is a great day for me, I said, being able to meet Orson Welles.

The producer looked as if he had just swallowed a frog. "I think we have a problem," he said. "Mr. Welles is not giving interviews today. Sorry."

But ... I said, I was on my way home from Bora Bora and I hung around in Los Angeles for four days specifically to talk to Orson Welles ... and to Kermit the Frog, of course.

"But nobody checked with Mr. Welles," the producer said.

Maybe, I said, if I could just sort of hang around, it would be great just seeing him work ...

"Mr. Welles always works on closed sets," the producer said.

On *closed sets?* Playing King Lear, maybe. But in a scene with a *frog?*

Jim Henson, who seemed like a kind and gentle person, looked pained at that.

I mean of course Kermit isn't just *any* frog, I said.

The producer looked morose.

The press agent asked if I would like to interview Kermit.

No ... I said. No. Kermit is a wonderful frog, but he is not a great creature.

And so I walked out alone into the sunshine and got on an airplane and flew back to Chicago and the telephone was ringing.

It was Michael Kutza, the director of the Chicago International

Film Festival.

"Here's a scoop!" he said. "This year's festival is going to be dedicated to Orson Welles."

What about Kermit the Frog? I said.

"Who?" said Michael Kutza.

Kermit the Frog, I said. He's a TV star. Gonna be big one of these days. Orson Welles is in his new picture.

six

A case of do or die

This section speaks for itself.

I wrote the second Belushi article a year after the first, in anger at all the nonsense that was being written about the Woodward book. I should have included an additional observation: You can read Wired *carefully and find no passages in which Woodward empathizes with the incredible suffering that Belushi must have endured through hangovers and withdrawals. His binges are described dispassionately, as if they contained no euphoria and, especially, no misery. Belushi is often described as dysfunctional, but pain is not indicated. To begin with the walking-around pain he must have felt so often, and to push so much humor out through it, Belushi must have had great courage.*

Rainer Werner Fassbinder

Let's hope we meet again, in your heaven, or my hell.

Montreal, 1983

Late on the night of June 9, 1982, the West German film director Rainer Werner Fassbinder made a telephone call from Munich to Paris to tell his best friend he had flushed all his drugs down the toilet—everything except for one last line of cocaine. The next morning, Fassbinder was found dead in his room, a cold cigarette between his fingers, a videotape machine still playing. The most famous, notorious and prolific modern German filmmaker was dead at thirty-six.

To those who knew him well, the death was not a surprise. Fassbinder had been on a collision course with drugs. He had long been a heavy drinker and user of drugs, but in the final two years of his life cocaine came to rule him completely, and he became reclusive and paranoid, a stranger to his friends.

Daniel Schmid was one of those friends. Schmid is a forty-two-year-old Swiss filmmaker who met Fassbinder when they were both young students in Berlin. They became lovers, and remained friends until the end. It was Schmid who received what was probably Fassbinder's last telephone call on the night of his death.

"I think the last line of cocaine killed him," Schmid said. "It was the final pebble that broke the sheet of glass. He could simply not believe that his heart was weaker than his head—that his body was weaker than his will to live."

The story of Fassbinder's last months of life became clouded with controversy, as his divorced parents waged a bitter fight in West German courts over his estate. Schmid, who says sadly that Fassbinder at the end was living an existence like Howard Hughes in his penthouse or Adolf Hitler in his bunker, was a powerless bystander during his friend's disintegration.

In August of 1983 in Montreal, as Schmid and I both served on the jury of the World Film Festival, the ghost of Fassbinder seemed almost like another presence in the city. Fassbinder had attended the 1981 Montreal Film Festival, nine months before his death, and I remember him at dinner, unshaven, defensive, ignoring the food and ordering a bottle of Cognac to be placed before him. This year at Montreal, his name came up again and again in conversations among the half dozen West German directors at the festival. Schmid had spoken privately about his friend's dying, and I asked if he would break his silence and talk publicly about the life and death of Rainer Werner Fassbinder. He agreed.

The portrait he painted was of a magnetic young artist who was the best and the brightest of his generation, who made more than forty films in less than fifteen years, and who died alone and lonely, addicted to cocaine, tormented by the suicides of two lovers, bitterly asking in late-night telephone calls how other people could possibly be so happy, so lucky.

"At the end, he stayed all the time in his room," Schmid said. "He was naked, sleeping on a mattress on the floor. The room was always kept overheated. His only contact with the world was the telephone. The room was filled with money, books and all his videotapes. There was a police guard outside: He had received death threats after his fifteen-hour television film *Berlin Alexanderplatz,* and he always had one or two people who would do anything for him, to keep the world away. When he died there was a cigarette in his hand and he was watching a tape of *Twenty Thousand Years in Sing Sing.*

"During the last two or three weeks of his life, he would call me in Paris at three in the morning, talking very slowly. I think he was very much aware in the final weeks that the drugs could actually kill him. He liked to *play* the passed-out one in public, but now he had really lost control. He was bleeding all the time from the nose, from cocaine, but he said he would buy one of those plastic noses like you hear the Hollywood stars have.

"He was obsessed with bank notes. At the end, when the money was coming in and he was a box-office success at last, he wouldn't get out of bed without the producer bringing him ten thousand dollars in the morning. Most of it went for drugs. All over his room, money was thrown, and people would steal from him all the time. He had become obsessed with Steven Spielberg, who had made so much money, and he would shout into the phone, *I want to make millions! I want to be rich like Spielberg!*"

Schmid and I were talking in the conference room where the Montreal jury held its meetings. It was a quiet Sunday morning. He smoked and drank coffee and recalled all of the different sides of Fassbinder's complex personality, not just the shadow at the end. He began by opening a book.

"Look at this," he said, pointing to a photograph of Fassbinder taken when he was nineteen. "That is how he looked when I first met him. Now look at this." He took a matchbook and used it to cover first the left side of the photograph, and then the right. The result was startling. The right side of Fassbinder's face was of a happy, clear-eyed, even warm young man. The left side seemed to show a more tired and bitter face.

"And he was always showing those two sides of himself," Schmid said. "When he wanted to convince you of something, he would play every role, acting like a kabuki dancer, leaping around the room. When he was unhappy, he shut himself off completely and went behind a wall.

"I met him in 1966, when we were both taking an exam for the film school in Berlin. I came from the Swiss countryside and arrived late at the exam because I missed my train. When I opened the door of the room, there were two hundred people inside, but somehow the only one I saw was this one guy, sitting back in the corner, pimples on his face, not very attractive, but he had this aura about him. I went and sat next to him.

"Of course Fassbinder failed the exam. All of his life, he failed all of his exams. He didn't even have a driver's license. He was *unable* to be examined. All doctors, professors, policemen, were for him a focus of hate. His mother had raised him calling him ugly, monstrous, an idiot, an unwanted souvenir from his father—who left before he was born. I think he had what the Freudians call a Monster Complex—a feeling that he was incapable of loving, or being loved. To be *tested* was unbearable to him."

Schmid said that he and Fassbinder became friends in West Berlin, where Fassbinder quickly gained a reputation as an *enfant terrible.* He formed a radical theater group. He made movies on a shoestring. When he screened his first film, *Love is Colder than Death,* it was rejected by the Berlin tastemakers because it dealt with unfashionable subjects like love, lust, unfaithfulness and jealousy. His taste for lurid melodrama clashed with the socially responsible films that were fashionable at the moment. "He was a hate object, right from the first," Schmid said. "He almost seemed to desire disapproval."

But already the publicity apparatus had discovered Fassbinder and started to create an image that became famous in the film world: The "bad boy" in his leather jacket, sneering at the world, deliberately rude on occasion, but incredibly prolific, turning out three or four films a year on invisible budgets, high-handedly ruling a repertory company of actors and technicians, friends, lovers and slaves.

Among the company members were the future star Hanna Schygulla, the future director Schmid, and the actress Ingrid Caven, who was to become Fassbinder's wife. "After they were married, he wanted her to be *only* his wife," Schmid said. "He gave her no roles in his movies. He introduced her not as an actress, but as 'my wife.' When I hired her to act in my film *La Paloma*, Fassbinder was so angry he split with her. But later he wrote *Shadow of Angels*, which was more or less about all of us, and asked me to direct it, and he played opposite her.

"The three of us made an agreement," Schmid said. "There were Fassbinder, myself and Ingrid. We said we would each take turns making one film and then working on a film of the other two. Fassbinder made *The Merchant of the Four Seasons*. Then it was my turn. *No*, said Fassbinder, *first I will make another film*. That was the day I quit. Ingrid quit, too. Rainer, of course, admired this. He admired people who resisted him, who stood up to him when everybody seemed willing to go along with him. We all remained friends up until the end. He once said that the people he would have liked to spend his life with ... couldn't take him."

In the seventies the moribund West German film industry, essentially dead since the most important filmmakers of the thirties fled Hitler, was reborn as the New German Cinema. A young generation of directors became famous around the world. Their names included Volker Schlondorff, Werner Herzog, Wim Wenders, Alexander Kluge, Margarethe von Trotta—but none more famous than Rainer Werner Fassbinder. He became a familiar figure at the world's film festivals, always roughly dressed in jeans and leather jackets, always with a drink and a cigarette.

It seemed almost a paradox that he went to so many festivals, because once he was there he refused interviews, rejected praise and responded rudely to compliments. Still, he went; Schmid says it was because he could not stand to be alone. The bad boy image was in contrast with a remarkable body of work. Films poured from Fassbinder's imagination, and he made more of them in less time than any other major director in history, usually about deliberately uncommercial subjects.

Those subjects often included eerie projections of his own final years. In *The Bitter Tears of Petra von Kant* (1972), an alcoholic lesbian isolates herself in her room and lives on the floor with a gin bottle after being rejected by her lover. In *Merchant of the Four Seasons* (1972), a fruit peddler, insecure and cuckolded, deliberately drinks himself to death. In *Fox and his Friends* (1975), a simple-minded young homosexual wins the lottery, becomes the lover of the owner of a bankrupt factory, is taken for all of his money, and finally dies alone in an underground station. In *Fear Eats the Soul—Ali* (1974), a Moroccan immigrant, desperately lonely, marries a cleaning woman twenty-five years older than he is, and then collapses of an ulcer.

Fassbinder's more recent films were more commercial, including the major box-office hit *The Marriage of Maria Braun* (1979). But they also returned again and again to the subjects of dependency, addiction, loneliness and self-hatred, as in *Veronika Voss* (1982), about an aging, drug-addicted actress who becomes the captive of a woman psychiatrist, or *Querelle* (1982), starring Brad Davis as a sailor adrift in a homosexual underworld.

"He was an unhappy man who hurled himself compulsively into his work but had a low personal opinion of himself," Schmid said. "The basis for his new friendships was always the same: *You are a pig and I am a pig. Let's start our relation there, both of us convinced the other will betray.* The two things all his characters know are dependency and rejection. Fassbinder *depended* on dependency and rejection. He depended on having around him at all times people who completely fawned upon him.

"The two people he loved the most in recent years both left and both hanged themselves. The first was Salim El Hadi, the star of *Fear Eats the Soul—Ali.* He couldn't take any more. He came out of the mountains of North Africa, Germany was a strange world to him, he started drinking, the tension built up, and one day he went to a place in Berlin and stabbed three people. Then he came back to Rainer and said, 'Now you don't have to be afraid anymore.' He hanged himself in jail. Fassbinder dedicated *Querelle* to him.

"The second person was Armin Meyer, a simple person. Fassbinder came to Paris for his birthday, to spend it with Ingrid and myself, and left Armin in Munich. When Rainer was not around, nobody came to the apartment. Nobody cared about Armin. He hanged himself, and Fassbinder's mother found the body three days later."

After the death of Armin Meyer, Fassbinder made what he called his most autobiographical film, *In a Year of Thirteen Moons* (1978), about a lonely homosexual: "It was inspired by anger and guilt about Armin's death," Schmid said. Then came *Maria Braun,* starring Hanna Schygulla, and *Despair,* starring Dirk Bogarde—and larger budgets, increasing fame, more money and more drugs.

"I ask myself, when did the turning point come?" Schmid said. "He was drinking all the time since the 1960s—those eternal Bacardi and Coke nights. And all the other things: uppers, downers, cocaine. But he was a gambler, not a suicide. Even in his last year, he didn't want to die. He wanted to see how far he could go. But they say every gambler really gambles to lose.

"I think I finally realized how dependent he was on cocaine when we took a trip from Europe to New York on the QE2, a couple of years before his death. That was an old dream, made up when we were twenty, to sail the ocean to America. Rainer took along no drugs, because he was terrified of customs. The third night, we played poker very late. He was friendly. The next morning, he had a dark look, a hateful look. Armin Meyer told me Fassbinder had become convinced that I had cocaine in my stateroom and was hiding it to torment him. *Knowing* that I did not use cocaine, he still believed this. And I realized that he had become a slave as well, to cocaine, to such a degree that he became paranoid even about his oldest friends."

Daniel Schmid lit a cigarette and looked out the window. He exhaled slowly, reliving old memories.

"He thought of me as the lucky one. He suspected me of being happier than he was. He thought he didn't know how to be happy. Always, every day, he was restless, switching things around, never able to sit still for a moment. In my apartment in Paris, he'd ask if we were going out. Then he'd take a couple of uppers. Then, *Maybe we'll stay here a while.* A couple of downers. *No, we'll go out.* More uppers and some cocaine. Then he would pass out. At the end, he kept cocaine by his bedside, to wake up in the night and snort it and go back to sleep. I'm still finding notes he left here and there in my apartment. One that I found the other day said, *Let's hope we meet again, in your heaven, or my hell.*"

There was a long silence. "I met him before almost anybody," Schmid said, meditatively.

There is, I thought, a line like that in *Citizen Kane: I knew him before the beginning ... and after the end.*

"He was shy when he was young," Schmid said. "All of his life he thought he was ugly. He tested people to see if they loved him. When it was clear to me that the drugs were dangerous to his life, I tried to help him. He was almost going to go into a hospital in Paris, but then suddenly he went back to Munich. I asked him, please come with me to the clinic. But if he would not come, what could I do? You can't control another person. He was too protected by all those who would do anything for him. It had become something I couldn't handle anymore.'

During the last weeks of his life, Schmid said, during those sad telephone calls at three in the morning, Fassbinder often repeated the same thing. "He would shout at me: *How are you able to just sit there and look outside the window? How can you? How can you just sit on a rock and look at the sea? How can everybody else be so lucky?*"

Kris Kristofferson I

Anyone with a ring in his ear is lying.

Los Angeles, 1975

Kris Kristofferson says he's spent most of his life living out of a suitcase, and today he looked it. He was wearing faded Levis and a ravaged leather flight jacket that looked ripped off of Jimmy Stewart in *Strategic Air Command*—and this was his uniform, you understand, for a meeting with Barbra Streisand.

He'd just come from Barbra. She wanted to talk to him about starring with her in a remake of *A Star is Born*. Kristofferson uncorked the bottle of Ballantine's Scotch on the table and had a healthy swig. He chased it with Coors beer. One hesitated to ask if he were interviewed for the James Mason role.

We were sitting by the side of the pool at the Sunset Marquis, which is the residential motel I was staying in halfway down the block from Sunset Strip. The California sun was casting late afternoon shadows over the pool, where groupies from the Elton John Band played water polo in astonishing bikinis. Kristofferson did not study them. He was speaking about the craft of acting.

"I never thought of acting as a creative process," he said. "Christ, I used to go to the movies and see Brando talking like he was trying to sell shoes and he was great. I thought anybody could do it. Then I tried it and I got *so* uptight. I'm limited as to what I can do on film. If I can suck myself into a scene, I'm OK. If I had to go on stage and raise my voice, I'd notice my voice was raised, and then I'd get to where I was thinking about that, and, man, it'd be all over ...

"I was on this last picture with Jan-Michael Vincent. He's a nice kid. I'll tell you how nice he is. He's spending all afternoon trying to talk to these forty foreign journalists who don't know six words of English, and I'm trying to sneak out to a bar. I used to tell him he cared too much. We'd be in an argument about something and I'd say, *God, man, look at me. Look me in the face and you can see yourself if you live ten more years.*"

Kristofferson let a little more of the Coors trickle into his glass. "He took a good hard look," he said. "I don't know what he decided. Suicide, probably."

No, probably not. He would have seen a bearded face with pale blue eyes, and a smile with little surprise in it, as if Kristofferson more or less expected the universe to amuse him. He once wrote a line in one of his songs that went: *Well if you don't like Hank Williams, why you can kiss my ass,* and philosophical variations on that theme might comprise the Kristofferson solution to the crises of life.

Kris stretched out at poolside, his cowboy boots crossed, his eyes narrowed against the sun, reflecting, perhaps, on the fates that had led him from a Rhodes Scholarship at Oxford to a career as a wandering minstrel ("I played every gas station between Denmark and Morocco") and songwriter ("Help Me Make It Through the Night"), and then to sudden popularity as a country singer, to marriage with Rita Coolidge, and finally to movie stardom in *Alice Doesn't Live Here Anymore.*

That was his fourth movie, after *Cisco Pike* and *Pat Garrett and Billy the Kid* (he was Billy) and *Blume in Love,* and by far the most successful. It's even gotten him into hot water with the theoreticians of the women's movement, who argue (and I summarize): What the hell kind of a liberated woman is Alice, anyway, if she strikes out on her own to build a career for herself as a nightclub singer and winds up falling in love with (italics theirs) *Kris Kristofferson?*

"Hell's fire!" Kristofferson said, leaning forward for another shot of Ballantine's. "Alice wasn't exactly falling into the seat of passion with *me.* That musta been some women's libber *fan* of mine. The guy I played wasn't exactly Mr. Right. She wasn't gettin' no bargain. He was narrow-minded, for starters. The only way I see it their way is if she runs away with Clark Gable, which would have been the way it would have happened except for Marty."

Marty is Martin Scorsese, the director. "He'll be a great director," Kristofferson said. "He's got the great ego for a great director. People came around, said, *where's the director? That's him! Him? Yep!* Looked like this little kid who just lost his ball on the mean man's roof. *Hey, Marty, we'll get you a new ball!* If I could work with Marty all the time everybody'd think I was a *great* actor."

Kristofferson also worked—on *Pat Garrett and Billy the Kid*—with Sam Peckinpah, legendary mean man, master of violence.

"The studio screwed him so thoroughly on that picture that he got sick. There were days when he couldn't raise himself up from his chair. I had something to do with talking Bobby Dylan into being in the picture, and Dylan would have been great, take my word for it, except there Sam screwed himself. He got the idea the producers were trying to shove Dylan down his throat. I don't even know if Sam knew who Dylan *was*.

"The atmosphere on that picture was so incredibly macho, they even had *me* claiming I wanted to do my own stunts. I didn't want a stunt man to do a stunt, and he wanted to do it, and everybody was strutting around and getting knocked out and having concussions to prove nothing to nobody. It was real self-destructive. And to see the picture, you'd never know Bob Dylan did a great job in it."

He shook his head and took another swig of Ballantine's and popped the top of a Coors and allowed that one of the hardest things in the music business these days was following Dylan.

"Hell, even Dylan can't be Dylan, the legend's so big. That's John Prine's single biggest problem. Prine is so good ... I remember this night the first time I heard him. Steve Goodman brought me over to this club in Chicago, the Earl of Old Town, I had heard Stevie, who was great, and now Stevie insisted we get there about the crack of dawn and here's Prine sleeping on the goddam *floor*.

"I mean, I was so embarrassed. I didn't want to hear anybody. They kick Prine awake and he stumbles to the mike to perform for the so-called stars, and I'm drowning my embarrassment in bourbon, and about halfway through the first song something catches my attention. And then his next song was 'Donald and Lydia.' And Goodman says that ain't nothing, wait'll I hear 'Sam Stone.'"

Prine, said Kristofferson, is the next singer who ought to try movies. "The guy's so funny, he tickles himself. Like the other day he's laying around the house with Rita and me, and he's reading the *National Enquirer,* and suddenly he starts reading us this story about some guy down in Tennessee who has himself a sixty-second memory. He can only remember what happened for the last sixty seconds. Prine starts figurin' what the guy's problems would be. Like, he's in the sack, and not only does he forget *who* he's in the sack with, he forgets *why.*"

Kristofferson let out a belly laugh. "Johnny's working on that song right now, bet you a million," he said. "That's how his mind works. There's a word for him—bemused. Anyway, thank God for the *National Enquirer,* and thank God too, I say, for Jackie and Cher and the other poor mopes who get maligned every single day of their lives to take the heat off the rest of us."

The shadows were growing chilly now, and the water polo game was over, and the level of the Ballantine's bottle had fallen to such a point that there should have been a line reminding us to reorder. Kristofferson sighed, divided the remaining Scotch between two glasses, and toyed with his.

"If there's one thing I've learned in this town," he said, "it's this—if you don't know nobody, you ain't goin' nowhere. All the rest adds up to, freedom's just another word for Datsun."

The poolside was deserted now. Suddenly a couple appeared. They were perhaps in their mid-fifties. They wore expensive white tennis clothes and Adidas shoes and carried rackets.

"I say," said the man, immediately perceived to be British. "Can you direct us to the courts?"

There were no courts. Only rooms surrounding the pool.

"Try lobbing one into the pool," Kristofferson advised.

"And get these good balls *wet?"* the man said. "But you know ... I *do* know you. You're married to ..."

"Rita Coolidge."

"That's right. And didn't we see you on ..."

"Television."

"I thought so," said the man, leaving with his friend.

Kristofferson finished the last of the Scotch. "He came closer than most," he said. "He almost knew who he was talking to. He thought Bobby Rydell. That ain't too far off."

Another silence fell. Through it, from the far shadows, another man appeared: swarthy, imposing, an earring in one ear, maybe in his middle fifties. It was Jose Ferrer, on his way to the ice machine.

"I remember you," Kristofferson said. 'You were in that great comedy about a man and a something-or-other."

"I'm afraid I was largely in tragedies," Jose Ferrer said.

"I remember it!" Kristofferson said. "You were in it with Rosemary Clooney!"

"I was *married* to Rosemary Clooney," Jose Ferrer said, "but I never did a *movie* with her. You can't have everything, you know."

He smiled philosophically and filled a bucket with ice and disappeared back into the shadows. Kristofferson turned his glass upside down and found, as he expected, that it was empty.

"Anybody with a ring in his ear is lying," he said. "I've never forgotten a single record I cut or a song I wrote. I admire the guy's spirit, but he's wrong." A long pause. "I'm *sure* the sneaky S.O.B. was in that movie." A longer pause. "And," said Kris Kristofferson, brightening visibly, "he was good in it, too."

Kris Kristofferson II

The road of excess leads to the palace of wisdom.

New York, 1981

For many long years, Kris Kristofferson was one of the legendary drinkers of his generation. When he was filming *A Star Is Born*, the director of that picture remembers, he got through one scene although he could hardly stand. Kristofferson liked to call himself "God's own drunk," and he romanticized himself as a "silver-tongued devil," and everybody's last memory of Janis Joplin has her sucking on a bottle of Jack Daniel's and singing Kristofferson's song "Me and Bobby McGee." The most famous line in that song is, of course,

Freedom's just another word, for nothin' left to lose.

Kristofferson stopped drinking about five years ago. Hasn't had a drop since. But he didn't stop getting high. He just switched from alcohol to marijuana. "I knew I was never gonna drink again," he was explaining to me not long ago, "but *grass* ... I thought I wouldn't give that up until I died."

On the day we talked, he had given it up for thirty-two days.

"Booze, five years. Grass, thirty-two days. Finished. I'm clean. Totally clean as a whistle. The progression was, first I stopped drinking. Then, not long after, I stopped the pills. Now grass. It's important for me to remember that I was still a drunk as long as I was getting stoned on grass. I finally had to face up to that."

Kristofferson and I were sitting in his hotel room in New York, one of a series of hotel rooms he'd inhabited since he hit the road last June. He was traveling with his sidekick and unofficial manager, Vernon White. Vernon came away from the icebox with little green bottles of Perrier and handed them around. Since everybody was into anniversaries, Vernon gave his credentials: "Booze, five years. Grass, ninety days. I stopped before Kris."

Earlier in the day, Kristofferson had faced a cross-section of newspaper and television reporters who interviewed him about his new movie, *Rollover*. He plays an international banker. Jane Fonda is the rich woman who falls in love with him. The interviews had gone OK, he thought. Now they were behind him, and he was talking frankly and honestly about his thirty years of drinking and drugging.

"I could *do* the interviews today, straight," he said. "I used to need grass to get up in front of people. Before that, I needed booze. Hell, I thought I always needed something. In looking at TV interviews with myself, I could always see the grass in my eyes. I could hear the long pauses. There he is, God's own drunk. Oh, Christ! Is that guy gonna remember what he started saying? I was doing verbal tap-dancing, trying to get my words and my thoughts lined up. Now, today, I just went out and did it. It's simple if you're not paranoid because of the stuff you've smoked to keep from gettin' paranoid."

I remembered previous times I'd talked with Kristofferson. Down in Durango in 1974, when he was shooting a Peckinpah picture. One long afternoon in Los Angeles, when he brought along a bottle of Ballantine's. There were stories that his wife, Rita Coolidge, was threatening to leave if he didn't stop drinking. Then reports that she had left. Then reports that he had stopped drinking, and was raising their child by himself.

But then there was that cover story in *Esquire* magazine, ironically titled "Kristofferson the Indestructible," reporting that what he had done was replace vast quantities of booze with unlimited amounts of marijuana. Toward the end of the interview, a stoned Kristofferson took *Esquire's* interviewer down to the beach, and then passed out in her lap.

I asked Kristofferson about the *Esquire* piece. He was defensive at first. "Parts of it were an invasion of privacy," he said. "Information about my domestic arrangements. But the part about the dope I didn't care that they mentioned, because dope was exactly what we were doing, and talking about. To me, smoking dope was as much a means for me to get comfortable, to open up for an in-depth interview. I thought it was a cheap shot for her to go ahead and write about it. But ... it was the truth."

Here there came a painful pause, as if he were evaluating something inside himself.

"I didn't like what I saw about myself in that article," he said. "To the extent I looked at that article and felt shitty about it, to that extent ... I decided to stop smoking dope. That was part of it. Another part was a deal I made with God, concerning an unrelated matter."

You gave it your best shot, I said. You were one of the most notorious boozers of your time.

"One of the most notorious to *live,*" he said. "Sooner or later, I suppose you come to the point where you have to say to yourself, either I'm gonna keep this up and die, or I'm gonna decide I want to live. With me, it was almost a conscious thing: *Hey! I'm gonna live.*

"At the beginning, you know, I didn't know diddly about grass. I was a drinker. When I made my first movie, *Cisco Pike,* I was playing a drug dealer, and the fact is, in real life I didn't even know how to roll a joint. What's more, I wasn't interested. Alcohol was my first choice. Later on, booze and pills. I didn't really get into grass in a big-time way until after I stopped drinking.

"At first, I enjoyed it to the fullest, just like booze was great at first. Grass enhanced the experience. Hey, isn't that a great smell! A great sunset! A great sexual experience! But eventually it dawned on me that grass was shutting things out instead of enhancing them. The irony was that grass was creating the exact opposite emotional state than the one I was theoretically smoking it for.

"It was like, I started out getting drunk to release my inhibitions. Booze gave me the courage to kiss a girl. To sing a song. But at the end, after thirty years ..."

Kristofferson paused. This was going to be hard to say.

"Well, one night I'm sitting there in the audience in a bar. Ronnie Hawkins is on stage. He sees me in the first row and says, *Come on up, Kris!* And grass had me so tied up in a paranoid knot that I was afraid to do it. I *couldn't* do it. Goddammit, I couldn't do the things I used to love. I had to be forced up on the stage to sing 'Bobby McGee' with my *own goddam band.*"

Part of the folklore, Kristofferson said, is that singers, writers, artists, all need to get stoned to find inspiration. "That's bullshit. Getting high was supposed to be a method of opening the doors of perception for me, and what it was doing was shutting them. Rather than easing problems for me, it was aggravating them. And with grass, paranoia goes right along with it."

Being sober feels so different, Kristofferson said, that he is beginning to reevaluate things in the light of what he is now beginning to understand about being stoned.

"On *Rollover,*" he said, "I was straight during the week and then I'd smoke on weekends. Sometimes on Mondays I'd be puffy-eyed. And I'd get angry a lot. Close into myself. Turn the anger onto myself and say, *OK, shoot the son of a bitching scene,* and then I'd sit back like a rock. They could start without me. I was mad about everything. About not having a beard. About wearing a tie. My voice would even change, I'd be so angry, I'd sound like a porpoise. Jane Fonda helped me a lot. She had a way of pointing out that what I was doing was self-destructive, without making me defensive."

What about Streisand, on *A Star Is Born?*

"What about her?"

How did she react? Was she as helpful?

Kristofferson smiled. "It ... wasn't as obvious to me at the time." He laughed. Reports of his feuds with Streisand and her producer boyfriend, Jon Peters, were widespread during the making of that movie.

"In retrospect," Kristofferson said, "I have a lot of gratitude to Barbra for some of the decisions she made on that movie. We were both fighting to protect the integrity of different territories. Looking at the movie today, I can see a lot of opportunities she gave me, that weren't as obvious when I was drinking a quart and a half of tequila and half a case of beer every day."

That's what it was like then, I said. What's it like now?

"I feel like I'm getting ready to do my best work. I feel as good as when I made the decision to get out of the Army and go to Nashville and become a country and western singer. I think better, I'm running better, I'm writing better. The only thing is, I wake up real early.

"The other day I took my little girl up to Marineland. We went to swim with the dolphins. When I was still using, I would have smoked some grass to make it feel better. Now the joy was in being there with my daughter—not because of a pill I had taken or a joint I'd smoked."

During his trip to New York, Kristofferson said, he went to visit a place called Phoenix House, a halfway house for teenage alcoholics and drug abusers. "They were so honest," he said. "I felt strange, coming in there after years of being a high-profile drinker. It's great that they can face the situation and see what it is. It took me thirty years to admit I had a problem. I told them that whatever worked with booze, worked better without it. I told them booze made me think depression was a permanent part of my life, because I was an angst-ridden poet, y'see. With teenagers, there are so many influences in the opposite direction, everybody telling them to get stoned, pass the joint around ... I felt like I was pissing in the wind.

"Still, I had paid my dues and I knew what I was talking about. You ever read Blake? You know what he wrote? *The road of excess leads to the palace of wisdom.*"

Kristofferson stood up and looked out his hotel window. There are at least two ways to look out a window. One way involves fierce resentments against all the strangers out there who are conspiring to make life miserable and impossible for you. The other way involves a cheerful curiosity about the possibilities still unexplored in the city. Kristofferson looked curious.

Richard Harris

Don't come near me. Not for two weeks. I may be dead.
Don't even come to disturb my corpse.

Toronto, 1983

"If this is so bloody safe," Richard Harris was saying, "why is he putting on a bloody face mask?"

The professional marksman pulled the mask down over his face and took aim at the left front rearview mirror of a Toronto police car. Richard Harris was sitting in the driver's seat, and this was one of those artsy-fartsy shots where the camera photographs Harris' reflection and then the mirror is shot out with a bullet.

"Did anybody check to see if this could be done?" Harris asked.

The marksman took aim. Two men began to bounce up and down on the back of the car, to make it rock. The marksman fired. The mirror splintered. The shot was over. It was time for lunch.

"I didn't even flick an eye," Harris said, getting out of the car. "I deserve the hero's medal for the week." He examined the mirror. "Bloody hell!" he said. "It went right through the metal! If I had known it was going to be done like this, I wouldn't have *done* the shot."

Is that really true? I asked him a few minutes later. We were sitting in his trailer, drinking herbal tea. It occurred to me that there was probably a story in the fact that Richard Harris was drinking tea, but I thought I'd start with the mirror.

"No, it's not true," Harris said. "I would have done it anyway. I have no sense of danger. I have no particular fears. A few years ago, during my period of not taking anything seriously, I was making a movie called *High Point* in Toronto. One of the scenes took place at the top of the C.N. Tower."

The tallest man-made object on Earth, I said.

"Or elsewhere. The shot called for me to roll down the slanted roof of the observation deck and hang onto the edge. The producer said, *You wouldn't do that yourself, would you?* I said *Sure!* And I did."

But there was a net?

"No net. I had to save myself. If I fell, I fell. I think you could call it great carelessness on my part, to do such a stupid thing. I must have been out of my mind at the time."

I sensed this was a good time to bring up the herbal tea. I notice, I said, that you are drinking herbal tea. Isn't that sort of a departure for you?

"Two years," Harris said. "To be exact, two years since August 11, 1981, when I had my last drink."

That must have been a momentous decision for a man long known as one of the champion boozers of the Western world.

"It was stop, or die," Harris said quietly. "And the hangovers were so painful. I used to look forward to hangovers as the start of a wonderful day, because they meant I could start drinking again—to cure the hangover, you know. But it got to the stage where it was horrible."

How is it, being dry?

"You get used to it. I miss the occasional glass of wine with dinner. I don't miss waking up next to the ugliest girls in the world. I was lucky to stop when I did. Some of my old mates have been practically crippled."

And as for you, you've just finished a stage tour in *Camelot* and now you're making this movie called *Martin's Day.*

"The tour's not finished. I'll gear up again after the first of the year for some more engagements in the United States. *Camelot* has been a huge success in America. Not so successful when I took it to London last winter."

I saw you in *Camelot* in London, I said.

"Bloody disaster, eh?"

I thought it was okay. I've always been a pushover for *Camelot,* anyway.

"The press had a field day: *Here's that bastard Richard Harris coming back to the British stage, a pint of lager in his hand.* I surprised them. I was on my good behavior. But the casting was a bit off. The girl couldn't sing. And the Lancelot was very odd. I had approval of the cast, of course, but I was off making a film and I left it to them. When I came to rehearsals and heard the girl singing, I thought they were sending me up. *Well look,* I said, *I can't sing. We all know that. But two out of three in the cast ought to be able to sing.* They didn't see it that way."

What else do you have in the works?

"A novel, a screenplay and a stage tour. About the novel I will tell you nothing, except that it is about two schizophrenic sisters and their obsession with a pop singer. It may someday become a film."

Who will play the singer?

"Not I, that's for sure. My days of teenage pop idolatry are over."

And the screenplay?

"Called *Himself Speaking.* Have you ever heard of *The Ginger Man?"*

The novel by J.P. Donleavy. The story of the mad drunken American named Sebastian Dangerfield, making a legend of himself in postwar Dublin.

"The very one. I played the Ginger Man on the stage in London, you know. Well, this screenplay is rather as if the Ginger Man were still alive, but he had dropped out of sight, you know. The Ginger Man in middle age."

Was there ever a real Ginger Man? I asked.

"Oh, most certainly. His real name was Gaynor Crist. He attended Trinity College in the late 1940s, which is where Donleavy met him. Donleavy didn't put into the book half of the things that Crist did. He's dead now, poor fellow. When I was going to do *The Ginger Man* on stage, I went to Dublin and took an ad in the paper, asking if all those who remembered Gaynor Crist would kindly step forward. *Hundreds* did! And they all had their stories. And two-thirds of them had a tear in their eye. He was much beloved by all, except for the establishment."

Harris poured himself another cup of herbal tea.

"One of the great things he did," he said, "was to dress up in the archbishop's vestments and wait in the sacristy until the precise moment when it was time for the sermon. This was at twelve o'clock Mass on a holy day in Dublin. Then he marched out to the pulpit, drew himself up, regarded the congregation, and said, *Has it come to your attention that you cannot buy contraceptives in Ireland?*"

Harris shook his head in wonderment. "Well, that was the end. After that one, he was asked to leave Ireland by the American consulate. He had already been thrown out of Trinity College."

Harris leaned forward and spoke in a conspiratorial tone. "Do you remember," he said, "the character in the book named O'Keefe?"

I think I do, I said. Wasn't he the guy who never had any luck with women?

"Exactly! No matter what he did, he could never get laid. Well, O'Keefe was based on a real person, you know. A famous American movie director who was at Trinity."

Can you tell me his name? I asked.

"Of course I can," Harris said, and he did.

Did his luck ever change?

"It finally did. He went to bed with the Ginger Man's wife one night. Then the Ginger Man came home unexpectedly, turned on the light and discovered them, much to (name deleted's) discomfiture. But the Ginger Man turned off the light, got into bed and went to sleep. And never mentioned it again."

Maybe he was too drunk to notice, I said.

"Or too kind."

Whatever happened to the Ginger Man?

"He went to Spain and taught English for Berlitz. He died on board a boat coming back to England, where he planned to take the cure for alcoholism."

How, I asked, did you finally stop drinking?

"I knew I had to. I was up to two bottles of vodka a day. Plus the brandies in the evening. I kept meeting people I didn't know I already knew. I telephoned my brother and told him, *Don't come near me. Not for two weeks. I may be dead. Don't even come to disturb the corpse.* Then I locked myself into my house in London, which has ten rooms. In every room, I placed two bottles. A bottle of vodka and a bottle of tonic. Also, a bottle opener, of course. And I challenged myself not to drink. For days and days I went through sheer agony, madness, withdrawal. I was in a terrible state. But at the end, I had broken it."

David Bowie

Fundamentally, I am a shy lad.

Cannes, 1983

This was not the David Bowie I was expecting. This was not the enigma hiding behind a bizarre rock 'n' roll mask, the androgynous Ziggy Stardust. This was a soft-spoken, amusing, thirty-six-year-old British artist wearing a yellow tie, a tan suit, a shirt with tiny checks and Gucci sunglasses placed neatly next to his knife and spoon. Bowie had the best manners of anyone at the table.

We were having lunch one afternoon in May during the Cannes Film Festival, six reporters and David Bowie. He was on the brink of a world concert tour, but he had taken this time out to bow in the direction of his screen career. One of his new films was in the official competition, and he had three other movies playing the film marketplace in the backstreets of Cannes. He chooses his films on the basis of their directors, possibly because he wants to watch them work; he confesses that he plans to direct a film himself.

The official entry was *Merry Christmas, Mr. Lawrence,* a film by the controversial Japanese director Nagisa Oshima, whose *In the Realm of the Senses* (1976) stirred up a worldwide storm with its obsessive relationship between a businessman and the geisha who castrates him in the name of love. That was a film the former David Bowie might have felt at home in, but the current David Bowie was more conventionally cast, as a British prisoner of war, in Oshima's *Mr. Lawrence.*

Elsewhere in the theaters in Cannes, Bowie could be seen playing an aging vampire in *The Hunger,* a pirate in *Yellowbeard* by Monty Python's, Graham Chapman and as Ziggy Stardust himself, in a 1972 concert film that he put on the shelf for years and recently decided to re-edit and release. Even though Bowie currently has his first chart hit in some time ("Let's Dance"), can this be the end of Bowie as a rock singer and the beginning of a new career as an actor?

"I'm a jack of all trades, but I no longer quite think of myself as a master of them all," Bowie said. "I do seem to be in a lot of movies at the moment, but I'm also doing my first world tour since 1978, so I definitely haven't put stage performance behind me. I think the difference between me *now* and me *then* is that I am more myself on the stage, and I'm saving the masquerades for film roles."

Bowie is quite frank about the difference between *now* and *then.*

"Six years ago, I decided I really didn't want to continue with a rock 'n' roll existence," he said. "Rock 'n' roll had become a particular crowd of people and the lifestyle that came along with them. I couldn't cope with it. I removed myself from that lifestyle."

A waiter placed fresh asparagus in front of him, and he looked down at the plate with a grave neutrality. Across the table from him, a British journalist with a malfunctioning tape recorder banged his Sony hard on the table to make it start. "How so?" the journalist asked. Bowie lifted an uncertain eyebrow. "How did you remove yourself, and from what?" the journalist asked.

"The simplest thing," Bowie said, "is to say I removed myself from drugs and Bel Air. I was killing myself. I was going to die. It's not so much the music, as the surroundings and the associates. They used drugs. I fell into their habits. I overdosed a couple of times. I scraped the surface of putting myself out of it completely. I went through a stereotyped seventies experience and somehow survived it. Two or three people saw me, physically and mentally, for what I was. They got me away. I have removed myself, absolutely, from drugs for six years now. And I moved to Berlin, which seemed like a much safer place to live than Los Angeles."

He spoke quietly, almost diffidently, as if he didn't want to bore us with these details about how he had saved his life. He suggested that at one point, all sorts of things had been connected in his life—drugs, rock 'n' roll, his onstage masquerades and a lifelong shyness—but that after kicking drugs he was learning that he could also let go of the masquerades.

Bowie for years was known as a conceptual rock 'n' roll artist, a performer who came out of a street mime tradition and created new characters for every tour. "I was very shy," he said. "I couldn't get up and sing my own songs. I found that if I created an outrageous character, I could sing his songs. Now, with this tour, I think you're going to see more of me on stage for the first time, and more positive songs. I have a more positive view of life."

"David," said the British journalist, tapping his Sony, "was it that bad? Tell us how bad it really was." Reporters for the trashy Fleet Street papers have a way of sounding simultaneously solicitous and insulting. Bowie nodded attentively.

"Apart from the possibility of killing myself with an overdose, I was approaching a serious breakdown. My thinking was fragmented. There was complete disorientation. It took the form mainly of hallucinations. I was unable to sleep. I developed a sudden interest in mythology. I got on an Arthurian kick ... the Holy Grail ... and it occurred to me that I was waiting for King Arthur to return."

He smiled, wanly. "It took me two years to get completely over all of that. I was disgusted with myself and my wasted life. What a waste it all was. There were large parts of the 1970s I have no recollection of. During my recuperation period, my recovery pivoted around my son. I held onto this: If he had a future, then I did, too. There was a time when I thought my life was over. Now I feel a good, healthy thirty-six, and I'm looking forward to the tour."

His son, christened Zowie, now called Joey, attends a private school in Switzerland. Bowie is a single parent. Of his former wife, Angela, he says, "I believe she lives in California. I sometimes vaguely remember being married."

Fleet Street: "But would you marry again, David?"

Bowie: "Yes, if I fell in love."

Fleet: "And how much longer do you think you can keep on singing? Ready to retire? Can you see yourself (chuckle) still onstage at fifty?"

Bowie: "At fifty? Most definitely. Of course! I never thought I was writing or performing for a 'generation,' or that my songs were topical. They're more along the lines of observations. Rather than still addressing myself to the same aging generation, at fifty I'll be doing whatever I'm doing *then.* Oh, good lord, yes. If Picasso could paint at eighty, I damn sure can still sing at fifty."

The thing that will be different, he said, is that he'll project more of his own feelings into his songs: "Before, they were remote, from a synthetic point of view. Now it will be me singing."

What about you directing?

"Well, I've done some short video films for the music channels, promotional films, things like that. A couple of them I'm pleased with. I've just about decided that the irresponsible people are in rock, while the crazy people are in film. I have to be realistic about my prospects as a film director. I know that I'm damn good at what I do in music. But in other areas I'm quite willing to relinquish the role of supreme being. When I was using drugs, I had a very inflated opinion of my importance and abilities. That's typical of rock 'n' roll and the chemically induced mood of the time."

I asked Bowie if the subject matter of his songs would change, now that he was off drugs.

"One thing I've never written," he said, "is drug music. I never saw drugs as an interesting subject. With me, they were more something to keep me working. Amphetamines and cocaine seemed to give me energy, but they didn't interest me except as something to reach for. You don't write songs about cigarettes, for example. I think my songs are more about observations of things, visions that strike me, attitudes that are interesting."

He smiled. "Fundamentally," he said, "I am a shy lad. At parties, I would get drunk. Onstage, I invented characters to play, so I wouldn't have to play myself. I had to overcome all that. I'm not shy now. I feel at ease with my situation. I'm more relaxed with people. Before, I think I had an unwillingness to recognize my emotional drives. One doesn't reveal one's feelings, does one? It wasn't the thing to show how one felt about things. Drugs and sex were a release for all that inhibition. For the first time, I don't feel I have to reach outside of myself for contentment."

About his new movies, Bowie was philosophical.

"I was dissatisfied, on the whole, by *The Hunger,*" he said, speaking of the box office disappointment in which he played the latest in a long string of self-destructing husbands of the vampire Catherine Deneuve. "It isn't very much like the script. It's certainly not my vision of what the film would be like. It's also too bloody. But the director had a good eye, and the film looks interesting. And it was fun working with Dick Smith, the greatest makeup artist in the world. I'd get up at three and spend four or five hours being aged. I love makeup, and now that I'm wearing less of it on the stage, I suppose I'll be wearing more in the movies."

After seeing Oshima's *Merry Christmas, Mr. Lawrence,* Bowie said he was struck by the stylization of both the Japanese and the British characters. (Each side in the movie behaves like the other side's caricatures of them.) "If the English had interpreted the Japanese the way Oshima has in the film," he said, "they would have been accused of racism. Oshima was fascinating to work with. He took only one or two takes of each scene. He edited in the camera. There were no daily rushes. A rough cut was ready within four or five days after the film was finished." He smiled. "I write songs like that."

During your world stage tour, I asked, how are you going to deal with the drug thing?

"No drugs," Bowie said. "Very simple."

But if people connected with the tour are using drugs?

"If I caught anyone with drugs on my tour," he said, "they'd be fired instantly. Just as there are road crews to hire *if* drugs are being used, so there are people to hire who do not use drugs. I've talked to Pete Townshend of the Who about this very thing. It's not that I'm a preacher in any terms, but this comes to putting other people in danger."

Fleet Street: "Are you a happy man, David?"

Bowie: "I feel content."

Fleet: "How would you measure your success?"

Bowie (smiling): "Well, for the first time, I'm self-sufficient. I've never made a great deal of money, as these things go, and I've spent a lot, as those things went, and I've been on the point of bankruptcy many times."

Fleet: "What do you want to make at this point in your career?"

Bowie (wry smile): "A lot of money."

John Belushi I

The spin cycle

Chicago, 1983

Death is the slamming of the door in your face, and the sound of bolting on the inside.—C.S. Lewis

It was just a year ago, on March 5, that John Belushi went to his last party. According to the fragmented reconstructions of his last night on earth, it began as pretty much a routine evening, for Belushi, of drinking and rock clubs and cruising the Sunset Strip and, at some point in the evening, making a drug connection that would be blamed as the cause of death.

The images from a year ago still are fresh in the memories of those who loved Belushi: the faded Hollywood glory of the Chateau Marmont residential hotel, where his body was found; the pasty-faced "unidentified woman" being led away in handcuffs by police; his best friend, Dan Aykroyd, dressed in a Chicago cop uniform, leading the funeral procession on a motorcycle. Soon the flowers of a second spring will bloom near John Belushi's grave.

Hardly a week goes by without a reminder of John's death. He's there on the TV every weekend, on the reruns of "Saturday Night Live." A poster from his movie *Continental Divide* hangs in my office. That was the one where he played a Chicago newspaper columnist, and on the poster, he's poker-faced and maybe a little sad, with a copy of the *Sun-Times* jammed under his arm. Every once in a while somebody will be talking about some comedian, and they'll say he does something "like Belushi used to do," and then I think that Belushi would have been only thirty-four years old if he still were alive today. And then I think, damn it all, John, why did you slam that door so soon?

I think I know the answer. The answer is not that John slammed the door and bolted it shut from the inside. The answer is that the door slammed shut on him. The kid from Wheaton whom I met in the early 1970s, who drank in the bars of Old Town and went to New York and became a star, and who came back to Chicago and opened his own private saloon, where he could drink all day and all night, was one of the most talented comic actors of his time, but he drank too much and drugged too much and it killed him. That's pretty much what happened.

Belushi liked to party, but there were a lot of bartenders in his old Chicago neighborhoods who were not overjoyed when they saw him coming. Some places were thrilled to have a guy like Belushi in the house, especially after he got famous. Other places asked him not to come back again.

When you are in your late twenties and making hundreds of thousands of dollars a year, there is an answer to a problem like that: Open your own bar. Belushi and Aykroyd took over a place near the corner of North and Wells that used to be named the Sneak Joynt, and they renamed it the Blues Bar. In the right circles in Chicago, the word spread quickly when John was in town, and his friends, or those who thought of themselves as his friends, dropped in to have a drink with John.

He loved to play host. For some reason, he seemed driven to be there, to be available for hours on end—in case somebody else might turn up or another crowd might come in. I think, in a way, he saw it as paying his dues. Although he probably never consciously put it into words, he basically was saying that even though he was a millionaire, he still was one of the guys and still ready to party all night with his old friends—or his newfound friends, as it often turned out. One night I saw him chugging from a bottle of Jack Daniel's and then plunging his face into the tub of ice behind the bar. Here's an irony: I was in pretty bad shape myself that night, and the question I asked myself was not *why* does he do it, but *how?*

That would have been during the time he was shooting *The Blues Brothers* in Chicago. It was common knowledge around town that a lot of cocaine found its way onto the set of that movie, as it found its way onto the sets of other movies Belushi made. The theory was that you couldn't get physically addicted to cocaine, but as George Carlin once explained, "The way cocaine makes you feel is like having some more cocaine."

Belushi sometimes thought he knew the answer to that dilemma. He thought the answer was control, also known as not partying too late when you gotta work the next day. I remember one Saturday afternoon during *Blues Brothers* when he came over to my house with his wife, Judy, and ate a microwave pizza and drank 7-Up and was, as he put it, "in training." In the hierarchy of the Belushi legend, Aykroyd was his "best friend" and Judy was his "wife," but the way I read it, Judy was John's best friend in the life-and-death things, and maybe it was no accident that he seemed to get into more trouble when she wasn't around. That afternoon he talked about a movie he wanted to make about a Chicago newspaperman —a guy something like Mike Royko, who had been a friend of his family since before he was born.

The filming schedule of *The Blues Brothers* ran into a lot of delays because of problems with "talent," as they call the people who appear in front of the cameras. John was trying to go full-speed twenty-four hours a day. It cannot be done, but let it be said that he gave it a better shot than most people. He had such talent and such energy, and such a natural rapport with Aykroyd, that, problems or no problems, they made a big, funny, aggressive, entertaining movie.

After *Animal House* and *Blues Brothers,* both big winners at the box office, John could have continued to make the same kinds of movies indefinitely. But he turned down the various proposals for *Animal House* sequels and went ahead with plans for the newspaper movie, *Continental Divide.* After it was finished, he and Aykroyd committed themselves to a very strange project called *Neighbors,* which was like nothing they'd done before and which they changed even more by "switching roles," so that Aykroyd played the weirdo guy in the movie, and Belushi, the weirdo expert, played the middle-class homeowner.

Belushi shot scenes from *Continental Divide* here in the *Sun-Times* features department, where I ran into him one Saturday afternoon. He looked great. He was thinner, he seemed bouncier, his eyes were clear and he was in a good mood. I told him he looked in pretty good shape. "Yeah," he said, "I'm in training. No more booze." I told him I'd stopped drinking, too. "Great," he said. "Way to go. My system is, no booze, no drugs, watch what I eat and work out a little. This is the new me." That would have been a year or so before he died.

When *Continental Divide* was released, it got so-so notices and did disappointing business at the box office. *Neighbors,* which was released for Christmas, 1981, got a more complicated reception. During a lackluster holiday season, it was one of the top grossers in early returns, maybe because Belushi and Aykroyd fans expected a rerun of their "Saturday Night Live" and Blues Brothers relationship. Then the movie dropped off; its eccentric charms were lost on the Belushi fans who cheered when he mashed beer cans against his head in *Animal House.*

Three months later, he was dead. He had stayed fairly straight after Christmas, his friends said, but when he went out West, away from Judy and Dan, to talk to Paramount about a script, he fell in with the Hollywood version of his Chicago friends, with the druggies and groupies and drunks and punks. After Belushi's death, Aykroyd said in an interview that John called his partying periods "the spin cycle"—that after getting off the booze and other stuff while making a movie, he was inclined to reward himself afterward. When he hit Hollywood that last time, he also was depressed because of the relative failure of his two attempts to break out of his *Animal House* image, and because Paramount hadn't liked his screenplay.

What actually happened on the last night of Belushi's life still is a matter of controversy. The last woman to see him alive told her story on television, and as I watched her I felt mostly pity, because it was clear from her voice, her manner and her bearing that she was not a villainess but just another victim, a person who met John while they were on the same merry-go-round. Some people blamed that sad woman for Belushi's death, but, watching her, I couldn't believe she made him do anything. She was just part of a system that enabled him to do drugs that last night, if he had the money and the inclination.

If it is true that nobody can really make anybody else take drugs, let it be said that another thing also is true: After a certain point, the drinker and drug user is no longer really free to make a decision about his own usage. By that I don't mean that John was so stoned on his last night that he didn't know what he was doing when he popped his last balloon. I mean that he was completely helpless in the face of the *first* drink or the *first* drug, because he had become trapped in a vicious circle: "in training" and "the spin cycle."

People tried to help him. From everything I've heard, his wife did her best. Aykroyd said he had talked to Belushi a few days before his death, had sensed an unhappiness and perhaps even sensed the approaching tragedy, and told him he needed some time to get away, be alone, be quiet, get the stuff out of his system. Aykroyd was planning to get together with Belushi and try to help him do that when the news of his death came.

John Belushi was a talented man who gave so generously of his talent that now, a year later, people still remember that he made them happy and resent the fact that the door slammed shut on him. What could have saved him? Who can say. A lot of movie stars have serious drug and booze problems. They say drug addiction and alcoholism are progressive diseases—that they always get worse, never better, that "moderation" is a joke and that the only answer is to get off the stuff and stay off the stuff.

A lot of stars have been able to do that; *Rolling Stone* seems to be featuring the Recovering Alcoholic of the Month on its covers these days. A lot of others, however, have not stopped, and sooner or later, many of them have died.

There was that macabre "Saturday Night Live" sketch where John Belushi went to visit the graveyard of dead SNL veterans and danced on their graves. After John himself was found dead, some TV stations used ironic excerpts from the sketch in their obituaries. Was that in bad taste? I don't know. Think about it. The message in the sketch was one of victory—the victory the living always have over the dead, the victory Belushi had over Jim Morrison, Janis Joplin, Elvis, Jimi Hendrix and the others who lived as if they were immortal. "They may be dead," the deeper symbolism went, "but I, John Belushi, still party, am still alive, still get away with it, still survive." It was the same careless shout of victory that all of those dead legends carried with them to the grave.

John Belushi II

Drugs can be fun.

Chicago, 1984

Who is right about John Belushi?

Bob Woodward has written a book named *Wired* that portrays Belushi as a man out of control, whose life came to be ruled by cocaine and other drugs.

Judy Belushi, his widow, has attacked Woodward's book for a number of reasons, of which the most heartfelt is: That's not John in the book. Woodward's portrait doesn't show the life, the humor, the courage, the energy. He wasn't just a junkie.

Yet the cops who removed his body from a bungalow at the Chateau Marmont on March 5, 1982, were brutally frank: He looked, to them, like just another dead junkie.

Judy Belushi remembers the good times. She argues that "drugs can be fun," and that she and John had a lot of ups along with the downs. The difference was that John never knew when to stop.

Woodward portrays a man who, at the time of his death, was throwing away a career and alienating key people in the movie industry by a pattern of uncontrolled drug abuse.

Judy Belushi speaks of the pressures of show business, of John's need to find energy and inspiration in drugs so that he could deliver what was expected of him.

In all the important ways, Woodward's book is apparently reliable. Judy Belushi quarrels with some dates and interpretations, but basically the facts are there, and documented.

Their real difference is over the interpretation of the facts. Beginning with the same man and the same life, Judy Belushi sees a lifestyle, and Bob Woodward sees the progression of a disease.

Was John Belushi an addict? Friends shy away from the word, and yet on the evidence in Woodward's book he was a classic addict, a textbook case of drug and alcohol abuse. You don't get much worse and live, as indeed he proved.

The protests over Woodward's unflinching portrait of Belushi's last days reminds me (not with a smile) of an old Irish joke. The mourners are gathered around the dead man's coffin.

"What did he die of?" one asks the widow.

"He died of the drink," she says.

"Did he go to AA?"

"He wasn't that bad."

John Belushi did try to stop, many times. It is just that he never tried to stop in a way that would have worked. He tried resolutions and willpower. Every addict knows that willpower hardly ever works in the long run, since when the will turns, the game is over. He tried changing his environment, with retreats to Martha's Vineyard. Recovering addicts talk cynically of "geographical cures," as if a habit you carry within yourself can be left behind. He tried placing himself under the discipline of others, and even submitted to "trainers" who were to guard him twenty-four hours a day. That made his drugs their problem, not his. He tried switching from one drug to another, or to "only beer" or "only pot." All mood-altering substances are interchangeable to the abuser, and the drug of substitute leads inevitably back to the drug of choice. He tried health kicks, with Judy mixing her husband "health shakes" in the mornings, all filled with yogurt and bananas and wheat germ. An abuser's body is incapable of efficiently absorbing nutrition. He talked to doctors who issued their dire warnings while writing him prescriptions for tranquilizers. He talked to psychiatrists who wanted to get to the root of his problem, as if today's drug abuse can be treated by understanding the traumas of childhood.

All of these attempts were valiant. When Judy Belushi speaks of them, she speaks from the bottom of her heart. But they were all doomed. All but the very luckiest of drug abusers and alcoholics have tried and failed at most of those strategies. Those who have been successful at stopping are almost unanimous in describing what finally worked:

1. Complete abstinence from all mood-altering substances.
2. Admission of defeat, and willingness to accept help.
3. Use of a support group, such as AA.

The odds against successfully stopping by going cold turkey and using willpower are so high, according to the Harvard Medical School study *The Natural History of Alcoholism,* that it's hardly worth trying—except as a prelude to an admission of defeat.

From the evidence in *Wired,* John Belushi was rarely away from one drug or another for more than a few days. Using Valium or Quaaludes as a "substitute" was just his way of putting his drug of choice on hold. When he did occasionally get clean, it was almost always in response to a specific challenge (doing a movie, meeting a deadline), and it often involved some kind of external control, like a bodyguard who would act as a substitute for Belushi's own will.

When he went back to drug use, it was also often in response to a challenge like a movie or a deadline; whether he was using or abstaining, he connected drugs with his ability to work

I remember a day here at the *Sun-Times* building when Belushi was shooting scenes for *Continental Divide.* I had known him for years on a casual basis; our paths crossed occasionally, from early days of Old Town bars and Second City parties to later interviews and show-biz occasions. I had rarely seen him looking better than he looked that day. He told me he was in great shape. He was off the booze and the drugs. He was exercising.

A man was standing next to him, and he introduced him as "my trainer." Well, what was he going to call him? "My drug guard?" Alcoholism and drug abuse are characterized by denial and an addict will substitute almost any conceivable illness or weakness for the one he must deny; John seemed to place the entire situation in the category of "losing weight" and "getting in shape." An alcoholic who has temporarily stopped drinking but does not yet admit his problem will frequently do what John did, which is to describe abstinence as a training program or a diet.

His career was coming apart. *Continental Divide* did not do well at the box office. There were arguments and major problems during the shooting of *Neighbors.* Work was at a standstill on the screenplay for Belushi's next project, titled *Noble Rot.* All the career setbacks are described by Woodward. They were accompanied by episodes of drug and alcohol abuse that grew increasingly alarming to his friends and family.

Judy Belushi, in describing those episodes, often links them with their "causes." For example, she differs with Woodward on his interpretation of Belushi's drug use during the filming of *Goin' South,* one of his early films, which starred Jack Nicholson. In the Woodward version, Belushi's drug use created problems with the shooting schedule. In Judy Belushi's version, John had flown to New York for a heavy "Saturday Night Live" taping schedule, had exhausted himself, was diagnosed as having "walking pneumonia," should have been hospitalized, was nevertheless advised by his lawyer to fly back to the movie location in Mexico—and only *then,* after being kept on hold for several days in Mexico, began to use drugs. Well, she seems to be asking, can you blame him?

The disagreement over the facts of this episode are unimportant, now that Belushi is in his grave. Judy's interpretation is revealing. Her rationale, if I follow it, is that John used drugs in response to an intolerable situation, and that drugs were his means of coping with it. He was not just irresponsibly going on a blast.

That is true, but it is half of the truth.

It is true, that for someone with a dependency on drugs or alcohol, there will be situations that literally cannot be gotten through without drugs or alcohol.

But the other half of the truth is: The situations that cannot be gotten through without drugs or alcohol are invariably situations caused by drugs or alcohol. Booze fixes a hangover. Then booze causes a hangover. If a non-drinker woke up with a normal hangover, he would go to an emergency room. A surprising number of drug and alcohol abusers walk around every day for years with symptoms that a healthy person would equate with "walking pneumonia," or worse.

Some reviews of *Wired* say it describes John as a tragic figure. But disease is not tragic, it is just very sad. And what is sad in John's case is that he was not lucky enough to find, or be able to accept, help. In the book, Dan Aykroyd cries out that John must be hospitalized, that he needs professional help. John Landis says, "We've got to get him formally committed if necessary." Judy was in agreement, but wondered how they'd ever get John to go along with it. They were right. At the time of John's death, his friends were apparently mobilizing to "enforce" such help—to intervene.

They were on the right track, but a little too late. John Belushi himself, on some pages of this book, pounds his fists, cries out against his demons and vows to straighten himself out forever. If he had gone the route of detox, drug counseling, therapy and AA, there is a possibility that he could have stayed drug-free long enough to come down to normal speed, to look soberly at his life, and to accept help. But in the years covered by this book, Belushi was never clean long enough to see very clearly.

To me, the tragic figure in the book is Judy Belushi. Tragedy is when you know not only what was, but what could have been. No matter what she thinks of the Woodward book, for me she comes across in it as a courageous, loving, generous and incredibly patient woman who stood by John as well as she could, who put up with a lot of hell, who did what seemed to be right, and who is not content to have his epitaph read "junkie."

Yet her behavior toward her husband, as described here, is often an example of "enabling." Almost all active alcoholics and addicts have "enablers" in their lives—people who make excuses, hold things together, assume the roles of bodyguard, parent, nurse, accountant and alibier. Enabling is obviously done out of love—usually out of a deep and stubborn love that refuses to admit defeat. But groups such as Al-Anon, the organization for friends and associates of alcoholics, argue that the best thing an enabler can do is stop enabling.

Judy tried that on occasion, threatening John with divorce as a last resort. Unfortunately, her battle was not only against her own enabling, but also against the army of enablers that flocked around Belushi in the years of his fame. This was possibly the most enabled man of his generation. The angriest pages in Woodward's generally dispassionate book are devoted to the friends, fans, agents, producers, employers, groupies and general scum who competed with each other to supply Belushi with drugs.

I remember John from the early 1970s, in Old Town, where, to put it cruelly, you'd put drinks into him like quarters into a jukebox, and he'd entertain everyone in the room. He was eventually "eighty-sixed" (barred) from most of those bars, though, and at the end was frequenting his own private saloons in New York and Chicago.

In Chicago during those early days, we were buying him drinks. In Los Angeles and New York in the later days, Woodward reports, money for cocaine was built into some of his business deals, and his associates were giving him hundreds of dollars in cash, on demand, day or night, to buy drugs. For that matter, what difference would it have made if they hadn't? Friends and sycophants were sneaking him drugs because it boosted their own images: There are long, painful passages in the book in which Judy is asking people not to give John drugs "because I know you don't want to hurt him." The same people are hiding drugs for him in stovepipes, toilet bowls and his pockets.

John Belushi was an actor and a comedian, but the book could have been written about a pilot, a plumber, a taxi driver or a journalist—if their diseases commanded $600,000 advances from Simon and Schuster. Judy Belushi is wrong, I believe, in confusing the progression of John's disease with the "demands" and "pressures" of show business.

Life involves a lot of pressure. It is easier to handle without the incalculable pressure of drug abuse. The comedian who cannot be funny, the pilot who cannot fly, the journalist who cannot meet a deadline, the mother who cannot be patient with her child, feels demands and pressures that are exactly the equal of Belushi's—since there is no measuring the intensity of the intolerable. *Wired* is essentially not a show-business biography, but just the sad natural history of a disease.

seven

The fundamental things apply

Linn Ullmann is still a daughter, no matter that her mother is Liv Ullmann and her father is Ingmar Bergman. Charles Bronson is still a husband and father, no matter that he was once the highest-paid movie star in the history of the world. Muhammad Ali is still the most famous man alive, no matter that even Apollo Creed has retired. William Hurt is not yet sure just who or what he is, and that is the most fundamental thing about him.

Linn Ullmann

He's ... you know ... he's Bergman.

Montreal, 1983

When you see them standing together, in the hotel lobby or at a reception, or waiting for a movie to start, you don't at first assume they're mother and daughter. They have the easy ways of friends. This began a couple of years ago, according to the daughter, when she was fourteen or fifteen years old and made the conscious decision to stop being a kid. Now that she is seventeen, she sighs, it is too late to turn back the clock.

Her mother is Liv Ullmann, the famous Norwegian actress. Her father is Ingmar Bergman, the famous Swedish director. She is Linn Ullmann, a tall, slender New York teenager with shoulder-length blonde hair and her mother's warm smile. (Her father, who has made the human tragedy his life's subject, is not known for his smile.)

Linn would be a senior in the fall at New York's Professional Children's High School, which was, she explained with a grin, "for professional kids." She has modeled for *Seventeen* magazine and has just signed with a modeling agency that is looking around for a product for her to be identified with, the way Brooke Shields sells Calvin Kleins. She hopes to study drama at New York University. All she has ever wanted to be is an actress.

Linn and her mother were at the World Film Festival in Montreal, where Liv's new film, an Australian version of Ibsen's *The Wild Duck,* was having its premiere. There was just the hint that Linn might be having *her* premiere here, too, as if her mother were gently introducing her to the rigors of being a public person.

Although Linn has been in a few movies (she played her mother as a child in Bergman's *Autumn Sonata),* she has not led the life of a movie star's child; her mother avoids glitter and works as an ambassador for UNICEF. Unlike world-weary Hollywood kids, Linn is sometimes even a little shy: "We actually lead a pretty quiet life."

On the morning after the premiere of *The Wild Duck,* Linn was reading in her mother's hotel suite. She had her finger marking her place in the paperback edition of Sidney Sheldon's *The Other Side of Midnight* ("You know, airplane reading"). She said she needed time to clean up her room, and there was the sound of drawers slamming before she threw open the door. She sat on the bed, her long legs curled up beneath her, wearing a light tan dress with a broad black belt and a small coffee stain. I asked her about her career as a model.

"I wouldn't call it a career, up to now," she said. "So far I've only done a little modeling, mostly for fun. I've just signed with the Eileen Ford Agency, which will be a big step up. I'm kind of ambivalent about modeling. It's fun, like being a little girl and dressing up like a princess. But the images aren't really true, all that beauty and richdom isn't really how life is. I've had a couple of roles in my father's movies, little things. Before I do something bigger, I want to study drama and theater. I'd like to go to NYU and audition for the Royal Academy in England. Some of the kids in my high school have been in movies already, some of those teenage pictures, but I'm not awfully crazy about those movies and I wouldn't want to do one."

You wouldn't take a role in a high school exploitation film like *Private School* or *Going All the Way?*

"It's difficult." She bit her lip. "I have my father and my mother, who are very big artists. I have to live up to that. I am also my own person, and have to live up to myself. I wouldn't want to just be in some movie to get a job. Acting's in my blood. I've never wanted to do anything else, so I want to do it right. My biggest dream is actually to be on the stage, more than to be in movies."

I got a feeling, I said, from the way you talked about "airplane reading," that you're a serious reader.

"I love to read, all the time. Lots of plays. O'Neill, Ibsen, American literature, Norwegian. Norwegian is my first language, but I think I'm beginning to think of myself more as European than specifically Norwegian ... God, I've been lucky, going to so many different schools all over the place. I'm not sure I really belong anywhere."

Tell me about your mother, I said.

"She is ... hmmm. A very typical mother, in many ways. I've never felt that she was a movie star. No rushing off to Hollywood for the weekend. She's strict, she worries about the same things other mothers worry about. As I'm becoming older, we're becoming more and more friends. When I was fourteen or fifteen, there was more of a crisis relationship, but I think all teenagers go through that stage. It's been ... interesting. The most fun is when we travel together."

Linn's father, who is considered by many people to be the greatest living film director, had a tempestuous love affair with her mother that Liv Ullmann chronicled with unadorned honesty in her 1978 autobiographical book, *Changing*. Tell me about your father, I asked.

"He's ..." She smiled and shrugged a little. "He's weird. He's a wonderful man, but I think of him more as an older ... as an uncle, more than a father. I know he'll always be there for me. But he's no a father-father, the way Mother is a mother-mother. He's a genius at his art. I love him very much." She smiled. "He's ... you know. He's *Bergman.*"

You could hear the italics as she said the name. She spends some time every summer with him, she said, on the Baltic island of Faro where he has his famous stone house and his own movie studio, and where he has shot many of his films.

"It's a family gathering. All of his kids are there. I have seven brothers and sisters on my father's side, and there's his wife, Ingrid, and her kids, and wives and husbands and boyfriends and girlfriends of kids, it's quite a crowd. Most of them are quite a bit older than me. I'm very good friends with Daniel, one of the youngest. I like Anna Bergman, who has had problems ... she ended up in the wrong kind of movies ... it's too bad, she's a very sweet girl. They all seem to be in show business somehow."

Your father has made such a specialty of analyzing human identities, I said, that I'd like you to analyze his.

She pursed her lips very seriously. "What it comes down to," she said, "is that my father is very, very insecure and a very big child. He forgets he's a genius. Because of course he's *aware* that he's a genius, so it's sometimes nice to see him questioning himself. And yet he is very wise. When I have a problem he knows so much about me that he can tell me exactly what I'm feeling. And he's always right. He knows people ... better than he knows himself."

Tell me about yourself, I said. Here's a dumb question: Do you have a boyfriend?

"Yes. But that's all I'll say about it, is 'yes.' About myself ... I don't feel like a teenager. I've never been to a high school dance. I've never hung out drinking milk shakes or whatever it is teenagers are supposed to do. My life isn't a bit like 'Happy Days.' When I was fifteen, I refused to be a child any longer. Now I'm seventeen, I sometimes want to be a kid. I can finally be childish without being embarrassed. Sometimes I think back and I think, God, I'm seventeen. Next year I'll be eighteen. Did I miss anything?"

Charles Bronson

It's just that I don't like to talk very much.

La Junta and New York, 1974

Charles Bronson is said to be the world's most popular movie star. Not America's. He will grant you Robert Redford in America. But in the world it is Charles Bronson. There is a sign in Japan, his publicist says, that displays Bronson's name a block long (one does not ask how high).

Bronson's eyes are a cat's eyes, watchful and guarded. They are the eyes of a man of fifty-one who once was a coal-town juvenile delinquent, spoke broken English, and embraced the draft in 1943 as a way to escape from the mines. These eyes were watching me one afternoon from across the dining room of the Capri Motel in La Junta, Colorado. They pretended not to, but they did. Their owner knew that I was in La Junta to interview him. What other mission would have drawn me to the cantaloupe capital of Colorado, where Bronson was shooting *Mr. Majestyk*, a movie about a melon farmer with union troubles? He had no great eagerness to be interviewed. He seemed to be sizing me up, with a sort of survivor's instinct.

It is conventional to say of movie stars that they are very private people, but Bronson has contructed a privacy so complete that it seems out of keeping with his occupation as a performer. He exudes an aura of privacy; I did not feel like approaching him. He sat at the head of a table with his wife of six years, Jill Ireland, at his left hand. Their children ranged around them: three by Jill's previous marriage to David McCallum, two from Bronson's first marriage, and their daughter, a perfect little blonde born in 1971.

Bronson finally sighed and handed his daughter to his wife. He came to be interviewed, after all. He does not mean to be difficult, but it is in his nature. He does not volunteer information, does not elaborate, and has no theories about his films ("I'm only a product like a cake of soap, to be sold as well as possible").

To make everything harder, *Time* had printed a hostile review only that week of Bronson's latest movie, *The Stone Killer*. The writer, Jay Cocks, dismissed it as another "Charles Bronson-Michael Winner picture." To Bronson, that was a personal attack: "First it was a novel, then it was a screenplay, and there was a cinematographer involved and a lot of other people. That makes it personal, when he picks on just two people, and that gets me mad." An ominous pause. "One way or another," he said, "sooner or later, I'll get that man. Not physically, but I'll get him."

There is that about Charles Bronson, and it is unsettling: He really does seem to possess the capacity for violence. It is there in his eyes, and in his muscular forearms, and in the way he walks. Other actors can seem violent in their roles; Lee Marvin, certainly, and Robert Mitchum and Clint Eastwood. But they don't seem violent in person. Bronson does. Maybe that's because he has been there, and violence isn't strange to him: back when he was Charles Buchinsky from the coalfields of Ehrenfeld, Pennsylvania, he did time twice, once for assault and battery and once for robbing a store. There were hard times early on in Ehrenfeld, and in the Air Corps, and working in mob gambling joints in Atlantic City. Director Michael Winner once told me: "After we've been on a picture a few weeks, the crew starts coming around and asking, *When does it happen? When does he blow up?* Actually I've never seen him blow up. But he seems to contain such a *capacity* for it that people tend to brace for it."

The breath of menace blows over as *Time* is forgotten, and in a moment Bronson is talking about his favorite pastime, which is painting. "When I was a kid," he says, "I was always drawing things. I'd get butcher paper or grocery bags and draw on them. And at school I was the one who got to draw on the windows with soap. Turkeys for Thanksgiving, that kind of thing. It seemed I just knew how to draw. I could draw anything in one continuous line without lifting the crayon from the paper. I had a show of my stuff in Beverly Hills and it sold out in two weeks—and it wasn't because my name was Charles Bronson, because I signed them Buchinsky."

He will talk about his painting, but not about his acting. In action pictures like Winner's, he says there's not that much time for acting.

"I supply a presence. There are never any long dialogue scenes to establish a character. He has to be completely established at the beginning of the movie, and ready to work. Now on this picture, *Mr. Majestyk,* there's something I haven't done for a while—acting. It has that, too, besides the action."

This sounds like modesty, but one senses it is not; it is just Bronson's description of what he does. He seems to consider himself a professional who can get the job done without investing a lot of ego in it. And apart from his pride of craft, the job is important not because it produces great movies but because it permits him to provide an extraordinarily comfortable life for his family.

He points out that as the eleventh of fifteen children of an illiterate coal miner who died when Bronson was ten, as a coal miner himself between the ages of sixteen and twenty, and as mailman, baker and onion picker at various other times, he has had great good fortune to arrive at his current condition: He is allegedly the highest-paid movie actor in the world. That is a claim more than one actor is usually making at any given time, and so later I put the question point-blank to producer Walter Mirisch, who was paying him: Is he?

"Some of the other guys *might* make more per picture," Mirisch said, "but Charles makes more pictures. And they never lose money." How much *does* Charlie make? I asked. "On this picture," Mirisch, sounding like the afternoon market report from Hornblower and Weeks—Hemphill, Noyes, "Charlie is making twenty thousand dollars a day for a six-day week, plus ten percent of the net, plus twenty-five hundred a week walking-around money. On his next picture, he'll probably make more."

I saw Bronson again several months later in New York, where he was working once more with Winner (who also directed him in *Chato's Land, The Stone Killer,* and *The Mechanic).* The new movie was *Death Wish,* about a middle-aged New York architect who is repelled by violence until his own daughter is raped and his wife murdered. Then the architect becomes an instrument of vengeance. He goes out into the streets posing as an easy mark, and when muggers attack, he kills them.

Death Wish was being shot in New York in late, cold February, and for openers I observed that the character seemed to have the same philosophy that's been present in all of Bronson's work with Winner: He is a killer (licensed or not) with great sense of self, pride in his work, and few words.

Bronson had nothing to say about that. "I never talk about the philosophy of a picture," he said. "Winner is an intelligent man, and I like him. But I don't ever talk to him about the philosophy of a picture. It has never come up. And I wouldn't talk about it to you. I don't expound. I don't like to overtalk a thing."

We are in the dining room of a Riverside Drive apartment that is supposed to be the architect's home in the movie. Bronson is drinking one of the two or three dozen cups of coffee he will have during the day and, having rejected philosophy, seems content to remain quiet.

Could it be, I say, that it's harder to play a role if you talk it out beforehand?

"I'm not talking in terms of playing a role," Bronson said. "I'm talking in terms of conversation. It has nothing to do with a role at all. It's just that I don't like to talk very much."

He lit a cigarette, kept it in his mouth, exhaled through his nose, and squinted his eyes against the smoke. Another silence fell. All conversation with Bronson has a tendency to stop. His natural state of conversation is silence.

Why?

"Because I'm entertained more by my own thoughts than by the thoughts of others. I don't mind answering questions. But in an exchange of conversation, I wind up being a pair of ears."

On the set, I learned, he doesn't pal around. He stays apart. Occasionally he will talk with Winner, or with a friend like his makeup man, Phil Rhodes. Rarely to anyone else. Arthur Ornitz, the cinematographer, says: "He's remote. He's a professional, he's here all the time, well prepared. But he sits over in a corner and never talks to anybody. Usually I'll kid around with a guy, have a few drinks. I think there's a little timidity there. He's a coal miner."

Later in the day, Bronson *is* sitting alone again. I don't know whether to approach him; he seems absorbed by his own thoughts, but after a time he yields. "You can talk to me now. I wouldn't be sitting here if I didn't want to talk. I'd be somewhere else."

I was wondering about that.

"I had a very bad experience on the plane in from California yesterday. There was a man on the plane, sitting across from me, and they were showing an old Greer Garson movie. He said, *Hey, why aren't you in that?* The picture was made before I even became an actor. I said, *Why aren't you?* I think I made him understand how stupid his question was.

"When I'm in public, I even try to hide. I keep as quiet as possible so that I'm not noticed. Not that I hide behind doorways or anything ridiculous like that, but I hide by not making waves. I also try to make myself seem as unapproachable as possible."

More silence. Phil Rhodes, the make-up man, is leafing through a copy of *Cosmopolitan.* Suddenly he whoops and holds up a centerfold of Jim Brown.

"Will you look at this," he says.

"Would *you* ever do anything like that, Charlie?"

"Are you kidding?" Bronson said. "What a bunch of crap. Look at that. Old Jim. People are so hung up on sex."

And, inexplicably, that sets Bronson talking. "I've been trying to make it with girls for as long as I can remember," he says. "I remember my first time. I was five and a half years old, and she was six. This was in 1928 or 1929. It happened at about the worst time in my life. We had been thrown out of our house ..."

The house was in Ehrenfeld, known as Scooptown, and it was a company house owned by the Pennsylvania Coal and Coke Company. When the miners went out on strike, they were evicted from their homes, and the Buchinsky family went to live in the basement of a house occupied by another miner and his eight children.

"This would have been the summer before I started school," Bronson says. "I remember my father had shaved us all bald to avoid lice. Times were poor. I wore hand-me-downs. And because the kids just older than me in the family were girls, sometimes I had to wear my sisters' hand-me-downs. I remember going to school in a dress. And my socks, when I got home sometimes I'd have to take them off and give them to my brother to wear into the mines.

"But, anyway, this was a Fourth of July picnic, and there was this girl, six years old. I gave her some strawberry pop. I gave her the pop because I didn't want it; I had taken up chewing tobacco and I liked that better. I didn't start smoking until I was nine. But I gave her the pop, and then we ... hell, I never lost my virginity. I never had any virginity."

He remembers Ehrenfeld well, and has written a screenplay with his wife about life in the mining towns. He worked in the mines from 1939 to 1943, and getting drafted, he says, was the luckiest thing that ever happened to him: "I was well fed, I was well dressed for the first time in my life, and I was able to improve my English. In Ehrenfeld, we were all jammed together. All the fathers were foreign-born. Welsh, Irish, Polish, Sicilian. I was Lithuanian and Russian. We were so jammed together we picked up each other's accents. And we spoke some broken English. When I got into the service, people used to think I was from a foreign country."

Five boys in his family were drafted into the Army. An older brother, the one who took him into the mines for the first time, was part of the European invasion. "He was a Ranger, and he won a medal," Bronson said. "He was under fire constantly. And he said he'd rather do that than go into the mines again."

Bronson would not talk about his hometown screenplay, called *$1.98*, except to say it was fundamentally a love story with a mining town as the environment, but the next afternoon he met with two VISTA workers to discuss possible locations in Appalachia for the film. The towns he had scouted, he told them, looked too good. There were streets, there were lawns where things grew ...

"I remember the old company towns. There was no neon, except for the company store. Nothing was green. The water was full of sulphur. There was nothing to put a hose to. There were unpaved streets covered with rock and slag. You had the rock dumps always exploding. They were always on fire, down inside, and if it rained for a long enough time, the water would seep down to the fires and turn to steam and the dump would explode."

The VISTA volunteers asked if Bronson's movie would deal with black lung disease.

"No, it's a love story. But it will be ... beneficial to the miners, I hope. Right now it isn't a finished script. There are too many empty, dull places. And it's naive. But it will be accurate about mining. You had a feeling about mining. It was piecework; you didn't get paid by the hour, you got paid by the ton, and you felt you were the hardest-working people in the world.

"When I worked, the rate was a dollar a ton. You spent one whole day preparing so you could spend the next day getting it out. The miners felt bound together; they knew how much they could get out, how much they could do. And they *worked.* With the new machines, it's easier. Not more pleasant, but easier. But in those days, that was pure work. It wasn't a man on a dock with a forklift or any of that bullshit. It was pure *work.*"

After the war Bronson went back home, but not to the mines. The veterans were given three months, he recalled, to decide if they wanted their old jobs back. Bronson did not. He picked onions in upstate New York, and then got his card in the bakers union. He worked on an all-night shift at a bakery in Philadelphia and took art classes in the evenings. He decided he knew more about drawing than the instructor did. He dropped the classes and quit his job (he still holds cards in both the miners and bakers unions), and went to New York City with the notion that he might try acting. Why acting?

"It seemed like an easy way to make money. A friend took me to a play, and I thought I might as well try it myself. I had nothing to lose. I hung around New York and did a little stock-company stuff. I wasn't really sure at that time if I even *wanted* to be an actor. I got no encouragement. I was living in my own mind, generating my own adrenaline. Nobody took any notice of me. I was in plays I don't even remember. Nobody remembers. I was in something by

Molière—I don't even know what it was called.

"I have no interest in the stage anymore. From an audience point of view, it's old-fashioned. The position I've been in for the last eight years, I have to think that way. I can't think of theater acting for one segment of the population in just one city. That's an inefficient way of reaching people."

After New York, he tried the Coast. Spent some time at the Pasadena Playhouse. Got his first movie role in *You're in the Navy Now* because he could belch on cue, a skill picked up during Ehrenfeld days. He worked for years as the heavy, the Indian, the Russian spy. He had two TV series, "Man with a Camera" and "Meet McGraw." And he was getting nowhere fast, he decided, so he went to work in Europe, where they didn't typecast so much and he had some chance of playing a lead or getting the girl.

His first great European success was in *Farewell, Friends*, opposite Alain Delon. That made him a lead, and then movies like *The Dirty Dozen* and *Rider on the Rain* made him a star. Although he worked for years in Europe, he refused to live there; he always maintained his home in America. He met Jill Ireland on a set in Germany in 1968, three years after her separation from McCallum and a year after her divorce. And now, he says, "I don't have any friends, and I don't want any friends. My children are my friends." And in Europe, Asia and the Middle East, he is said to be the top box-office draw. "One of the ironies," he observed, "is that I made my breakthrough in movies shot in Europe that the Japanese thought were American movies and that the Americans thought were foreign."

That night in New York, the *Death Wish* company gathered to shoot a scene outside a grocery store on upper Broadway. Bronson said that, since he was here anyway, he would do some shopping. He began with a box of cookies. An old man, a New York crazy, was berating a box of Hershey bars because it wouldn't open. *What the hell's going on here?* he shouted at the box. Bronson opened it for him. The man hardly noticed.

While the location was being prepared, Michael Winner drank

coffee across the street and talked about his enigmatic star.

"It's unnecessary for him to go into any big thing about what he does or how he does it," Winner said, "because he has this quality that the motion-picture camera seems to respond to. He has a great strength on the screen, even when he's standing still or in a completely passive role. There is a depth, a mystery—there is always the sense that *something* will happen.

I mentioned a scene in *The Stone Killer* in which Bronson has a gunman trapped behind a door. The gunman fires through the door, and Bronson, with astonishingly casual agility, leaps to the top of a table to get out of the line of fire.

"Yes," said Winner. "His body projects the impression that it's coiled up inside. That he's ready for action and capable of it. You know, Bronson *is,* as a human being, like that. That's not to say he goes about killing people. I'm sure that he doesn't."

A pause. "That's not to say he *hasn't,* in his day. Now he seems to have gotten a reputation for blowing up and hitting people on pictures. In my experience, he's not like that. He's a very controlled and reasonable person." Pause. "But there is a great fury lurking below."

The next afternoon, Bronson taped an interview for exhibitors with some people from the publicity department at Paramount. Bronson described the character he plays in *Death Wish*: "He's an average guy, an average New Yorker. In wartime, he would be a conscientious objector. His whole approach to life is gentle, and he has raised his daughter that way. Now he has second thoughts, and he becomes a killer."

Did you prepare for this character in any special way?

"No, because to play him I draw upon my own feelings. I *do* believe I could perform this way myself."

Chapter Seven

Muhammad Ali

Stallone doesn't have the moves. It's perfect acting though. The regular average layman couldn't see what I see.

Los Angeles, 1979

Right here in the middle of Muhammad Ali's mansion, right here in the middle of the mahogany and the stained glass and the rare Turkish rug, there was this large insect buzzing near my ear. I gave it a slap and missed. Then it made a swipe at my other ear. I batted at the air but nothing seemed to be there, and Muhammad Ali was smiling to himself and studying the curve of his staircase.

I turned toward the door and the insect attacked again, a close pass this time, almost in my hair, and I whirled and Ali was grinning wickedly.

He explained how it was done: "You gotta make sure your hand is good and dry and then you rub your thumb hard across the side of your index finger, like this, see, making a vibrating noise, and hold it behind somebody's ear, sneak up on 'em, and they think it's killer bees."

He grinned like a kid. "I catch people all the time," he said. "It never fails."

A long black limousine from NBC was gliding up the driveway, and Ali was ready to go to work. This was going to be Diana Ross' first night as guest host of the "Tonight" show, and Ali was going to be her first guest. And then, after the taping, Ali had a treat for his wife, Veronica, and their little girl, Hana. They were going to the movies. What movie were they going to see? *Rocky II,* of course. A special screening had been arranged, and Ali was going to play movie critic.

"Rocky Part Two," Ali intoned, "starring Apollo Creed as Muhammad Ali."

The taping went smoothly, with Ali working Diana Ross like a good fight. He kidded her about her age, leaned over to read her notes, got in a plug for his official retirement benefit, and made her promise to sing at the party.

And then the heavyweight champion of the world was back in another limousine, a blue and beige Rolls-Royce this time, heading back home to a private enclave off Wilshire Boulevard. It was a strange and wonderful trip, because during the entire length of the seven-mile journey, not one person who saw Ali in the car failed to recognize him, to wave at him, to shout something. Ali says he is the most famous person in the world. He may be right.

He gave his fame, to be sure, a certain assistance. He sat in the front seat, next to the driver, and watched as drivers in the next lane or pedestrians on the sidewalk did their double takes. First, they'd see the Rolls, a massive, classic model. Then they'd look in the back seat: no famous faces there. Idly, they'd glance in the front seat, and Ali would already be regarding them, and then their faces would break into grins of astonishment, and Ali would clench his fist and give them a victory sign. This was not a drive from Burbank to Wilshire Boulevard—it was a hero's parade.

Back home, waiting for Veronica to come downstairs so they could go to the movies, Ali sat close to a television set in his study. His longtime administrative assistant, Jeremiah Shabazz, talked about crowds and recognition: "The biggest single crowd was in South Korea. I think the whole country turned out. Manila was almost a riot; they almost tore the airport down. All over Russia, they knew him. But Korea was amazing."

Ali ignored the conversation. He is a man who chooses the times when he will acknowledge the presence of others, and the times when he will not. There are moments when he seems so intensely self-absorbed, even in a roomful of people, that he seems lonely and withdrawn. He was like that now, until his daughter, Hana, walked in and demanded to be taken into his lap, and then he spoke to her softly.

"What's Veronica say?" he asked Cleve Walker, an old Chicago friend who was visiting.

"She's coming right down," Walker said.

"Then let's go."

The five cars pulled out of the mansion's driveway like a presidential procession. Ali drove his own Mercedes, second in line, following an aide who was leading the way to United Artists' headquarters out on the old MGM lot. All five cars had their emergency flashers blinking the whole way: It was the day's second parade.

Rumors of Ali's visit had preceded him to the studio and a crowd of young kids was waiting for him in the parking lot. He shook their hands, told them to hang in there, touched them on the shoulders, and left them standing as if blessed by royalty.

And then he was inside a private screening room and settling down to watch the most popular movie of the summer—the sequel to the movie that won the Academy Award as Best Picture two years ago, and made Sylvester Stallone into a star as Rocky Balboa, the Philadelphia club fighter who took on the black heavyweight champion of the world. Ali, who said he'd really liked the original *Rocky*, settled down in the back row, Veronica and Hana next to him, and if he was reflecting that *Rocky* itself might very likely not have been made if he had not restored the fading glamour of boxing, he did not say so.

He watched the opening scenes of *Rocky II* in silence, not speaking until the scene in which Apollo Creed, the heavyweight champ, delivers a televised challenge designed to taunt Rocky back into the ring.

"That's me, all right," Ali said. "Apollo sounds like me. Insulting the opponent in the press, to get him psyched out. That's me exactly."

Back home at Rocky's new house, the doorbell rang.

"You know who that's gotta be," Ali said. "That's gotta be his trainer." And, yes, Rocky opened the door and his old trainer, Mickey, was standing there on the doorstep.

"That's how Angelo Dundee used to get me," Ali remembered. "A good trainer knows a good fighter can't stand to have people talk about him bad on television."

Mickey was giving Rocky advice: "We got to get you fighting with your other hand. Use your right, save your left, protect that bad eye...

"It just maybe could be," Ali said, "that if you started on a kid at seventeen or eighteen, by the time he was twenty-two you could change the hand he leads with. But not overnight it can't be done."

Now Mickey was drawing on his ancient store of boxing lore, making Rocky chase chickens to improve his footwork.

"That's one that goes back to the days of Jack Johnson and Joe Louis, chasing chickens," Ali said. "You don't see chickens at a training camp anymore except on the table."

Mickey was leaning fiercely at Rocky, who was pounding a bag. "Jab! Jab! Jab!" he was shouting.

"With a great fighter," said Ali, "you don't have to tell him that. He goes at the bag like a robot. I never had anybody tell me to jab. If you don't want to jab, what are you doing being a fighter?"

Now there was a wider shot showing Mickey's gym, with Rocky in the foreground and the background occupied by a dozen fighters working out, jumping rope, sparring.

"What you see here, if you know how to look for it," Ali explained, "is the difference between real fighters and actors. A real boxer can see Stallone's not a boxer. He's not professional, doesn't have the moves. It's good acting, but it's not boxing. Look in the background. Look at that guy in the red trunks back there. You can see he's a real fighter."

Now Rocky was in the ring with a sparring partner. 'The other guy's a real fighter," Ali said. "Stallone doesn't have the moves. It's perfect acting, though. The regular average layman couldn't see what I see. And the way they're painting the trainer is all wrong Look at him there, screaming, *Do this!* and *Do that!* I never had anyone telling me what to do. I did it. Shouting at the fighter like that makes him look like an animal, like a horse to be trained."

Is there any way, I asked, that the character of Rocky is inspired by you?

"No way. Rocky doesn't act nothing like me. Apollo Creed, the way he dances, the way he jabs, the way he talks .... *That's* me."

On the screen, a moment of crisis had appeared in Rocky Balboa's life. After giving birth to Rocky Jr., his wife had slipped into a coma. Rocky had just left the bedside and was praying in the hospital chapel.

"Now he don't feel like fighting because his wife is sick," Ali said. "That's absolutely the truth. The same thing happened to me when I was in training camp during one of my divorces. You can't keep your mind on fighting when you're thinking about a woman. You can't keep your concentration. You feel like sleeping all the time. But now at this point, I'm gonna make a prediction. I haven't seen the movie, but I predict she's gonna get well, and then Rocky's gonna beat the hell out of Apollo Creed."

Back in the hospital room, Rocky's wife opened her eyes. Ali nodded. "My first prediction is proven right," he said.

Rocky's wife turned to him and said, "There's one thing I want you to do for me: Win."

"Yeah!" said Ali. "Beat that nigger's ass!"

Little Rocky Jr. was brought into the room by a nurse. The baby had a head of black hair that would have qualified him for the Beatles. Ali laughed with delight: "They got a baby to win the Academy Award. Look at that Italian hair! Rocky couldn't deny the baby in court in real life!"

Now there was a montage, as Rocky Balboa threw himself into his training regime with renewed fury. "That's right," said Ali. "He's happy now. He's got his woman back. I'm gonna further predict that in the big fight, they're gonna make it look at first like Rocky's losing, and his eye will be cut and it will look the worst before he wins, and that after the movie the men will be crying louder than the women."

Rocky was weight-lifting: "The worst thing a boxer can do. It tightens the muscles. A fighter never lifts weights. But it looks good in the movie."

In an inspirational scene, Rocky was running through the streets of his native Philadelphia, trailed by a crowd of cheering children who followed him all the way up the steps of the Philadelphia Museum of Art. Rocky gave his trademark victory salute, repeated from the most famous moment in the original *Rocky*.

"Now that's one thing that some people will say is artificial, all the crowds running after him, but that's real," Ali said. "I had the same kinda crowds follow me in New York."

And now it was time for *Rocky II*'s climactic fight scene—longer, more violent and more grueling than the bravado ending of the original *Rocky*. In his dressing room, Apollo Creed, played by Carl Weathers, was jabbing at his image in a mirror.

"Weathers told me he got the dancing and the jabbing, the whole style of Apollo Creed, from watching my movies," Ali said. "The way he's fighting in the mirror, those aren't real fighting moves, but for the movie they look good. And the motivation here is right. Apollo, he won the first fight, but some people said Rocky should have won. If you lose a big fight, it will worry you all of your life. It will plague you, until you get your revenge. As the champion, almost beat by a club fighter, he has to have his revenge."

Could a club fighter in real life stay in the ring with the heavyweight champion?

"No. What he might be able to do, he might be able to come in and absorb an amount of punishment and wait and get a lucky shot and knock him out ... with the odds being very high against that. But to stay in the ring, to stay with the champion, he couldn't do that."

And now, on the screen, Rocky Balboa had fallen to his knees and was praying in the locker room, and Muhammad Ali, his daughter Hana asleep in his arms, was completely absorbed in the scene.

As Rocky got back to his feet, Ali broke the spell: "The most scary moment in a fighter's life is right now. The moment before the fight, in your dressing room, all the training is behind you, all the advice in the world don't mean a thing, in a moment you'll be in the ring, everyone is on the line, and you ... are ... scared."

Apollo Creed and Rocky Balboa came dancing down the aisles of the Philadelphia Spectrum, and shots showed Rocky's wife at home, nervously watching television, and Apollo's wife at ringside, nervously watching her husband.

"Even Apollo's wife favors my wife Veronica," Ali observed. "They're both light-skinned, real pretty girls ....."

Apollo was taunting Rocky: "You're going down! I'll destroy you! I am the master of disaster."

"Those first two lines, those are my lines," Ali mused. "That 'master of disaster' ... I like that. I wish I'd thought of that."

And now the fight was under way, Rocky and Apollo trading punishment, Apollo keeping up a barrage of taunts, and dancing out of Rocky's way. Between rounds, in the fighters' corners, their trainers were desperately pumping out instructions.

"My trainer don't tell me nothing between rounds," Ali said. "I don't allow him to. I fight the fight. All I want to know is did I win the round. It's too late for advice."

How long do you predict the fight will last?

"Hard to say. Foreman they stopped in eight, Liston they stopped in eight ... the movie might take something from that. I can't predict. But look at that. There's Apollo using my rope-a-dope defense."

In the tenth round, Ali nodded: "Here's where the great fighters get their second wind, where determination steps in." On the screen, Rocky was taking a terrible beating, and his eyes, as Ali had predicted, were badly swollen.

"In a real fight," Ali said, "they would never allow the eyes to be closed that much and let the fight keep going. They would stop it."

But in *Rocky II* they didn't stop it, and the fight went the full distance, Ali observing that in real life no fighter could absorb as much punishment as both Apollo and Rocky had, and then the theater was filled with the *Rocky* theme and the lights were on and Ali's entourage was applauding the movie.

Muhammad Ali got up carefully, so as not to wake Hana, and handed his daughter to Veronica.

"A great movie," he said. "A big hit. It has all the ingredients. Love, violence, emotion. The excitement never dulled."

What do you think about the way the fight turned out?

"For the black man to come out superior," Ali said, "would be against America's teachings. I have been so great in boxing they had to create an image like Rocky, a white image on the screen, to counteract my image in the ring. America has to have its white images, no matter where it gets them. Jesus, Wonder Woman, Tarzan and Rocky."

William Hurt

You could actually go out and play in the smaller typhoons.

Chicago, 1981

"This is an experiment," William Hurt said. "Frankly, I'm more interested in how it goes than in what happens. I want to discover what I think of you, and what I think of all this. I'm vastly curious about this time we'll spend together."

All this?

"All this. It's a fantasy, sitting here looking at Lake Michigan, in a hotel suite with my name on the matchbook covers. But what can I say? How can I express my feelings? What does it matter what I feel? The characters I perform in a movie have no connection to me, and so what you think about them has no connection. Your feelings about those characters are valid but they're *your* feelings. They have nothing to do with what I feel."

I agreed. I settled down deeper into my corner of the big overstuffed couch in Hurt's suite at the Ritz-Carlton. Hurt was a very hot young movie star, with a box-office hit as the tortured scientist in *Altered States,* and possibly another one as a janitor who stumbles across a crime in the thriller *Eyewitness.*

I had heard that Hurt was a difficult interview—indeed, an impossible one, who refused to give interviews on the grounds that he just simply did not understand what it was that was supposed to take place between himself and the interviewer. I also had heard that his speech tended in the direction of large metaphysical insights.

Sample:

Hurt: "Do I have to wear makeup for the television interview?"

Press agent: "Do you want to?"

Hurt: "I don't care. I just wanted to experience how you would respond to such a question."

Now here I sat, interviewing the metaphysician. William Hurt's appearance is remarkably engaging. He is tall, fair, handsome, with round rimless glasses and an easy smile. He looks so open and carefree that it is a little startling to hear the way his speech turns in on itself in tortured introspection, as if every statement must have a meaning, and every meaning must be distrusted.

"I don't *want* to be a movie star," he said, lighting a cigarette. "I want to be a member of the ensemble. I don't want the loneliness of the star, or the presumption. I was happy before I got here. They told me, *you're gonna be real big*. My answer was, *what's the matter with my size?* One of the most difficult problems is trying to figure out why they now want to pay me more money for what I have always done, and for which I used to be paid next to nothing at all."

Why not? I said. If you are going to do it, and they are going to pay you, then, all else being equal, why shouldn't they pay you more instead of less? From your point of view, of course.

"Exactly! Remember the Yale undergraduate, or was it the Harvard undergraduate, who went in to take the philosophy examination. And on the paper was written one question: *Why?* And so he answered, *Why not?* and turned in his paper. He got an A on the paper."

William Hurt. I got up, poured myself some black coffee, and sat back down. I was thinking to myself: In some ways, this interview is going very well. He is a pleasant, intelligent, sensitive actor, and he is talking a lot, so I don't have to be primed with dozens of questions. On the other hand ... well, on the other hand, what is he saying? Lost in a sea of abstractions, I decided to put some concrete questions to the test. I asked him when he made *Eyewitness*.

"When?" he said. "When was it made? That is a difficult question. Although I have a perfect sense of spatial orientation, I have no sense of time. People get mad. I don't care about celebrations much, and, when I forget Christmas, people get angry with me."

Did you make it after *Altered States*?

"Yes. After *Altered States,* and after playing Hamlet in the Circle Repertory Company in New York. Circle Rep is my true home, the place where everything is right. Hamlet is a role you live with all of your life. You spend time with great roles, but you don't compare them. Comparison is odious: *NO! I am not Prince Hamlet, nor was meant to be ...*"

Ah, yes! I said. *I am an attendant lord, one who will do to swell the progress of a scene or two ...*

Hurt lit another cigarette. "Plays seek us," he said. "We don't seek them. What would a library be without readers? Who was it who said, you know, Napoleon's adversary at Waterloo? Wellington! The Duke of Wellington once said, *Never apologize and never explain.*"

I have an Irish friend, I said, who says, *Never apologize, never explain and keep 'em guessing.*

"That's even better," said Hurt.

Is the stage your first love, or film? I asked. It was a question I somehow knew was going to get me into trouble.

"In terms of the knowledge of acting," he said, "where do you go to learn about film acting? When I was in school, there were no such classes. And all the great studio contract players were dead. The biggest problem is to develop a film technique when they are always stopping everything to stick a finger up your nose or into your ear. Your space is invaded. And it was very hard for me to learn to act out of sequence. On stage, the challenge is different: to remain on your breath in your body. I made an enormously important discovery about stage acting: The focus is not on me. The attention of both myself and of the audience should be on the subject, which is the play. In here, on the other hand, the implication is that the focus *is* upon me. The implication is ... what do you want to know about me?"

It was a valid insight. What *did* I want to know about William Hurt? I wanted to know, well, something about his life. I plunged right in.

Where do you live? I asked.

"New York, Upper East Side. Oh, yes, I *am* a New Yorker!"

Were you born there?

"Washington, D.C. I lived there for six years, and then in the South Pacific for several years. My father was in the State Department. The South Pacific was wonderful for a boy. You could actually go outside and play in the smaller typhoons."

What do you think, I asked, about the fact that *Altered States* is a big hit and you are now a movie star?

"I went to see *Altered States*," he said slowly, "and I thought, how trivial. It's just a movie. It's a great movie but, still, I had put myself through hell on account of it. It took me to the brink of death."

I asked: You were almost killed making the movie? But, of course, my question was too literal.

"One doesn't kill oneself just because of a movie," he mused. "I had become very self-destructive. I forgot that you do not kill yourself just because of a film."

In *Altered States* you played a scientist, and now in *Eyewitness* you play a janitor, I said.

"But they both look exactly the same," he said. "I decided against any differentiation in physical characteristics. I wanted to look the same as I do look. The same glasses, the same hair because I had too much to learn about movie acting without worrying about my physical appearance. So I look like those characters, but I am not those characters. I am not that guy on the screen. What you think about that guy is important to you, but not to me. Actually, doing the work is all-important to the actor. But having done it, why dwell on it? I have a deep and perturbing problem about the nature of the glory that's given to actors, but not to teamsters. Teamsters perform every day, too. Our notions of what constitutes creativity are primitive in these times."

What do you do in your spare time?

"Sometimes I drop out. I race off on my motorcycle. I fly-fish, read books, talk to people on the streets, start new hobbies like bird watching. It was amazing to me how many birds were on the beach at Malibu. In the mornings, after I had stayed in bed as many hours as I could, I would walk out on the deck and strafe them with an imaginary machine gun."

eight

The world will always welcome lovers

Woody Allen belongs in the chapter with the other directors, but you find him here because he seems to fit in perfectly, right after Nastassja Kinski's poetic display of fiercely burning passion. Love is the all and more than all, yes, of course, but could we, on the other hand, do something about these chiggers?

Brooke Shields

She'll be with us for the rest of our lives.

New York, 1981

If nobody had ever heard of Brooke Shields, if there had never been a single Calvin Klein ad on television, if all of those movies and magazine covers had starred somebody else—if she were, indeed, a completely unknown sixteen-year-old girl, then it would have been necessary to discover her. It is impossible for a young woman so beautiful to remain unnoticed. She is one inch shorter than six feet tall, she has a flawless complexion, a friendly smile, astonishing eyes, an aristocratic carriage and a tawny mane of hair, and there is no doubt that she is a star. She would be a star under any conditions. She would be a star behind the counter at Burger King.

"Autographs!" she said. "Anybody got a pen?" I gave her mine. Brooke and her mother, Teri, were standing in a hotel suite reserved for the publicity staff of her new movie, *Endless Love.* Brooke was not complaining about autographs: She seemed to accept the necessity of signing them as something that went with the territory. She wrote "Best wishes, Brooke," handed over the glossy photograph, returned the pen and skipped out of the room.

Mike Maslansky, the famous Hollywood press agent, watched her leave, and then he made a statement that sounded like a formal prophecy. "She will be with us," he said, "for the rest of our lives. She will be like Elizabeth Taylor, a legendary beauty, human royalty. When I am eighty-five years old, I expect to pick up the paper and read about Brooke Shields' eighth marriage."

I thought about that. I asked: Surely you don't think she'll have *that* unhappy a life?

Maslansky shrugged. "Whatever she is doing when I am eighty-five, they will still be writing about it in the papers. Brooke Shields is a permanent fact of our lives.'

Even from a press agent accustomed to hyperbole, that sounded like some sort of ultimate claim. He was not saying Brooke Shields was beautiful, or talented, or a kid with a great future ahead of her. He was saying that she will be one of the greatest stars, someone like Bogart or Monroe or Taylor, someone who is not just a person but a human genre.

I wondered if that were true. I'd met Brooke before, on her twelfth or thirteenth birthday, on the beach in front of the Carlton Hotel at the Cannes Film Festival. A man named Melvin Simon, a shopping center millionaire who had become a movie producer, had just finished a movie named *Tilt!,* which starred Brooke and was destined never to be released. He was throwing a "typical American teen-age girl's birthday party" for her, with hot dogs, hamburgers and Cokes.

Brooke and her mother, Teri Shields, sat surrounded by what the Italians call *paparazzi,* a species that is half photographer, half vulture. Melvin Simon sat to one side, gazing out into the harbor where Stavros Niarchos' yacht swung at anchor. "Look at that yacht," he whispered to himself. "I wish I was *really* rich." I sat down near Brooke and asked one of those inane questions reporters ask kids: What do you think of all this? Brooke sipped on a

Coke and said, "I think it's neat."

Later that afternoon, Teri Shields got into a well-publicized fray with a waiter at the Carlton. The details of the disagreement remain unclear, but it was reported that Teri bit the waiter and was ejected from the premises. Stories in national magazines painted a picture of the relationship between mother and daughter: Brooke, really still just a kid, and Teri, the proud backstage mother with a tendency to drink too much.

At the time, Brooke struck me as being a beautiful young girl, yes, but somehow unfinished, uncertain, a little gangly. The Louis Malle film *Pretty Baby,* which starred her as a child prostitute, was released during that period and captured just those qualities, enlarging them into an unforgettable portrait. But now it was 1981 and years had passed. Brooke had grown into a very tall, very beautiful, very rich and famous teen-ager who got ten thousand dollars a day for modeling Calvin Klein jeans and who appeared on the cover of Time magazine, which described her as "The Look of the '80s." Brooke and Teri remain very close, and their relationship has grown less stormy since Teri stopped drinking. But is it fair to say Brooke has blossomed into another Elizabeth Taylor, into a world-class standard of female beauty?

I walked with Brooke and Teri out of the press suite and down the corridor of the Parker-Meridian Hotel to the suite where they were spending the weekend. The corridor was crawling with security men. This same weekend, the Parker-Meridian was hosting not only Brooke Shields but also the contestants in the Miss Universe pageant. The rent-a-cops looked like the kind of guys you'd want to hire rent-a-cops to keep out of the hotel.

In her suite, Brooke bounced her Calvins down on an overstuffed sofa. Teri sat down across from Brooke. I borrowed my pen back from Brooke, reflected for a moment or two, and made a mental note: It *is* fair to say that Brooke Shields has blossomed into a world-class standard of beauty.

Brooke made a little face. "My tummy made a noise," she said to her mother.

"Do you want some club soda? Some water?"

"No, it's all right. It's just noisy." She giggled. Our interview was beginning. I started with a question about Brooke's experience a few weeks ago, testifying before Congress. She had described herself as a possible model for other teen-agers. Wasn't it hard for a star to identify with other kids?

"Well, I'm flattered to think I could at least express my ideals," she said. "Since I do go to a regular private school, all of my friends are teen-agers."

She talked in a very direct, open way—like a kid. Her voice is pitched higher than you'd expect, given her height and the bold quality of her look, and the thought occurs that she is, after all, really only just sixteen. Nobody can be adult at sixteen, except perhaps for Jodie Foster. I asked about her anti-smoking TV commercials.

"I hate smoking," she said. "I thought the ads could help encourage kids not to start. The senators didn't know if the government should subsidize the commercials because of my image in some of the movies I've made. I said two things. That when I play those roles, I am an actress, I am not acting as myself. And secondly, the cigarette companies use glamorous people to promote smoking, so why not have just as effective ads that go the other way?"

How does a sixteen-year-old kid feel, testifying before Congress?

"At *first* I wasn't nervous. It was only later, remembering where I was and that those were senators, that I got a little nervous. I was just being myself."

Why do so many kids smoke?

"Maybe they think it's a time to rebel. I don't know. I know it's easier to start than to stop. I've given up arguing about it with kids I know, because I figure if they're dumb enough to start in the first place, they're just stupid, so nothing I could say would help."

Teri Shields leaned forward. "Brooke has so many other things to do with her time," she said, the proud mother. "She has horseback riding, sewing, all the little hobbies she has, and of course her career has helped."

That's no doubt true, I thought to myself, *but it sounds like a Hollywood cliché*: Teen-age star prefers sewing to boys. In your new movie, *Endless Love,* I said, you play a girl of sixteen who falls in love with a boy about her own age, and there are scenes in the movie where you make love. How does this fit into your thinking?

"I very strongly believe that nobody should make love until they're married," Brooke said. "But the character I played behaved differently. I think the real message of the movie is that the teen-age years are so crucial. It's a time when everything you do is so important to you, and makes such an impression on your mind, and adults sometimes forget that and act like kids don't have real emotions."

"I can remember as if it were yesterday," Teri Shields said, "the time when I was twelve and I baked a Valentine's cake and my father laughed at me."

"Of course," said Brooke, "it's very hard to be a parent."

How about being a teen-age star? I asked.

"It's been gradual," Brooke said. "I started when I was a child model, and so it's sort of grown on me."

"People forget that about Brooke," Teri said. "It's not instant overnight stardom. Some people are amazed to learn she's been in eight movies."

"What I'm starting to look for now," Brooke said, "are stronger roles." Her eyes began to sparkle. "I'd like to be a ... *heroine!* In something like *Star Wars* or *Raiders of the Lost Ark.* I'd love that. Also in comedies and musicals. People don't know I can sing, but I can. I was in a show once with Tom Jones. I especially like to sing country and western. I'd like to get some roles where they forget that I'm a kid, and don't cast me like a little girl."

Endless Love is probably the best role in Brooke's career since *Pretty Baby.* Both films were directed by Europeans, the first by Frenchman Louis Malle and this one by Franco Zeffirelli, whose most famous film is *Romeo and Juliet* (1967), another story about star-crossed teen-age lovers. How did Brooke and Zeffirelli get together?

Teri Shields answered. "It all started with our travel agent," she said. "He called up and said he was reading the novel *Endless Love* and Brooke should play the girl. We were in London doing *The Muppet Movie,* and I called Zeffirelli, but it was a year before he would meet Brooke. We kept seeing ads in the trade papers: 'Young boy, young girl, no experience, have to be nude ...' He was determined to find unknowns, which is what he did with *Romeo and Juliet.* Well, the nude scenes were a problem. Brooke doesn't do them. Finally, after a year, he saw Brooke and was just flabbergasted with her looks. He told us, 'I saw *Blue Lagoon.* I don't know why it's making so much money ... but I think we could improve upon your acting.' Well, this fit into our thinking. After *Blue Lagoon,* we thought Brooke should try something more extensive. More ambitious. But when we saw the screenplay, we were disappointed. There was nothing for Brooke to do but be beautiful. We asked for some additional scenes where she did some acting, and then we took the movie."

But without the nude scenes?

"Brooke never does her own nude scenes," Teri said. "There's always someone to double for her body."

"It's just me from the neck up," Brooke said. "People don't always seem to know that."

Were the sex scenes in *Endless Love* tricky, even from the neck up?

"I just try to think about the character and the dialogue. The love scenes are happening to the character, not to me. I'm an actress."

The love scenes in *Endless Love* were so steamy, however, that the Motion Picture Ratings Board shocked the producer, Universal, by slapping the film with an X rating—reportedly not only because of explicit photography but also because the participants were so young. The movie is now rated "R," after several cuts.

Brooke seemed mystified by the controversy: "They said ... there was *lingering.* What does that mean?"

"That the camera was lingering on your bodies when you were in bed," Teri said. "They shortened those scenes. And a scene watching your reflection in a mirror, I guess you were supposed to be making love like crazy in that scene. They shortened that."

Brooke grinned. "In real life, I don't even *have* a boyfriend," she said. "Sooner or later, I'll meet somebody, but ..."

She shrugged. I had my next question all ready: Then what about those reports that you stayed out too late with John Travolta and your mother got mad and went looking for you?

Brooke and Teri both laughed. "Actually," said Brooke, "John took me to a Bruce Springsteen concert, and the *paparazzi* found out about it and camped out in front of our door hoping to get a picture of the two of us together. But John is just a friend. We're not in love or anything like that."

"And also," said Teri, "with them both having new movies coming out, it didn't seem fair. So I phoned Brooke and told her to go to John's hotel and I'd come and pick her up. *Then* when we got home, the *paparazzi* were still there, and Brooke almost killed Ron Galella, who is the most persistent photographer in New York, by pushing the electric garage door opener and banging him in the head with the garage door."

"It was funny," Brooke said. "I was pushing on the button and he was pushing on the door. Sometimes life really gets crazy. Like going out with John Travolta; I told him I thought more people recognized him than me, but he said he thought we were about equal."

"He's a wonderful boy," Teri said about Travolta. "They're such good friends."

"He's sweet, he's cute, and we can talk to each other," Brooke explained. "He's such a good friend. I could just chew on him."

"It's hard for Brooke, being recognized everywhere she goes," Teri said. "She tries putting on sunglasses, but then she just looks *more* glamorous, although not like Brooke Shields."

Do you have any private life?

"Horseback riding, sewing—I want to go to college. Maybe to a good Ivy League school."

"Brooke loved West Point," Teri said.

"Yes, but not to go to *school* there!"

You know, I said, with the Miss Universe contestants in the hotel, when they see Brooke in the elevator, it must discourage them.

"I hope so," Teri said.

"Some of them," said Brooke, "are really gorgeous."

Nastassja Kinski

It was like bathing with Perrier

Cannes, 1984

The riots were Wednesday. Kinski was Thursday. Relative calm returned by the weekend. But it is safe to say that few entrances in the history of the Cannes Film Festival have rivaled the reception of Nastassja Kinski when she arrived here for the premiere of her latest film, the luridly stylistic *Moon in the Gutter*. The film was not a success, but Kinski was a triumph—not because of her performance, but because of herself. Has there ever been an actress in the history of the cinema who has so fascinated so many people without yet having appeared in a single truly great movie?

The day began early, with the sun still rising over the old harbor of Cannes. Municipal workers with buckets and brushes were scrubbing away the political slogans sprayed all over the Palais des Festivals the day before by rioting medical students. Meanwhile, the world's film press was having a quiet little riot of its own, trying to get into the Palais for the early critics' screening of *Moon in the Gutter*, the second film by Jean-Jacques Beineix—the young man whose *Diva* was the most successful French film in United States box office history.

There was not enough room in the two-thousand-seat press screening theater, and so the movie was moved to the grand auditorium, where three thousand or more journalists, clutching their credentials like the keys to the palace, shoved in to see a melodramatic story of love, lust, doom and obsession. The movie starred Gerard Depardieu, the brawny French star, as a dock worker haunted by the death of his sister, who cut her throat after being raped. In a sleazy waterfront dive, Depardieu meets a rich young playboy and, through him, the playboy's passionate sister—played by Kinski, of course. Depardieu lives in a Cannery Row flophouse with a tempestuous prostitute (Victoria Abril) and assorted other flotsam, and cannot understand why Kinski returns to the docks night after night in her red Ferrari convertible to offer him love and ecstasy.

If this description sounds a little overblown, the film itself is utterly without restraint. It is one of the most flat-out exercises in romantic excess I have ever seen, a poem made from neon, jazz, blood, revenge and moistly parted lips. And Kinski throws herself into this cauldron with joyous abandon, providing the kind of uninhibited, risky, overblown performance that legends are made of.

Moon in the Gutter is not a successful film, and it was greeted by enthusiastic boos at the morning screening, but it is certain to further the legend of Kinski—who, at twenty-two, managed to get herself on the covers of *Time, Playboy* and *Vogue* in the same month for three different reasons (she is news, she is sexy and she is the hottest face in the world).

After the screening, there was another near-riot at the press conferences. Kinski, Beineix and Abril were late in arriving. The still photographers and television cameramen commandeered the first three rows, stood on the chairs and each other's shoulders and waited grimly, ignoring the cries of *"Assiz!,"* which is how the French say "Down in front!" A spokesman for the festival arrived briefly to say that the Beineix party had disappeared—lost apparently, in the labyrinth of the new festival palace. Then they arrived to a great ovation, thunderous roars of *"Assiz!,"* and a bewildering wall of flashguns.

All eyes were on Kinski. Beineix, seated next to her, was discovering what it feels like to have the attention of the world focused nine inches to the left of your ear. Kinski wore a simple black dress with a scooped-out white shawl collar. It was at once vaguely ecclesiastical and chastely suggestive. She wore a stainless steel Tiffany wristwatch with a steel expansion band, a ring from the trinket counter of a dime store and a smile that made it clear she was not bored by her first Cannes press conference. Some young actresses pretend to be blasé in the face of great attention. One of the charms of Kinski is that she is so obviously enjoying the limelight.

The first questions, gloomy ideological ones, were directed at Beineix, who defended the purity of the image over the corruption of dialogue, and said he was not in the least disturbed by the people who walked out of his movie, because his movies were made for the people who stayed. Faultless logic. Finally, somebody observed that Kinski's entrance in the movie had been accomplished with dramatic use of light, shadow, closeup and passionate classical music, and said that all her directors seemed obsessed with her, then asked her if she hoped someday to make an ordinary entrance and play an ordinary person. Her response was a breathless speech, delivered in a clear, loud, passionate voice:

"What does it mean, ordinary? We sleep, we dream, and our dreams are as real as real life. We must not deny our dreams. Obsession is the main reason for our living. That's what I live for. The other things—I wake, I sleep, I work, I smell—that's what we all live for. If a director shares my obsessions, that means he sees through me. My role is always someone ready to die for a moment of emotion."

I was not quite sure what that meant, but I got the feeling, all right, and I got the message: After a generation of actresses trained to analyze their roles and speak intelligently about them, here is the Isadora Duncan of movies. Kinski always was in motion on the stage, even while other people were talking. She lit cigarettes, puffed a few times, stubbed them out and leaned back in her chair to catch the eye of Abril, her co-star, so they could wink and giggle like two schoolgirls during a boring lecture.

An hour later, I joined Kinski for lunch on a private terrace of the Gray d'Albion Hotel. I do not remember a single thing about what we ate, except that the miniature bird eggs reminded her, for some reason, of her boyfriend. I struggled to keep up with the torrent of her declarations. I remember telling her at one moment that I thought she was a romantic. "I am happy for that," she replied, simply.

She said that some of the questions at the press conference seemed to object to the lyrical romanticism and high style of *Moon in the Gutter,* a movie not above shots where we see the moon reflected in the gutter and then blotted out by a stream of blood.

"Here is all I am saying," she said. "We're born, we're children, we're here in this incredible free world, we grow up, we're told to be afraid, we see that here we have been given this body and soul and sex and dreams but we have not been given the reason for our existence. We're unhappy, and it is very rare in life that we find a moment of ecstasy, a moment like being born, or dying. It is like I said at the press conference, if we are not ready to die for a moment of emotion, what is the use of life?"

I nodded. The critics, I said, were too intellectual in their analysis of the film. They wanted to think it, not feel it. She nodded. A faint mist from an indoor water fountain drifted between us, and she brushed it aside as a sprite would comb the dew.

"They rejected it so violently that their rejection means something," she said. "The film touches something they don't want to have touched. There are certain emotions so deeply buried they never come up, things like death and rebirth. They are so strong we deny them. Like when someone we love is dead, and we can't even cry."

You are, I said, obviously much in sympathy with the approach of Monsieur Beineix.

"Sometimes when he said 'Action,' I felt like exploding," Kinski said. "I wanted to cut myself in half and give something great, you know. It's wonderful when you are in such a visionary film, it pushes you toward another planet. I have never felt so cold and so hot as during this film."

What was it like, I asked, working with Gerard Depardieu? He is a large-boned, rough-and-ready leading man, not a matinee idol....

Kinski could hardly find the words. "He was totally unpredictable," she said. "At one moment, he would turn on. At the next, he was—away. There was nothing in the middle. When he is on, he looks at you, and it goes through you. In the scene where I met him for the first time, when I walked into the cafe and saw him, I have never had such a sensual experience in my real life as I had in that scene from cinema. There was no past, no future, only now. It was like ... like ... like being bathed with Perrier. Everywhere, you know?"

He was ... extraordinary? I asked.

"Totally unpredictable," she said. "When he is there, he gives and is tender and it is wonderful. Then he goes away somewhere into his own head, and it's like just putting the knife in you. When he was there, it was like we were diving into each other's souls."

I cleared my throat. You are talking about making the movie? I asked. Or ... some more personal relationship?

"What relationship," she asked, "can be more personal than making a movie?"

I came back to my typewriter after lunch, clutching my notes, a little dizzy. I felt like bathing in Perrier—everywhere you know? It is possible, I suppose, to be a little amused by Nastassja Kinski's passion, her grand and idealistic visions. But I have talked to many actresses, and I know that sooner or later most of them come down to earth and talk about their last picture and their new deal and their agent and what new vitamins they're taking and what their astrological sign portends ... and I hope Kinski stays inside her dream for many long and breathless years.

Woody Allen

An intellectual rationalist is also an animal who lusts after women and is not above drawing blood in the throes of passion.

New York, 1982

It looked like a shrink's office. The sun was filtering through the curtains and the air conditioner hummed reassuringly, and, after a subtle moment of jockeying for position, I got the couch and Woody Allen took the big overstuffed, black leather chair.

We were in Woody's office, on Fifty-seventh Street, just a little to the left of the Russian Tea Room. I had just come from a screening of Allen's new film, *A Midsummer Night's Sex Comedy,* and I was in the strange position of talking to him before I had sorted out my own thoughts about the movie. Even though I was on the couch, I began with the kind of question an analyst might use.

Your movie seems to be saying that women are more resilient than men. That we can count on them for support and encouragement.

Woody nodded. "I've always felt more sanguine about women than about men," he said. "They're more mature, less bellicose, more gentle. They're closer to what life's supposed to be about. They bring up kids. Men are stiffer, don't cry, die of heart attacks. Women are just more into nature. They know what sex *should* be. They never dissociate sex and love. A guy will pick up a girl, telling himself all he's looking for is a fling for the weekend, but what he's really always after is the woman of his dreams, someone to spend the rest of his life with. Women are looking for the same thing in a man, only they're honest enough to admit it."

Woody's new movie is about just such insights, filtered through a gentle pastoral scene occupied by three couples who circle one another's egos for a weekend. The movie, lushly photographed in ripe greens and yellows and browns, takes place somewhere in upstate New York, sometime around 1906. The couples are Woody Allen, as a stockbroker and self-described crackpot inventor, and Mary Steenburgen, as his sweet and secretive wife; Jose Ferrer, as a behavioral scientist and self-described genius, and Mia Farrow, as his sweet and secretive fiancee; and Tony Roberts as a doctor and self-described satyr, and Julie Hagerty as his sweet and oversexed nurse.

During the course of the weekend, all three of the men suffer the pangs of unrequited lust. Roberts falls in love with Farrow, Allen kicks himself for not having seduced Farrow when he had the chance, and Ferrer, who is to marry Farrow the next day, tries to seduce Hagerty. Meanwhile, Allen discovers that Steenburgen has had an affair with Roberts, and Roberts' wife turns to the nurse for advice and comfort.

This spare plot summary makes *A Midsummer Night's Sex Comedy* sound like a steamy melodrama, but, in fact, the tone of the movie is gentle, whimsical and forgiving, and it is strangely appropriate that Woody Allen furiously pedals through some of the key scenes on a bicycle. It also is somehow easy to accept his claim to have invented a sphere that foresees the future, eavesdrops on the past and reminds us of all our lost opportunities.

"I started with the notion of making one of those beautiful summer films," Woody said, crossing his arms against the chill of the air conditioner. He looked like your standard-issue Woody Allen, with his black horn-rimmed glasses and khaki pants, his work shoes and oxford cloth shirt, grown slightly frayed at the collar. But he also looked somehow different: He seemed thinner and more composed and his hair was combed.

"I wanted to portray the country the way I want it to be, with golden vistas, and flowers, animals, moon, stars, all in 1906, a perfect setting to deal with problems of love and romance. I saw it as a chance to get in some of my philosophy, that there's more to life than meets the eye, that an intellectual rationalist is also an animal who lusts after women and is not above drawing blood in the throes of passion. He can explain the cosmos, and his friend the doctor can play God and watch people die, but all of these men are ... wistful. Wistful, because they haven't met the right woman yet."

I nodded. You love the country? I said.

Allen recoiled. "No! I hate the country! This Fourth of July weekend, when everybody else has gone out to the country, I stayed in Manhattan. I worked, I went to see *Poltergeist* at Eighty-sixth and Third Avenue and I walked around the empty streets. The country is great as it appears in one's fantasies, in Shakespeare's *Midsummer Night's Dream,* with all the little forest spirits, but when I go to the country to shoot a movie, we have to have a nurse for snakebites and poison ivy. They have gnats and mosquitoes. It's awful."

But when you were making this movie in upstate New York, I said, you had to put up with the country?

"Not at all. I drove back to New York every night and stayed in my own bed. Oh, I can take a little of the country. Sometimes I reluctantly visit Mia Farrow in her country home in Connecticut, but I always come back the same day. I would never think of staying overnight."

In other words, I said, your penthouse view of Central Park is about as sylvan as you like to get?

"I like the view just from the window, through glass. I like it best in the winter. I'm not crazy about the green of leaves. At the beginning of our film, when we shot the montage of the leaves and the ponds and the little deer running past, I was hiding behind the camera."

When you were a kid, you never went to the beach?

"I got sun poisoning. It was terrible. I preferred staying home in Brooklyn and playing baseball in the streets. I was a very good athlete, good at baseball, football, from growing up in the streets, but I didn't get to like nature that way. I think we all miss the point that when Shakespeare was talking about summer, he was writing from a land where summer was a lot more like spring is here. He didn't know about dust and ticks. I personally prefer gray, overcast days to sunny ones. That's one reason I don't like it in Los Angeles. I really can't stand the climate."

As I quote Woody Allen saying these things, he has a tendency, I suppose to sound like the Woody Allen persona that has become familiar in his movies, his books, even a comic strip based on a scruffy little horn-rimmed intellectual. But he was saying them sincerely, not for comic effect, and I realized that he'd slipped a crucial autobiographical fact past me: *He was good at sports!*

Really? I said. Really good at sports?

"Very good at sports," he said.

That's certainly not my image of Woody Allen, I said. I think of you as a nearsighted little kid who was always dropping the ball.

"A lot of people would get that idea from my movies," he said, "but actually I was very good at sports. You shouldn't confuse me with the characters I play."

But I do, I said. After I saw your last movie, *Stardust Memories,* I found myself leaving the theater and saying to myself that this was the first time I didn't *like* Woody Allen.

"Well, then one of us made a mistake," he said. "Actually, a lot of people had your reaction. In all fairness to the movie, some critics did like it, but most people probably would have agreed with you. Everybody assumed that what I was doing was showing myself. In fact, I was showing a fictional character who was not a wonderful person, who had money and fame and yet was unhappy and hated his fans. Everything seemed to irritate him. Nothing in his life gave him any happiness. And perhaps what I was trying to say in that movie was that at the end of life, it may not be fame that we remember with pleasure, not money, but just a few moments of happiness set aside from the emptiness of life, when, in the case of that movie, the character spent some time listening to Louis Armstrong, and was delivered from his misery, and was happy."

I almost wanted to sigh.

"I've always had this theory about films," he said, "that they're more mythological than the stage, that we have almost this need to believe that the people on the screen are like the people they play. I've played a lot of characters that aren't me. 'Woody Allen,' whatever that means, isn't necessarily me. Some guy will walk up to me at Michael's Pub, where I play jazz, and ask me why I'm doing it, since I don't need the money. He has some idea of me that misses the possibility that I like to play jazz.

Allen was drifting into such an introspective, thoughtful tone that I paused a second and asked, Do you believe in God?

He was silent for a moment.

In this new movie, I said, you have an extraordinary closing scene which seems to suggest an afterlife, another plane of existence ...

"Yeah," he said. "Well, I don't think we know the answer to the question of whether there's a God or not. I think organized religions are silly. I think Sartre, who was an atheist, had more religion than a lot of clergymen who are essentially just practicing a lifestyle and a business. But I don't feel we know all the answers. In this movie, I have the scientific rationalist turn into a spirit of light. I remember once talking with Billy Graham, on a TV special I did, and I asked him, *What if you're wrong about God and the afterlife and everything? What if you die and there's nothing there?* And he replied that he *still* would have led a better life by thinking the way he did. And I thought to myself, he's right about that, if he's telling the truth. Of course, he's politically and commercially involved in religion, but ... if he does really believe that, he'll lead a richer life."

He sighed. "I'd love to be a genuinely religious person, not coerced, but freely religious. But it's like Ingmar Bergman told me: *Thought gets in the way.*"

Is there anything in your life that passes for prayer?

"No. I try to make the right choices, that's as far as I go. I always have the fear that if I were to be tested, I would not come through. If I had been in the concentration camps, if I'd been in the French Resistance, would I have just caved in to everything to save myself pain? I fear that I would have. I fear I'm a coward."

The movie persona of Woody Allen has a lot of coward involved in it, I said.

"Yes, it does. And I got some of that from Bob Hope. He is my favorite comedian—not the Bob Hope of the last fifteen years, but the movie Bob Hope, the star of movies like *My Favorite Brunette,* which I saw for fourteen cents in Brooklyn when I was growing up. He was so funny And he played such a great coward."

I interviewed him once, I said, and when I asked him what he thought about the fact that Woody Allen admired him, he seemed pleased, but he also seemed to be still in competition ... as if the two of you were still going up for the same jobs.

"Yeah. He gives me ninety percent acceptance. He'll say things like, *Woody Allen is a wonderful kid, and a near genius.* Instead of that automatic, meaningless use of the word 'genius' that everybody in show business throws away all the time, he makes it a point to add the 'near' to the genius."

There seemed to be just a ghost of insecurity there, and, if it was only a ghost, that was progress for Woody Allen, whose years in psychoanalysis have become part of his legend.

He is, in a sense, the ideal if flawed Manhattan man, successful, brilliant, rich, neurotic, sincere, and always searching, like the man in his anecdote, for the perfect woman that he can live with happily for the rest of his life. The problem with women, even perfect ones, however, is that there is nothing that quite complicates a life like the addition of another whole life to it. In other words: Can a man who hates the country and appreciates Central Park best when it is seen through glass, in the winter, easily adjust to the daily messiness of a relationship? I put it to him this way:

Are you getting along any better with children these days?

"You mean Mia's kids?"

For example.

Mia Farrow, the love in Woody's life, has seven children altogether.

"Well, I've always gotten along OK with kids. They're not one of my hangups. You should probably also take into account the fact that Mia and I have been seeing each other for the past two years, but we do not live together. So I haven't been put to the absolute test of becoming the father of seven children overnight.

"She lives with them. She loves them immensely and is a very good mother. I participate with them. I've always been good with kids. Being a good athlete, I can play games with them, basketball, things like that. I did magic tricks when I was a kid, and I can still do some of them. I have an endless amount of patience."

He sort of grinned. "You've got to realize," he said, "that a relationship is always better if you don't actually have to *live* with the other person."

Really?

"Oh, of course. That means you can be in a constant state of courtship. Mia loves the kids beyond anything, and she takes care of them, and then, in the evenings, we'll meet, and it's like a date, and some days we'll stay together but I almost always come home to my house at night. It's ever so much easier to get along with somebody if you aren't always having to go to bed with them, when you're tuckered out, and get up with them, when you're still sleepy. I can't see why people won't let sex be a daytime activity."

Is that what your next movie is going to be about?

"No. Or rather, I don't exactly know what my next movie is going to be about. I discover the themes in my movies while I'm filming and editing them. This one is almost finished, and it will come out at Christmastime. It will be in black and white, and it doesn't have a title yet. You know, I don't *hide* my titles. When I know the title to one of my movies, I'll say it. Like *Love and Death* for example. But with *Annie Hall* and *Manhattan,* and now this one, I honestly didn't know what to call them until the last minute."

So what's the working title? *Woody Allen's Christmas Picture*?

Woody grinned. "Actually," he said, "the working title is *Woody Allen's Fall Picture."*

Is there any symbolism in that?

"Not that I know of."

And you really would prefer to walk around the empty streets of Manhattan and go to see *Poltergeist* than spend the weekend in the country?

"It seems perfectly normal to me."

nine

As time goes by

Two kinds of time are at work here. The Charlie Chaplin and Ingrid Bergman pieces are about lifetimes. The other two are about downtime. Bob and Ray kill some time in a coffee shop during a day of rehearsals. Three teenage movie stars have lunch at a Chinese restaurant. So it goes.

Bob and Ray

Good gravy! It's as empty as the day it was made.

New York, 1970

"It all goes back, maybe, to a farm expert from the Pioneer Valley in Massachusetts, getting red in the face while being interviewed about artificial insemination," Ray Goulding said. "The wife and kids are at home glued to the radio, and you ask him the key question, and he looks at the microphone and says, *Well, Ray*... and turns red. What we do is basically based on observation, on watching people. It's not necessarily a style."

Bob Elliott nodded gravely. Ray cleared his throat and began to pour cream into his iced coffee. He kept tilting the little stainless steel container until finally it was upside-down.

"Hey! There isn't any cream in this container," he said.

"I'll bet you feel like a fool," Bob said.

"Good gravy," Ray said, lifting up the lid and looking inside. "It's empty as the day it was made."

"Jacques Tati couldn't have done it better," Bob said. "There you were trying to pour cream and the little stainless steel container was *empty.*"

"I'll have to admit the joke's on me, all right," Ray said, grinning ruefully. "Oh miss? Miss? May we have some cream in this container, please?"

"Why don't you sample some of those Parker House rolls with rich creamery butter from nearby farms?" Bob asked.

"No," Ray said. "Just the iced coffee is enough for me today ..."

"It's sort of a back-and-forth style," Bob said. "We started doing it when we were morning radio announcers in Boston, after the war. I guess you could say it just sort of grew on us. Wouldn't you say that, Ray?"

"Yes, I'd say that," Ray said. "I don't see how I could improve on the way you've expressed it, Bob."

"Watch that water, miss," Bob said. The waitress was filling his water glass. She left a new container of cream and disappeared.

"Looks like she poured some water into your salt shaker," Ray said. "Luckily you won't be needing the salt since you're only having water."

"Came through like a sluiceway," Bob said.

"We made some changes in the show every night during the previews," Ray said. "We're babes in the woods when it comes to Broadway; we have twenty years of material to choose from, and a lot of new stuff, and the question is what will work on a stage. But Joseph Hardy, our director, brought us along very well."

"Very well indeed," Bob said.

"We finally had to drop the soap operas," Ray said. "We were doing Mary Backstayge, Noble Wife, but it wasn't working. There was something too static about sitting there looking at a radio. Hardy had us try it live one night, and that didn't work either. We kept the news bulletins about Ralph Crusader, though ..."

"And we've added a David Chetley instant news analysis after the Sore Loser broadcast," Bob said. "After the candidate says we won't have him to kick around anymore, David Chetley remarks on his absynthian vehemence and complete amphigory."

"Robert Downey says that when you see Nixon on TV he looks about eight frames out of synch," Ray said.

"Yes, but he's not lacking in a certain degree of circumlocutory agility," Bob said. "Did you notice the other night, when we did the Sore Loser broadcast, a lady walked out of the theater?"

Ray sipped his iced coffee. "Yes, I noticed that," he said. "Of course you never know. She may have been one of those radicals you read about, or on the other hand maybe she just had gas cramps."

Ray nodded thoughtfully. This was during a coffee break across the steet from the Golden Theater and their first Broadway show, *Bob and Ray: The Two and Only.* Bob did most of the thoughtful nodding, and Ray did a lot of talking, but somehow it was Bob's occasional sober asides that made Ray's seemingly sober remarks transform themselves into a Bob and Ray routine.

Hugh Downs mentioned once that, after becoming a Bob and Ray fan, he had a great deal of difficulty in conducting a straight interview. He'd ask a question and think, *good gravy, that's a Wally Ballou question.* That's part of the delicate genius of Bob and Ray; their material is removed by only the slenderest of margins from the actual situation in interviews.

"Ralph Crusader has turned up some really interesting information," Ray was saying. "Several thousand pairs of socks have been dumped on the market with a faulty stitch in the heel. A 1968 type of stitch in a 1970 sock. They're looking into the sock people, the shoe people ... the thread people apparently don't have altogether clean hands, either."

"We all owe a lot to Ralph Crusader," Bob said. "Give me a good soft drink of brominated vegetable oil, or whatever they're putting into it now, any day. Good gravy."

"Were you watching TV a few weeks ago, when the Mets and Cubs were rained out?" Ray asked. "Jack Brickhouse and Ralph Kiner had to ad-lib for an hour. It was one of the great spontaneous broadcasts in recent television history."

"It reminded me," Bob said, "of those interviews that used to be conducted by our character Elwood 'Pop' Hedge, the veteran old baseball announcer."

"There's a thin line between Elwood 'Pop' Hedge and Kiner and Brickhouse all right," Ray said. "Sports announcing particularly lends itself to self-satire. Here were these two guys sitting there trying to kill an hour describing the rain at Wrigley Field."

"Congratulating the ground crew," Bob said.

"By all means," Ray said. "The ground crew has certainly done a top-flight job in the difficult task of getting those tarps out there."

"You bet, Ray," Bob said.

"Were you watching when they brought in Peanuts Lowrey and started to interview him?" Ray asked. "They reminisced about that fight in Brooklyn in ... was it 1946? I wonder how many times Peanuts has relived that fight on rainy-day broadcasts."

"The part I liked," Bob said, "was when Brickhouse called Peanuts the best signstealer in baseball. And Peanuts grinned that you-better-believe-it grin ..."

"Then Kiner got to talking about the death threat he received in ... was it 1950? They even mentioned on the air the name of the guy who sent the threat, which wasn't very sporting all these years later."

"Kiner said he didn't take it very seriously," Bob said, "but all the same he found himself moving around a lot in left field."

"Now here comes General Manager Bob Scheffing," Ray said. "Come on in here, Bob, and have a word with the fans. That's an old soap opera device, remember? You couldn't see the character on radio, so he had to be introduced by title."

"Why hello there, Deputy Mayor Richard W. Halfwaithe," Bob said. "And what brings *you* to town hall today?"

"Reminds me of that soap opera we did on the Mutual program," Ray said. "Matt Neffer, Spot-Welding King of the World."

"Not to overlook the Life and Loves of Linda Lovely, featuring Ricky L. Lewellen," Bob said.

"We never did Linda Lovely, Boy Girl," Ray said, "but we would have liked to."

"Look over there, Ray," Bob said. "Isn't that the Glenn Miller Orchestra getting into its bus in preparation for another tuneful swing around the nation?"

"Yes it is," Ray said. "You go out humming that tune." They looked out the window at the Glenn Miller bus, which was indeed parked outside.

"We played with them up at M.I.T.," Bob said.

"I think I read in the paper," Ray said, "that they ran into some trouble up in Canada. Their instruments were stolen, their tuxedos, even their bus."

"I'd imagine a bus with 'The Glenn Miller Orchestra Directed by Buddy DeFranco' painted on the side would be difficult, even impossible, to conceal," Bob said.

"Looks like they've got it back," Ray observed.

"Linda Lovely," Bob said. "Wasn't she sponsored by those Chocolate Cookies With White Stuff in Between Them?"

"Kids eat 'em up," Ray said. "The Nabisco folks know what that white stuff is, but they're not talking. Kids love 'em! You know what kids do? See, if you eat the entire cookie at once, it's gone right away and doesn't last as long. But if you separate the wafers and eat them separately, the white stuff tends to stick to just one wafer. So kids slide the wafers around until the white stuff is evenly distributed."

"I get it. And then they eat the white stuff right off the cookie, right?" Bob said.

"No," Ray said, "they eat the chocolate wafer as well."

"There's the girl singer, getting onto the bus now," Bob said. "I wonder where they're headed. Probably one of the first college hops of the season."

"We're loyal to you, Illinois," Ray sang. *"We're orange and blue, Illinois* ... And now, Bisodol presents ..."

"Remember," Bob said, "that's spelled B-i-s-o-d-o-l."

"Whatever Arthur Godfrey recommends, that's what I use for pain and discomfort of stomach upset," Ray said. "Amotone comes in tablet or liquid form, I know that much. Bejabbers, I know it backwards."

"Bejabbers?" Bob said.

"And now it's time for the surly old investigator," Ray said.

Bob hummed "Someday I'll Find You."

"That used to be the theme for Mister Keen, Tracer of Lost Persons," Ray said. "I think Noel Coward penned it in one of his weaker moments. Arthur Godfrey used to have this morning simulcast, TV and radio and I'd listen on my way home from work. He said he liked a raw egg in a glass of milk in the morning. It sounded nauseating to me, let me tell you, but I told my wife that if Arthur could, I could. The secret is not to break the yolk."

"On the contrary," Bob said, "I'd think it would be ten times easier to get down if you stirred it up real well in the milk."

"Well now, you've triggered me," Ray said. "That frankly hadn't occurred to me. What would that be called, Bob? A prairie oyster? Or is that when you have the raw egg with Worcestershire?"

"Neither one would be called a prairie oyster out here in Marlboro Country," Bob said.

"Those old radio programs were great," Ray said. "Remember at the end of 'Gangbusters,' when they would describe one of the FBI's ten most-wanted criminals? And then the announcer would add: *Caution, kids, if you see this man, contact your local law enforcement agencies or the nearest office of the FBI. Do NOT attempt to apprehend him yourself!*"

"And now, from the air-cooled Terrace Lounge of the Hotel Statler, the melodies of ..." Bob said.

"In the early days of radio," Ray said, "you'd be listening and suddenly the program would go off the air. They always blamed it on difficulties 'west of Denver.' I kept imagining some crazed Mountie with a hedge clipper."

"And now," Bob said, "from the beautiful Cinegrill Lounge of the Hollywood Roosevelt Hotel on famed Hollywood Boulevard ..."

"Good gravy," said Ray.

Chapter Nine

Matt Dillon, Diane Lane and Vincent Spano

It will become an art film.

New York, 1983

A Chinese restaurant on Second Avenue in New York. One of those places where all the right demographic groups are seen eating dim sum with their Significant Others. In a corner by the window, three young people are studying the menu.

Clockwise from the seat nearest the giant ficus tree, they are:

MATT DILLON, *nineteen, "teenage heartthrob," although he makes puking noises when he hears that description. Matt has starred in* The Outsiders, My Bodyguard, Little Darlings *and* Tex. *He is dressed in jeans and a leather vest over a black T-shirt. He has been compared to James Dean, and specializes in playing tough, inarticulate teenagers.*

DIANE LANE, *eighteen, who appeared on the cover of* Time *two years ago for a story about the new generation of young actresses and on the cover of* The Movies *two months ago for a story about herself. A stage actress since the age of six, Lane has starred in* A Little Romance, Cattle Annie and Little Britches, Six Pack *and four made-for-TV movies. She is a stunning beauty, combining the best features of young Elizabeth Taylor and young Natalie Wood.*

VINCENT SPANO, *twenty, an Italian-American New Yorker, who shared the lead in* Baby, It's You *as a slick greaser named The Sheik, then played the son of a sheik in* The Black Stallion Returns, *and was a troubled kid in* Over the Edge. *His darkly handsome looks do not prepare you for his quick intelligence.*

The three actors are in New York to promote their new movie, Francis Ford Coppola's Rumble Fish, *which premiered two nights earlier at the New York Film Festival. Dillon and Lane are also the co-stars of the previous Coppola film about alienated teenagers,* The Outsiders. *It was a minor box-office hit. But on the basis of the audience reaction and early reviews,* Rumble Fish, *a black-and-white allegory about teen gangs, is likely to be more of a problem picture. Coppola calls it "an art film for teenagers."*

The curtain rises as the three prepare to order lunch.

* * *

Diane: "I walked past the theater on my way here. Did you see the publicity photos they put outside? Pure fantasy land. They're all in color, even though the movie is in black and white. They gave me eye makeup, but I didn't wear any in the picture. They gave me a scarf, and I didn't wear a scarf even once in the whole movie. And of course they put a boob shot on prominent display."

Vincent: "After we eat, we ought to go back and check out the theater."

Matt: "They got real long lines. I was gonna go in, but I didn't know ..."

Vincent: "It's good publicity to show you support the film."

Diane: "I got asked for my autograph. It's the first time that's ever happened, out of context. If they *know* you're there, and who you are, then I might be asked, but it was the first time anyone just recognized me on the street. I don't think I'm very recognizable, especially with my exquisite skin condition."

The waiter approaches the table.

Vincent (to the waiter): "Do you have any just like vegetarian dishes?"

Diane: "Speaking of not being recognized: A couple of years ago, I went to the Underground Disco with this girlfriend. We were both just seventeen, a couple of cosmetic queens out together. And Robert DeNiro was there with Joe Pesci. I recognized him. I was dying. And he made a pass. He didn't know who I was. I was so flattered, in one way. In another way, I thought I must really look like a wench. Now there's a possibility I'll appear with him in *On the Waterfront* on Broadway. On the first day of rehearsals, I'll say to him, *Remember me? You came on to me at the Underground Disco?*"

Vincent: "Would it be possible to prepare my food without using MSG?"

Waiter: "We use no MSG, sir."

Vincent: "And also no starch, sugar or salt, please."

Waiter: "But without that, how will the chef make the sauce?"

Matt (studying menu): "What do you recommend?"

Waiter: "Crispy beef with orange peel very good, sir."

Matt: "I don't like oranges in my meat."

Diane: "What else is good?"

Waiter: "Jumbo shrimp with snow pea pods very good."

Diane: "Ugh! I hate shrimp! They make me think of... underwater cockroaches."

Waiter: "Maybe chicken be better for you."

Vincent: "Could he just stir-fry some vegetables?"

Matt: "For me, maybe he could just cut up a steak and fry it."

Diane: "I'll have chicken and Chinese vegetables."

The waiter returns to the kitchen.

Vincent: "How is *Cotton Club* coming along?"

He is referring to the new Francis Ford Coppola picture, starring Richard Gere and Diane Lane in the story of a famous Harlem nightclub.

Diane: "Well, OK, I guess. Francis quit for a couple of days because he wasn't getting paid, but I think they got that straightened out. I think they got some Arabian money or something."

Reporter: "You're in that with Richard Gere?"

Diane: "Yes. He's really a nice person, except don't ask about his private life. He doesn't divulge."

Matt: "So you know nothing?"

Diane: "Except that he's living with a Brazilian woman downtown somewhere, and they don't come above Tenth Street."

Vincent: "Those big-budget movies. I was offered a role in *Sahara* with Brooke Shields, but I didn't take it. I wondered if it would be good for my career to play another sheik. Also, I didn't want to be standing around in the Sahara Desert waiting for Brooke to fix her eyelashes."

Matt takes a deck of cards out of the pocket of his vest.

Matt: "Pick a card, any card. This is a really good trick."

Diane: "I've been having nightmares based on the things HBO has been showing. First they had the deadly black mamba attacking Klaus Kinski. Then I saw a documentary on that terrible Cocoanut Grove nightclub fire. Just the thing to see while I'm filming

Cotton Club."

Vincent: "This morning they had an auto-racing documentary, with crashing cars spilling gas on the crowd."

Matt: "They torched the crowd? Pick a card, any card."

Vincent takes a card.

Matt: "Now put it back anywhere in the deck. Now shuffle the deck."

Vincent returns the card and shuffles. Matt fans through the deck.

Matt: "Is this it?"

Vincent: "No."

Matt (stage astonishment): "It isn't? Didn't you pick the six of hearts?"

Vincent (looking a bit surprised): "Yes."

Matt: "Then let's see."

He spells "six of hearts," peeling off one card for every letter. He flips over the eleventh card. It is the six of hearts.

Vincent: "Amazing!"

Matt: "It's a really good trick."

The food is served.

Diane: "When we did the press interviews, one thing I didn't know how to answer about *Rumble Fish* was ... why didn't Motorcycle Boy take Rusty-James to the hospital after he was knifed? It never occurred to me that he ought to, but it makes sense, doesn't it?"

Vincent (patient explanatory tone): "Motorcycle Boy couldn't take Rusty-James to the hospital because Motorcycle Boy is dead. He is like a failed prophet who returns to the scene of his defeat. He's the Christ symbol."

Matt: "You trying to tell me Motorcycle Boy is a spirit?"

Vincent: "He even pours a bottle of whiskey into your open wound. That is obviously an evil baptism."

Diane: "Did you talk to Susie [S.E. Hinton, author of the novel and screenplay] about this? I've been trying to improvise my way through explaining this movie for two days. Give me a break. What is this shabby attempt at significance?"

Vincent: "Motorcycle Boy has no identity. Remember when he looks at himself in the mirror? There is no sign of recognition on his face. It's like a fish looking into a mirror."

Diane: "Give me a break."

Reporter: "What about the scene where Rusty-James dies, and levitates out of his body, and floats around town looking at his friends? What did that signify?"

Matt Dillon, who plays Rusty-James, levitates his chopsticks in the air.

Matt: "It's like if you ever thought you were gonna die, you start thinking, *I wonder if they're still talking about me?* You know, like, *That Rusty-James ... he's one cool dude."*

Diane: "What was the significance when you hit the bum, Matt?"

Matt: "Partially, it was because he looked like a father. Hey, there's all sorts of things to learn about this movie."

Diane: "I was so confused, talking about it today."

Matt: "It will become an art film."

Vincent: "I got some great notes on it."

Matt: "Pick a card, any card."

The reporter picks a card.

Vincent: "See, what Motorcycle Boy did is, he went to California, and what he found was nothing, man, because California is dying. And so he came back, and Patterson, the cop, shot him, because he represents the devil. Jealous."

Diane: "Jealousy is the only completely destructive emotion there is."

Vincent: "And *after* he shoots him, he lights up a cigarette, see, because it was almost merciful, killing the Motorcycle Boy and releasing his spirit."

Diane: "Not releasing him. Fulfilling his destiny."

For a few moments, they concentrate on their food.

Diane: "Guess who I saw on the street today? Alain Delon."

Matt: "Delon? The French guy? Is he good?"

Diane: "We hit eyes. It was electric. I kept right on walking. But the effect was shocking. I freaked."

Matt: "The card was the three of clubs? Right? Let's see."

He spells out "three of clubs." The twelfth card is the three of clubs.

Reporter: "Amazing."

Matt: "It's a good trick. It's very simple. But you gotta know it."

Vincent: "I think we should go look in the theater and see how the movie is playing. This is it, after all. After today, we break up, we all go our separate ways, we're moving on. Let's let people know we are supporting it."

Diane: "I *love* the black-and-white photography. It's luminous. It looks like the light is coming *from* the screen. Color looks like it's projected *on* the screen."

Matt: "At the film festival, somebody shouted out that he shoulda stayed at home and watched 'Dallas.' Other people made rude noises. I figure they made up their minds before they saw it. I saw a drunk on the sidewalk; he said it stunk. I told him to get a job."

Their fortune cookies read: "You will make a good impression on a stranger" (Diane); "You have depths that others do not suspect" (Vincent), and "Wealth and a long life" (Matt). When they arrived at the theater, the manager did not recognize them and would not let them in until a press agent intervened.

Diane (as they were allowed inside): "Let's sit in the smoking section, with the grownups.'

Charles Chaplin

Look. There's Charlie Chaplin.

Chicago, 1977

Let me tell you two stories about Charles Chaplin, who died on Christmas Day.

Both stories take place in Venice, where every one of Chaplin's dozens of films was shown during a tribute at the 1972 Venice Film Festival. Day after day, for two weeks, Chaplin's movies were shown at the Palace of Cinema, and day after day the parents of Venice brought their kids to the free screenings, and the kids laughed with delight at these moments that were filmed fifty years before they were born.

And then one day Chaplin himself came to Venice. He was a very old man, snow-haired and frail, but this was the first complete retrospective of his work that had ever been mounted, and so he felt he should come. And on a night near the end of the festival, they did something in Venice that had never been done before.

They turned out all the lights in the Piazza San Marco, that vast square in front of the cathedral, and they told the orchestras of the sidewalk cafes to stop playing "Volare" and go home. And they put up a gigantic movie screen at the end of the square opposite the cathedral and showed *City Lights* on it. And the square was filled with ten thousand people. Italians and tourists, Venetians and people from the mainland, old couples and young lovers and little kids sitting on their fathers' shoulders.

The movie is about the Tramp, the character Chaplin created in those dozens of short comedies, and then developed in the longer films like *The Gold Rush* and *Modern Times,* and then turned into a savage satire on Hitler in *The Great Dictator.*

The Tramp was always the same, with his tattered clothes and frayed dignity, his cane and his battered hat, and the nobility of his soul. In *City Lights,* the Tramp fell in love with a blind girl who sold flowers in a little shop. And although he didn't have a penny to his name, he made it possible for her sight to be restored. At the end of the film, there is a moment when the girl and the Tramp meet again. She doesn't recognize him, of course, but then she reaches out her fingers and touches his face, and from the contours she knows who he is. And then she kisses him.

I had seen that moment before. But now, standing in the dark in Piazza San Marco with ten thousand other people, I felt the power of it so strongly that my eyes began to mist. And all of that enormous crowd was so quiet that you could hear the pigeons calling from their nests in the stones of the old buildings.

A single spotlight flashed out of the darkness. It shone across our heads and onto a balcony on the third floor overlooking the square. We all turned and looked at the balcony. The doorway was opened and an old man walked forward and stood on it. Charlie Chaplin. We did not applaud at once. We stood, still silent, in awe. The hush lasted three or four seconds, a very long time. And then we cheered and applauded and shouted "Charlie!" He raised his hand and waved to us, and then two people stepped forward to help him back into the room.

That is the first story.

I walked quietly out of the square and down to the landing in front of the Palace of the Doges. The vaporetto came—one of those little boats that run up and down the canals like buses. I took the vaporetto back out to the island of the Lido, where the film festival was being held, and I watched a little boy in his mother's lap as he looked through the Charlie Chaplin souvenir booklet she'd bought him. I thought to myself that I knew a lot about movies, but that the secret of Chaplin's greatness, the reason why *his* movies seemed to speak to everyone in every country, was one I might be able to understand but would never be able to explain.

The next day, in the dining room of the hotel on the Lido, I met some friends for dinner. I was seated so that I faced directly toward the dining room door. Half an hour or so after I sat down, I looked up and realized that Charlie Chaplin was standing there in the doorway. He was with a woman—his wife, Oona, I suppose—and a young man who was helping to support him. Maybe one of his sons.

I was the only person who had seen him. He looked around the room. He seemed unhappy in some way. I could not understand why. "Look," I said. "There's Charlie Chaplin." My friends turned to look. He saw them turn. He smiled. He did not know them, but he stepped forward one step, and smiled. Other people turned, and then everyone in the room knew that Charlie Chaplin was there in the doorway. Someone stood up and began to applaud, and then we all did. And Charlie Chaplin smiled again, and waved at us, and then he walked away.

What had I seen in his eyes, in the moment when no one else knew he was in the doorway? How can I possibly know? But did I see the child born in London in 1889, the child of the drunken father who died a few years later, and of the mother who carried him on stage in her arms, the mother who later went mad? The child beaten in orphanages? The child who could never remember a time when he had not performed on the stage? The child who became the single most famous performer of the twentieth century, and who had just been cheered by ten thousand people as he stood on a balcony overlooking Piazza San Marco, and who now, less than a day later, was standing in the doorway of a hotel dining room ... afraid he would not be recognized?

Of course the Tramp was universal. We were all kids once.

Ingrid Bergman

I remember every detail. The Germans wore gray. You wore blue.

You must remember this,
A kiss is still a kiss,
A sigh is just a sigh ...

I will always remember Ingrid Bergman as the most beautiful woman in the movies, and I will not think of her as gone because in her great roles she is still as young for me as on the day she finished them. The movies are like that. The bad ones age rather quickly. But the good ones are like time capsules, preserving forever those moments that create our fantasies. I have seen two of her films, *Casablanca* and *Notorious,* at least twenty times each, and her image in them—vulnerable, sad, strong and with an inner glow—is part of my life.

It's still the same old story,
A fight for love and glory ...

For many people, Ingrid Bergman's one unforgettable role was in *Casablanca* (1943). She played a woman who, out of all the gin mills in the world, had to walk into Rick's Place. And she had to walk in on the arm of a hero of the Resistance and meet a man she had fallen in love with years ago in Paris in a world at peace.

"Yeah," Humphrey Bogart told her, "I remember every detail. The

Germans wore gray. You wore blue."

Hearts full of passion,
Jealousy and hate.

It was a great performance in a great role in a great movie. But for me, the greatest Bergman role is not in *Casablanca* but in *Notorious,* a movie Alfred Hitchcock directed in 1946. The movie, like *Casablanca,* played Bergman between two men who both loved her. But while *Casablanca*'s irony was that both men were courageous and heroic (each after his fashion), the two men in *Notorious* were unworthy of her (each after his fashion).

The man she fell in love with first was Cary Grant, as an American spy. He knew she was the daughter of a Nazi, knew she was not a spy herself, and recruited her to marry into a postwar Nazi spy ring being operated by Claude Rains in Rio. Rains was indeed sincerely in love with her, but was no doubt a villain, and was under the thumb of his domineering mother. Grant did indeed love her, but thought she was "notorious"—the kind of woman who would cynically marry Rains. What Grant, blinded by anger and jealousy, did not understand was that Bergman married Rains because Grant wanted her to, and she was so desperately in love with him she'd do anything he wanted.

The movie's most unforgettable scene was the long kiss between Bergman and Grant—a kiss advertised at the time as the longest in the history of the movies. It began on a moonlit Rio balcony, continued inside a drawing room, continued while Grant talked on the telephone, continued while he walked to the door. All during that time, while he played aloof and cool (the bastard!), she clung to him with a love born of desperation.

It was that scene that made the rest of the movie work, and that emotion paid off at the end, when Grant finally realized that Bergman was not drunk but almost dead from arsenic poisoning—and they walked down that endless staircase past the gauntlet of Nazis who were powerless to stop them.

And man must have his mate,
That no one can deny.

But Bergman could not trust her mate in her other great movie role, in George Cukor's *Gaslight* (1944). She was the wife of a madman (Charles Boyer), who ostensibly left the house at night and then sneaked back into the attic to plan his nefarious deeds. She thought she was going mad as she saw the gaslight dim. And (the bastard!), rather than reveal that the lights dimmed because he had turned on the gas in the attic, he let her believe she was indeed losing her mind. Ingrid Bergman won her first Oscar in that film.

But she fell out of favor with the American public when she left her Swedish husband, Peter Lindstrom, and ran off in 1949 with Roberto Rossellini, the Italian neo-realist whose work she so passionately admired that she wrote him she would appear in anything he wanted.

The public, egged on by the dowager crones of film gossip, Louella Parsons and Hedda Hopper, made her unwelcome in Hollywood for several years. And when she returned, in 1956 in *Anastasia,* she may have won her second Oscar, but the magic was gone and it would remain missing in many other mediocre films: *The Inn of the Sixth Happiness* (1958), *The Yellow Rolls-Royce* (1964), most assuredly in *Murder on the Orient Express* (1974), for which she won the Oscar as best supporting actress and seemed to be quite sincerely saying the simple truth when she told the Academy she'd rather it had been given to someone else.

The fundamental things apply ...

And then, in 1978, she gave her best screen performance in more than thirty years, in a film and a role filled with great personal risk. The film was *Autumn Sonata,* directed by Ingmar Bergman, the Swedish filmmaker who had attained greatness in her homeland in the years since she had left it.

She played an internationally famous concert pianist. As the film opens, she has returned to visit her daughter (Liv Ullmann) after a separation of seven years—she has been too busy for her family. After she arrives, she learns to her horror that her other daughter also will be there. This daughter (Lena Nyman) suffers from a degenerative nerve disease, and the Bergman character has tried to forget her, to close her out of her life.

We had never quite seen Ingrid Bergman the way Ingmar Bergman saw her in *Autumn Sonata,* nor had most of us ever heard her speak her native language. We'd never seen her pushed so hard by a director whose commitment is to merciless honesty. Bergman was able to use not only her star qualities, but every last measure of her artistry and humanity. It was not just that *Autumn Sonata* was her last film. It was that she knew she had to make it before she retired. It was a great performance, inspiring thoughts of what other performances she might have given, if she had not lost so much time to love, scandal and Hollywood dreck.

But such thoughts are fruitless. From Ingrid Bergman we had a long and full screen career, containing the classic performances in *Casablanca, Notorious, Gaslight* (and some would add *Dr. Jeckyl and Mr. Hyde, Spellbound, For Whom the Bell Tolls* and *The Bells of St. Mary's).* She showed good timing by retiring after *Autumn Sonata*—we would not have wanted her in a cameo in another of those Agatha Christie omnibuses.

And she gave us irreplaceable moments: The look in her eyes when she asked Sam to play it again, and the look when she asked Bogart if he remembered Paris. The anguish that crossed her face when Grant cold-bloodedly stood by and let her marry Rains. The dread that she was going mad and Boyer simply did not care. And the pain in *Autumn Sonata* that said, "Yes, I should have loved you all better, but I, myself, should have been loved as well, and all I received was applause."

... as time goes by.

Epilogue

No matter what the future brings

Burns and Matthau

How can a dancer retire?

Chicago, 1975

"Where do you want to sit?" asked George Burns. "Over here, by the light? How about this chair?"

"How about the sofa?" said Walter Matthau. "You take the chair, George. Have the chair."

"I'll take the sofa."

"Sit down, sit down," said Matthau. "Those are modern pants you're wearing, George."

"It's a new pair of pants."

"I got a new coat today," said Matthau. "I went to Eddie Bauer, I got one of those coats that's good for the North Pole."

"I don't need a coat because for three days I'm not leaving this hotel," Burns said.

"I had a coat I thought was warm," Matthau said. "I got it at Aquascutum in London. Ingrid Bergman comes up. *Walter!* she says. *Remember me? I starred with you in* Cactus Flower!" I look at her. *For Christ's sake, Ingrid,* I say, *of course I remember you. How could I forget a nice Jewish girl like you?*"

"I've got a coat for Altoona," Burns said. "I don't have a Chicago coat." He lit a cigar. "I'm glad when people remind me of their names. I forget names all the time. I remember once I had a secretary for fifteen years. One day a director walks into

Chasen's, his name is Boris Petroff. I want to show off I remember his name. *Boris,* I said, *I want you to meet* ... then I forgot my secretary's name. Fifteen years."

"Look at this," said Matthau, paging through the movie ads in the morning paper. "Our ad is right next to the ad for *The Story of O.* They'll go to the wrong movie, they'll be sitting there looking at all that ass on the screen, they'll be saying, which one is supposed to be Smith and which one is Dale?"

"Those pictures," said Burns, exhaling his cigar. "They're showing too much these days. Let them look at each other and go into the bedroom and then cut to a sandwich."

"Or the next morning, they're having breakfast," said Matthau.

Burns drew on his cigar. "They have to have something," he said. "These days, people can no longer read or write. You have to leave them with a little something."

"What were they calling you?" Matthau said. "You were our technical advisor on *The Sunshine Boys*?"

"I'm still a performer, I'm a professional, a singer, I don't give advice," Burns said. "Let 'em find out for themselves."

"My father, he's ninety-one years old, he's a technical advisor for Hughes Aircraft," Matthau said. "He told me a story about this tomcat. All the tomcats are jumping over a picket fence, and the last tomcat jumps too low and castrates himself. When he gets to the other side, the other tomcats tell him not to worry: He can be the technical advisor."

Burns inhales. "I'm at that point now," he said.

"When does sex stop for you, George?" asked Matthau.

"For me ..." said Burns, rotating his cigar, "5:30 this morning."

"How many girls did you have in there?"

"Three. We did harmony. At my age, it's easier to sing."

"I'll bet you were a genius in your time," Matthau said.

"Gracie married me for laughs," Burns said. "I got more

laughs in bed than when I played Vegas."

"I'll bet you were a genius in the sack," Matthau said. "You were probably warm, quiet, faithful ..."

"This is me you're talking about?" said Burns.

"Yeah."

"Because I leave the door open. I like applause." He drew on his cigar, thoughtful. "What must be terrible," he said, "is a girl who's a sex symbol, everybody's always after her. What can she do? What can she invent? What can be different? At this late date, who's gonna invent a new exit or entrance?"

"I heard there's a book out that says Hugh Hefner has had two thousand women in twenty years," Matthau said.

"Two thousand?" said Burns.

"That's right."

"That works out to one thousand girls every ten years."

"That's right."

"A hundred girls a year. A different girl every three or four nights." He studied his cigar.

"Hefner has to be a very unhappy man," Matthau said.

"That's easy, that many girls," Burns said. "It's easy to do with two thousand different girls. What's hard is two thousand times with your wife."

"Hefner has to be living in the depths of despair."

"He's having more fun than my sister Goldie," Burns said. "I wish he'd talk to Goldie. I'd give him her phone number. She's older than I am."

Matthau got up to use the bathroom in Burns' hotel suite. When he was gone, Burns said, "You enjoy the picture? We got some good reviews. I got a darling letter from Cagney, he saw the reviews, he wrote a letter. I wrote him back. I said I was sorry he was retired. How can a dancer retire? He was a dancer, too, you know. An actor can retire, sure. But how can a dancer hang up his shoes?"

Matthau came back into the living room.

"They got a clothes line in the john," he said, "you can wash out your undershorts and hang them up to dry."

"I brought enough clean," Burns said. "I'd always be walking into wet shorts. That's not very stylish, especially with my head piece. How much you think a good toupee costs?"

"About thirty bucks?"

"Closer to three hundred and fifty. When I have five or six people in for dinner, I don't wear it. When I go out, I wear it. When I come home, I put it on the block, the block looks great, I look lousy."

"I've got a stand-in," Matthau said. "I went out and got a haircut. He's bald, he had his toupee trimmed."

"Not a very smart fellow," Burns said.

"A lot of people get silicone, face lifts, there's nothing wrong with a toupee," Matthau said. "Merle Oberon, she has silicone in her face, her behind ... she looks like she's been dead for nineteen, twenty-two years ..."

"Well," said Burns, "is she alive?"

"Medically speaking."

Burns inhaled his cigar. "She was a very pretty girl," he said.

"Did I hear you mention Cagney when I came in a moment ago?" said Matthau.

"He wrote me a nice letter," Burns said.

"He was offered my role," Matthau said. "He was the only non-Jew they were interested in."

"Cagney speaks excellent Jewish," Burns said. "He came from that section. Gracie and I ..."

"But he's retired and he wouldn't even consider it," Matthau said. "I didn't mean to interrupt your story."

"I keep them short," Burns said.

"Go ahead."

"We'd visit Cagney, the first thing he'd do was take out his dancing shoes, we'd do a few steps in the living room ..."

"I think I interrupt you a lot," Matthau said.

"I'll squeeze it in," said Burns.

Acknowledgments

These selections originally appeared in slightly different form with different titles in the following publications:

"Prologue," *Atlantic Monthly,* December 1980
"Robert Mitchum," *New York Times,* September 19, 1971
"Groucho Marx," *Esquire,* July 1972
"Lee Marvin I," *Esquire,* November 1970
"Kirk Douglas," *Esquire,* February 1970
"Charles Bronson," *Esquire,* August 1974
"Bob and Ray," *New York Times,* October 3, 1970

All other selections originally appeared in the *Chicago Sun-Times.*